McGraw-Hill

New York Chicago San Francisco Lisbon London Madrid
Mexico City Milan New Delhi San Juan Seoul Singapore
Sydney Toronto

To Barbara Gilson: brilliant editor, outstanding human being, dear friend

Library of Congress Cataloging-in-Publication Data applied for.

McGraw-Hill

A Division of The ***McGraw-Hill*** *Companies*

Copyright © 2003 by The McGraw-Hill Companies, Inc. All rights reserved. Printed in the United States of America. Except as permitted under the United States Copyright Act of 1976, no part of this publication may be reproduced or distributed in any form or by any means, or stored in a data base or retrieval system, without the prior written permission of the publisher.

1 2 3 4 5 6 7 8 9 10 11 DOC/DOC 0 9 8 7 6 5 4 3 2

ISBN 0-07-139923-2

McGraw-Hill books are available at special quantity discounts to use as premiums and sales promotions, or for use in corporate training programs. For more information, please write to the Director of Special Sales, McGraw-Hill, Two Penn Plaza, New York, NY 10121. Or contact your local bookstore.

This book is printed on recycled, acid-free paper containing a minimum of 50% recycled, de-inked fiber.

Information contained in this work has been obtained by The McGraw-Hill Companies, Inc. ("McGraw-Hill") from sources believed to be reliable. However, neither McGraw-Hill nor its authors guarantee accuracy or completeness of any information published herein, and neither McGraw-Hill nor its authors shall be responsible for any errors, omissions, or damages arising out of use of this information. This work is published with the understanding that McGraw-Hill and its authors are supplying information but are not attempting to render engineering or other professional services. If such services are required, the assistance of an appropriate professional should be sought.

Contents

Preface

I have the world's nicest students. They are polite, earnest, and sweet. They are fun to talk to and a delight to teach. Unfortunately, many of them are ill prepared for college. They are not ready for the onslaught of work and do not know how to study and budget their time. Many have not been taught critical reading skills or how to take tests.

After interviewing students across the country—including many at the nation's top schools—I have come to realize that this dilemma is not unique to my students. Far from it. Worst of all, a distressing number of students believe they cannot succeed. They have been shaken by years of low grades or grade inflation that results in artificially raised scores.

These problems are not restricted to college-age students. They are endemic among students of all ages, from 8 to 80. Elementary school students quake before standardized tests and fail to earn the scores they merit. Adult learners fear returning to the classroom, scarred by their experiences decades before.

This book is designed to help *all* students master the techniques they need to succeed in their studies. It will help everyone learn the skills to flourish in a classroom and learn with ease and self-confidence. It will teach you the strategies you need to earn your best scores on standardized assessments such as SATs, ACTs, and GREs so you can achieve your goals. Best of all, when you have the skills and confidence you need, learning will be fun—as it should be.

Thank you to the hardworking and dedicated people at North Market Street Graphics, especially Christine Furry and Christine Crocamo. You make me look good.

At McGraw-Hill, my thanks to Barbara Gilson (she's the best!) and to Maureen Walker and Maureen Harper.

—LAURIE ROZAKIS, PH.D.
THE STATE UNIVERSITY OF NEW YORK COLLEGE
OF TECHNOLOGY AT FARMINGDALE

Organization of the Text

This book is arranged in five sections for a total of 20 chapters. The chapters take you step-by-step through the process of becoming a master student and test taker. Each chapter ends with a series of review exercises. These help you reinforce and extend what you've learned. The exercises include true-false, fill-in-the-blank, and multiple-choice test items, because these are most often tested in high-pressure exams.

Here's how to use this book:

Option 1

- Read through the book from beginning to end as you would any book.
- Complete all the exercises at the end of each chapter to assess your progress. This gives you even more practice with test taking.

Option 2

- Pick and choose the chapters you wish to read, and read them in any order you like.
- Skim the exercises to find the ones that help you learn more about the areas in which you need improvement.

Option 3

- Use the book as a study guide immediately before and after major tests. Read and reread the chapters you need the most.
- Complete the exercises that directly match the types of tests you are taking now or plan to take in the near future.

PART 1

CHAPTER 1

Studying and Tests: Crucial to Success

You should read this chapter if you need to review or learn about

- Grade inflation
- Standardized tests, including SATs, GREs, and GMATs
- Common myths about studying

Let's start by probing the issue of grade inflation to see why it's becoming more and more important that you do well on tests, especially standardized measures such as SATs, GREs, and GMATs. Then you'll learn more about some of the most important standardized tests so you understand what you're up against. Finally, we shatter some common study myths about standardized tests. In later chapters, you learn effective study techniques, including ways to manage your time more efficiently.

Get Started

With grade inflation, grades have become less reliable measures of achievement. As a result, colleges, graduate schools, and employers are increasingly relying on standardized tests to rank candidates. Therefore, you must try to do your best on standardized assessments.

Understand Grade Inflation

In 1997, Professor Will Holmes of the University of Georgia discovered that only 5 of the 96 students in his American-history class had earned A grades. He knew that some students had to earn a 3.0 grade point average to keep their full-tuition scholarships from the state. "I just weakened," says Dr. Holmes. "My TAs and I participated in some pretty wholesale grade inflation." When the smoke cleared, Professor Holmes had raised the number of As from 5 to 23 (*The Chronicle of Higher Education*).

Did you catch these recent news stories?

- The principal of a poorly funded school admitted faking grades to help struggling students.
- Teachers around the country acknowledge raising grades to help students "feel good about themselves."
- Many professors concede they raise grades to prevent students from dropping out of poorly enrolled classes. The professors fear that if too many students drop the classes, the classes won't be offered the following semester.

"The administration would like to say it's all due to improved students, but part of it is faculty knuckling under to give higher grades," says Charles H. Keith, a professor of cell biology at the University of Georgia. Grade pressure even comes from an occasional enraged parent, such as one who told a foreign-language instructor, "I'm a lawyer. Now what are we going to do about this C you gave my son?"

Drinking, dating, and football no longer dominate the freshman experience as they once did; for many students, campus life now centers around making the grade. Check out these statistics:

- From 1993 to 1996, the proportion of As and Bs that freshmen received increased from 50.7 percent to 62.7 percent.
- Inversely, Cs, Ds, and Fs fell to 26.7 percent, from 40.3 percent.

The trend continues, as many professionals fear that Cs have become the new equivalent of Fs—unacceptable to students accustomed to receiving only As and Bs but really earning Cs.

Grade inflation is nothing new. In fact, it started during the Vietnam War, when professors gave students higher grades because those with low grades could lose their deferment and be sent to war. Many professors and researchers believe that today's grade inflation is based on the self-esteem movement. Because education must make students feel good about themselves, the argument goes, students' feelings can't be hurt. Therefore, everyone must receive a high grade—whether they earned it or not.

Explore the Call for Accountability

College and university admissions administrators are no fools; neither are employers. They realize that grades are being puffed higher than the Goodyear blimp. To counter grade inflation, savvy administrators are increasingly relying on standardized tests as a true measure of students' achievements. For example,

- When your transcript for admission to college is being evaluated, college counselors compare grade point averages to SAT and/or ACT scores. If grades seem absurdly high and SATs and ACTs absurdly low, you better believe they're going to wonder if grade inflation is a factor. In part, the SAT was created to give a more reliable measure of achievement than grades for students desiring to enter college.
- School district directors hiring new teachers often compare college transcripts to the applicant's score on the National Teacher's Exam or the Praxis to see if the scores indicate the same level of achievement. Both exams were created to give a more reliable measure of achievement than grades for candidates desiring to become teachers (or for teachers seeking tenure).
- School boards hiring administrators such as superintendents, principals, and grade-level directors look at scores on the School Leadership Series test. This test was created to give a more reliable measure of achievement than grades in graduate school.

There's been an ongoing debate about the reliability of standardized tests. Do they accurately measure achievement? Are they biased against women, minorities, and the poor? Do scores go up with coaching? Whether standardized tests are in fact a more reliable measure of achievement than grades isn't really the issue; what matters is the reality. And here's the reality: formal measures of assessment such as standardized tests are assuming increasing importance for students of all ages, from children to mature learners. Standardized tests are also becoming an important factor for job applicants in specific fields.

Therefore, you have to sharpen your study skills and test-taking techniques to a fine point to stay in the game.

Testing Terminology

The chart in Figure 1-1 defines the latest testing terminology. The terms are arranged in alphabetical order. Familiarize yourself with these terms so you understand the different types of assessments and skills that are being measured.

Term	Definition
Academic standard	A clear statement about what students should know and be able to do in certain subject areas at certain stages of their education.
Assessment	The measure of a student's skills or knowledge in a subject area. Tests and portfolios are both forms of assessment.
Criterion-referenced tests	Measurements of a student's performance based on a set body of content. State tests that match state standards (standards-based tests) are criterion-referenced tests.
High-stake tests	Tests used as the only criterion to make an important decision for a student or school. The test score may be used to decide whether a student graduates or whether a school is subject to harsh consequences, such as replacing the principal and much of the staff.
Norm-referenced tests	Tests that compare students' performance to a norm group of students. Scores are reported on a bell curve, with 50 percent of the students who take the test falling below average and 50 percent falling above.
Performance-based assessment (also called *authentic assessment*)	Students apply their knowledge in a hands-on task, such as writing an essay or conducting science experiments.
Performance standards	Criteria that describe how good a student's work must be, or what level of mastery is required, to meet the academic standards.
Standardized tests	Tests constructed so that the questions on the test and the way it is administered are uniform, or standardized, for the large number of students taking the test. The term *standardized* has nothing to do with academic standards. It does not mean that the tests are in any way aligned to academic standards.

Fig. 1-1 Testing terminology you need to know.

Scholastic Aptitude Tests (SATs) I and II

The SAT I is a three-hour multiple-choice test that measures verbal and math reasoning abilities. Administered by the Educational Testing Service, the SAT is used as an entrance exam to nearly all competitive colleges and universities in the United States.

According to the Educational Testing Service, every year about 2 million students who apply to college take the SAT. Nearly all competitive colleges require the SAT because it is believed that the test measures skills that correlate to academic success. The test is scored from a low of 200 to a high of 800. The test has a total of six types of questions, shown in Figure 1-2.

Quick Tip

The PSAT/NMSQT is a practice version of the SAT I. It is used to help students gauge their performance and is the criteria for scholarships administered by the National Merit Foundation. The PSAT is two hours long and contains the same types of questions as the SAT. The score is 20 to 80.

The SAT II is a one-hour subject area test administered by the Educational Testing Service. Most competitive colleges and universities require students to take at least three SAT IIs. The tests are scored from a low of 200 to a high of 800. Subject tests fall into five general subject areas (see Figure 1-3):

- English
- Languages
- History
- Mathematics
- Science

SATs I and II are administered nearly every month on a Saturday, although Sunday test dates are available for students who cannot test on Saturday because of religious obligations. SATs I and II are administered abroad as well as in America. Contact the Educational Testing Service for specific dates, times, and locations.

Advanced Placement (AP) Test

Advanced Placement (AP) is a program of college-level courses and examinations that allow high school students to earn advanced placement and/or college credit. The Advanced Placement program is administered by the College Entrance Examination Board, a division of the Educational Testing Service (ETS).

In May 1998, AP reached a milestone: for the first time in the history of the program, more than 1 million students took an AP exam. These students represent more than 3500 sec-

Verbal	Number	Math	Number
Sentence completions	19	Five-choice	35
Analogies	19	Quantitative comparisons	15
Critical reading	40	Grid-ins	10

Fig. 1-2 Types of questions on the SAT.

English	Languages	History	Mathematics	Science
Literature	Chinese	U.S. history	Level IC	Biology
Writing	French	World history	Level IIC	Chemistry
	German			Physics
	Hebrew			
	Italian			
	Japanese			
	Korean			
	Latin			
	Spanish			

Fig. 1-3 SAT II subject tests.

ondary schools; credit is accepted by more than 2000 participating colleges and universities. More than 100,000 examinations a year are taken in English alone.

Currently, AP courses and exams are given in 33 different subjects, including art, biology, calculus, chemistry, Chinese, computer science, economics, English literature, English language, environmental science, French, German, history (European, U.S., and world), Latin, music theory, physics, psychology, Spanish, statistics, and U.S. government and politics. The tests are scored from 1 (low) to 5 (high).

Each examination is three hours long. One hour is devoted to multiple-choice questions, two hours to essays. The multiple-choice questions count 45 percent of the grade; the essays count 55 percent of the grade.

CLEP Test

As with the AP test, the College-Level Examination Program (CLEP) test allows students to earn college credit, save time in earning a college degree, and save money on tuition. CLEP examinations cover material taught in courses that most students take as requirements in the first two years of college. A college may award the same amount of credit to students earning satisfactory scores on the CLEP examination as it grants to students successfully completing that course.

Many CLEP examinations are designed to correspond to one-semester courses; some, however, correspond to full-year or two-year courses. Unless stated otherwise in its description, an examination is intended to cover material in a one-semester course.

Each exam is 90 minutes long and, except for English composition with essay, contains primarily multiple-choice questions. (See Figure 1-4.)

Composition and Literature	Foreign Languages
Analyzing and interpreting literature	College-level French
English composition	College-level German
English literature	College-level Spanish
Freshman college composition	
Humanities	
History and Social Sciences	**Science and Mathematics**
American government	Calculus
History of the U.S. I: Early colonizations to 1877	College algebra
History of the U.S. II: 1865 to the present	College algebra-trigonometry
Human growth and development	Trigonometry
Introduction to educational psychology	College mathematics
Principles of macroeconomics	Biology
Principles of microeconomics	Chemistry
Introductory psychology	Natural sciences
Introductory sociology	
Social sciences and history	
Western civilization I: Ancient Near East to 1648	
Western civilization II: 1648 to the present	
Business	
Information systems and computer applications	
Principles of management	
Principles of accounting	
Introductory business law	
Principles of marketing	

Fig. 1-4 CLEP subject tests.

Graduate Management Admissions Test (GMAT)

The Graduate Management Admissions Test assesses analytical writing, quantitative reasoning, and verbal abilities. The test is presented on a computer, not on paper, and the questions are tailored to your abilities (as based on your response to the first question). The GMAT has the sections shown in Figure 1-5. The test is scored from 200 to 800, as with SATs I and II.

Area	Time	Contents	
Analytical writing	60 minutes	Writing two topics	Analyze an issue Analyze an argument
Quantitative	75 minutes	37 multiple-choice questions	Data sufficiency Problem solving
Verbal	75 minutes	41 multiple-choice questions	Reading comprehension Critical reasoning Sentence correction

Fig. 1-5 Contents of the GMAT.

Graduate Record Exam (GRE)

There are three Graduate Record Exams:

1. The General Exam
2. Subject area exams
3. The Writing Assessment

Each test is used as an assessment for admission to graduate school.

1. The *General Exam* is a computer-based test of general knowledge. The test is about two and a half hours long and is scored from 200 to 800. The test is structured as shown in Figure 1-6.

2. The *subject area tests* are also designed to help graduate school admission committees assess a candidate's strengths and weaknesses. Each test is 2 hours and 50 minutes long and is scored from 200 to 800. The eight tests are as follows:

- Biochemistry, cell and molecular biology
- Literature in English
- Biology
- Chemistry
- Computer science
- Mathematics
- Physics
- Psychology

3. The *Writing Assessment* consists of two analytical writing assignments: a 45-minute essay that requires you to argue your position on an issue and a 30-minute essay that requires you to analyze an argument.

Area	Time	Contents	
Verbal	30 minutes	30 multiple-choice questions	Reading comprehension
Quantitative	45 minutes	28 multiple-choice questions	Arithmetic, geometry, algebra, data analysis
Analytical	60 minutes	35 questions	Draw inferences, make conclusions, etc.

Fig. 1-6 Contents of the GRE.

Praxis Series: Professional Assessment for Beginning Teachers

There are three Praxis tests, as follows:

1. Praxis I: Academic Skills Assessment
2. Praxis II: Subject Assessment
3. Praxis III: Classroom Performance Assessment

Quick Tip

According to the Educational Testing Service, 80 percent of the states that include tests as part of their licensing process (currently 35 states out of 43) use the Praxis Series to assess teachers.

1. *Praxis I, Academic Skills Assessment,* measures reading, writing, and mathematical skills. The test is offered in paper-and-pencil format as well as on computer. Both test formats measure similar academic skills, but the computer-based tests (CBTs) are tailored to each candidate's performance.

2. *Praxis II, Subject Assessment,* tests the subject areas the candidate will teach, such as mathematics, English, and science. Currently available are more than 140 content tests in multiple-choice formats.

3. *Praxis III, Classroom Performance Assessment,* involves classroom observations. Trained observers sit in the classroom to observe and assess a teacher's performance.

Quick Tip

Test of English as a Foreign Language (TOEFL) measures the ability of nonnative speakers of English to use and understand American English as it is used in college and university settings. Scores on the test are required by more than 4300 two- and four-year colleges and universities, professional schools, and sponsoring institutions. The test is offered on computer throughout most parts of the world.

For additional information about any of these tests, you can contact ETS:

Educational Testing Service
Rosedale Road
Princeton, NJ 08541
Phone: 609-771-7300, 609-921-9000
E-mail: etsinfo@ets.org
Fax: 609-734-5410, 609-530-0482

Shatter Study Myths

Myth: You can't study for a standardized test.
Reality: Oh, yes you can.

Many people still believe that you can't improve your score on a standardized test because these tests are designed to assess the knowledge you have gained during many years of education. Although it is certainly true that you can't cram for an SAT, a GRE, a GMAT, or any other standardized test, you most certainly *can* significantly improve your score by studying. Follow these suggestions:

1. *Familiarize yourself with the test format.* By taking old tests to learn which format you will encounter, you'll know whether you're going to be asked to write an essay or to fill in multiple-choice items . . . or both. Obviously, studying old test formats helps save time, which increases your chance of earning your best possible score.

2. *Understand the scoring.* On some standardized tests, you are penalized for guessing. Therefore, you shouldn't fill in answers willy-nilly. However, you should *always* fill in an answer if you can eliminate one or more of the choices. Other standardized tests, in contrast, assess no penalty for guessing, so you shouldn't leave any blank answers at all.

3. *Learn the test directions.* Any time you can save is that much more time you'll have to spend answering questions. If you learn the test directions for each section ahead of time, you will save the time you would otherwise have spent going over the directions. This extra time will certainly help you earn a better score and could even make a crucial difference in your score.

4. *Take practice tests.* Practice does make perfect, especially when it comes to testing. As an added bonus, previously used questions are often recycled, so the real test may include a question that you have already answered correctly during your study time.

5. *Improve reading comprehension.* Read, read, read to pump up your vocabulary, reading speed, and overall understanding. More on this in Part 3.

6. *Review math skills, especially formulas and computation.* By studying the type of math you know you'll encounter on the test, you'll most certainly improve your score.

While we're here, let's blast these study myths:

Myth: Everybody knows how to study.
Reality: Just the opposite is true. In fact, most people waste a tremendous amount of time trying to figure out how to study.

Myth: The ability to study successfully is an inborn trait, like the ability to throw a great pitch.
Reality: Studying effectively can be taught, just as any other skill can be taught—and learned.

Myth: Cramming is a good way to get ready for tests.
Reality: Reviewing concepts at the very last second may help fix a stray idea in your mind, but for the most part cramming will simply result in brain overload. When you're overloaded, you won't understand what you're studying, so you're simply wasting your time.

- Grade inflation has lead to an increased reliance on standardized tests.
- Learn the specialized words that are applied to testing and assessment procedures.
- Popular standardized tests include the SAT I, SAT II, AP, CLEP, GMAT, GRE, and Praxis. They are all administered by the Educational Testing Service in Princeton, New Jersey (phone: 609-771-7300, 609-921-9000; e-mail: etsinfo@ets.org).

- You *can* (and *should!*) study for standardized tests.

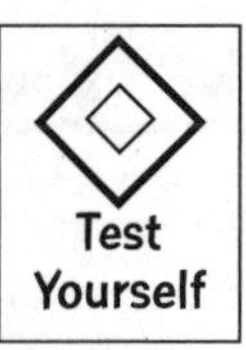

QUESTIONS

True-False Questions

1. Classroom grades are a very accurate measurement of a person's achievement and abilities.

2. Grade inflation is not new; in fact, some professionals believe that grade inflation dates back to days of the Vietnam War when professors were eager to help students maintain their student deferments.
3. There has been an ongoing debate about the reliability of standardized tests.
4. Performance standards are the measure of a student's skills or knowledge in a subject area.
5. Tests and portfolios are both forms of assessment.
6. Standardized tests are closely aligned to academic standards.
7. Nearly all competitive colleges require the SAT because it is believed that the test measures skills that correlate to academic success.
8. The SAT II is a three-hour subject area test administered by the Educational Testing Service.
9. The Advanced Placement test is scored from a low of 200 to a high of 800.
10. The Graduate Management Admissions Test assesses analytical writing, quantitative reasoning, and verbal abilities.
11. You can't study for a standardized test.
12. Cramming is a good way to get ready for all tests, especially standardized ones.

Completion Questions

1. To counter grade inflation, savvy administrators are increasingly relying on __________ as a true measure of students' achievements.
2. Some critics of standardized tests have argued that they are biased against women, __________, and the poor.
3. __________ are tests used as the only criterion to make an important decision for a student or school. The test score may be used to decide whether a student graduates or whether a school is subject to harsh consequences, such as replacing the principal and much of the staff.
4. The __________ is a three-hour multiple-choice test that measures verbal and math reasoning abilities.
5. SATs I and II are scored from a scale of __________ to __________.
6. __________ is a program of college-level courses and examinations that allow high school students to earn advanced placement and/or college credit.
7. As with the AP test, the __________ test allows students to earn college credit, save time earning a college degree, and save money on tuition.
8. There are three Graduate Record Exams: the General Exam, subject area exams, and the __________.
9. The __________ is the Professional Assessment for Beginning Teachers.
10. __________ measures the ability of nonnative speakers of English to use and understand American English as it is used in college and university settings.

Multiple-Choice Questions

1. Many professors and researchers believe that today's grade inflation is based on the _________.
   (a) Self-esteem movement
   (b) Push for more testing
   (c) Increased reliance on academics
   (d) Decline in student performance
2. Standardized tests can be used in all of the following instances *except*
   (a) Granting teachers tenure
   (b) Evaluating teacher performance in the classroom
   (c) Denying an employee health coverage
   (d) Admission to college and graduate school
3. Clear statements about what students should know and be able to do in certain subject areas at certain stages of their education are called
   (a) Norm-referenced tests
   (b) Academic standards
   (c) High-stake tests
   (d) Criterion-referenced tests
4. Tests constructed so that the questions on the test and the way it is administered are uniform for the large number of students taking the test are called
   (a) Assessment tests
   (b) Standardized tests
   (c) Norm-referenced tests
   (d) Authentic assessment
5. SATs I and II are
   (a) Tests of English as a second language
   (b) Graduate school admission tests
   (c) Tests given to teachers
   (d) College admission tests
6. About how many students take Advanced Placement tests every year?
   (a) A few thousand
   (b) 10,000
   (c) 1 million
   (d) 100 million
7. The GMAT contains each of the following sections *except*
   (a) The General Exam
   (b) Verbal

(c) Quantitative
(d) Analytical writing

8. The Graduate Record Exam (GRE) is used for admission to
   (a) Private schools
   (b) Medical and dental schools
   (c) Undergraduate colleges and universities
   (d) Graduate school
9. When you study for a standardized test, you should do all of the following *except*
   (a) Review math skills, especially formulas and computation
   (b) Take practice tests
   (c) Cram as much as you can the night before
   (d) Familiarize yourself with the test format
10. It is a myth that
   (a) You can study for standardized tests
   (b) Everybody knows how to study
   (c) The ability to study successfully can be learned
   (d) The ability to study successfully can be taught

ANSWER KEY

True-False Questions

1. F 2. T 3. T 4. F 5. T 6. F 7. T 8. F 9. F 10. T 11. F 12. F

Completion Questions

1. Standardized tests 2. Minorities 3. High-stake tests 4. SAT I 5. 200 to 800 6. AP, or Advanced Placement 7. CLEP 8. Writing Assessment 9. Praxis Series 10. TOEFL

Multiple-Choice Questions

1. a 2. c 3. b 4. b 5. d 6. c 7. a 8. d 9. c 10. b

CHAPTER 2

You *Can* Succeed!

You should read this chapter if you need to review or learn about

- ➔ Resolving to succeed in your studies
- ➔ Establishing study goals
- ➔ Setting up a study center

In Chapter 1, you learned all about grade inflation and the increased reliance on standardized tests. In addition, you surveyed the different types of standardized tests, including SATs, GREs, and GMATs. Last, you debunked common study myths, especially as they pertain to studying for standardized tests. This chapter covers adopting a positive attitude about studying and positioning yourself for success.

Get Started

How can you maximize your achievement?

1. Adopt a positive attitude.
2. Position yourself for success in your studies.

Assess Your Attitude

How would you rate your study skills and study attitudes? Fill out the following worksheet to see. Check all the statements that apply to you. Leave blank all the ones that don't apply.

____ 1. "I want to study more, but what's the use? I'm not going to do well, anyway."
____ 2. "I just don't know where to begin."
____ 3. "The teacher [professor, instructor] doesn't like me."
____ 4. "I can't get my head into studying because I'm not sure what I want to study."
____ 5. "I can never find my books and all the other supplies I need."
____ 6. "Because of family situations or job obligations, I keep missing class. I never seem to know what's going on in class."

Did you check several of these items? If so, you're not alone!

Read on to get the help you need to conquer these common study problems. Each of the following sections gives you strategies you need to deal with these situations.

Adjust Your Attitude

Many people check item 1, "I want to study more, but what's the use? I'm not going to do well, anyway." Do you feel this way? If so, have you ever used these excuses?

- "I'm not smart enough to learn all this stuff. I don't have the brains."
- "The teacher isn't good, so I'll never be able to learn what I need."
- "I don't have the time to get the grades I deserve. I am far too busy with my job [husband/boyfriend/wife/girlfriend/parents/children—fill in as many as apply]."
- "I'm just not meant for college [graduate school, this course]. They let me in by mistake."
- "I had terrible teachers when I was younger, so I won't be able to catch up now."
- "I never paid attention in class. That put me far behind the eight ball."

If you talk yourself into failing, you probably will fail. But if you talk yourself into success, you have a good chance of doing well. Study smart by having a positive attitude about school and yourself.

Start by . . .

- Being enthusiastic about learning
- Having discipline
- Deciding that you can do well on tests and papers
- Having self-respect
- Making friends with people who support your hopes and dreams
- Not being a quitter
- Preparing for the future
- Using your time wisely

Quick Tip

Never skip classes near exam time—you may miss a review session and other crucial information.

The connection between attitude and achievement is well documented. There's no question that your self-image has a very powerful influence on your academic achievement. If you see yourself as a successful learner, your academic performance will improve. To stop setting up roadblocks in the classroom, start seeing school as a positive force, not something deliberately designed to bring you down.

Remember, studying brings short-term and long-term rewards. Developing good study habits will help you learn more in your classes and remember the information better. Your self-confidence will soar as people praise your achievements. Studying more effectively also leaves more time for a life filled with friends, sports, and entertainment. Later on, those same good study habits will help you do well in your job. You'll find it easier to make smart life choices, too. So get the right attitude!

Get Started on the Journey of a Lifetime

How about item 2, "I just don't know where to begin"? Many people feel this way because studying *can* seem overwhelming.

Stop. Take a deep breath. Now take control. Here's how to do it:

1. List all the things you have to do in descending order, from most important to least important.
2. Break your workload down into manageable chunks. You can study algebra for 1 hour, not 10 hours. Likewise, you can learn grammar for 45 minutes, not 4 hours.
3. Schedule your time realistically. Begin studying early, and slowly build as the exam approaches.

4. Use all your time. For example, use the hour between classes to review notes. Use the 10 minutes while you're standing in line at the deli counter to do skim reading, review some vocabulary, or proofread a paper one more time.
5. Be sure to build in study breaks. You'll study more effectively if you take brief breaks, about 15 minutes each.

Time management skills are so critical to study success that I devote all of Chapter 3 to helping you develop effective time management techniques.

As you study, follow these steps:

- Get an overview of what you must do by surveying your syllabus, reading material, and notes.
- Identify the most important topics emphasized as well as any areas you still don't understand.
- Spend the most time on information that your instructor stressed in class.

Keep the following equation in mind (you might even want to copy it and place it over your desk!):

Subject skills + smart study = school success

Be a Class Act

"The teacher [professor, instructor] doesn't like me," you say. Actually, you may be right. Teachers are human, like you. They tend to judge students by the way they act in class.

When you treat your instructors with respect, they will treat you with respect. If you do your work to the best of your ability and take school seriously, your teacher will respond. Get with the program by taking an active and positive role in the classroom. Here's how to get started:

- Come to every class.
- Be prepared. Bring your books, notebooks, and homework.
- Sit in the front of the room. This reduces distractions and shows the instructor that you are serious about learning.
- Pay close attention in class.
- Take good notes.
- Raise your hand when you know the answer.
- Ask intelligent questions when you're confused.
- Treat your teachers with courtesy.

Reach for the Stars (They're Closer than You Think!)

Did you check excuse 4, "I can't get my head into studying because I'm not sure what I want to study"? If so, you have plenty of company. Many people aren't sure what career would give them the most satisfaction. Where do you see yourself in 5 years . . . 10 years . . . 20 years?

You might have firm career plans. Possibly you have a general idea of a job or career that suits your interests and abilities. Perhaps you already have a career but desperately want to change fields because you're burned out doing the same thing day after day, year after year. Maybe you love your career but you're being forced out of the job. You have no choice but to retrain. Maybe you don't have any plans for the future at all.

Setting goals can help you study more effectively to make your hopes and dreams become reality. You can set *short-term goals* and *long-term goals.* Short-term goals look ahead an hour, day, a week, or months. Long-term goals are set years in the future.

Good students set both short-term goals and long-term goals. Often, the two types of goals work together. For example, if you set a goal to learn three new words a week, you'll do better in class, on standardized tests, and in the workplace. This helps you earn higher grades, which helps your long-term goals of attending college, getting into graduate school, moving up in your job, or becoming more self-assured.

Study the sample timeline in Figure 2-1. How could you adapt it to suit your plans?

Goal: To raise my grades 5 points in three months.

September	October	November
Week 1: Write down all assignments.	Attend extra help.	Check my progress.
Week 2: No TV until homework is done.	Cut computer cybersurfing.	No music while studying.
Week 3: Take better notes.	Study with a classmate who earns great grades.	Visit the library weekly.
Week 4: Reread notes every night before bed.	Read one extra book a week.	Reward myself!

Fig. 2-1 Make a timeline to show your goals and the steps you'll follow.

Carve Out Your Own Space

Perhaps you checked item 5, "I can never find my books and all the other supplies I need." Organization is one of the keys to effective studying and test taking. In fact, good organizational skills can help you succeed in every part of your life.

I'm always astonished at the number of students in my college courses who come to classes unprepared. Then they're shocked when they fail! To avoid having this happen to you, Figures 2-2 and 2-3 offer checklists of materials you will need in school and for homework. Photocopy the list and use it to check off your supplies each day. Then you won't forget anything important.

The famous British novelist Virginia Woolf claimed that every writer needs a "room of one's own" in which to compose. The same is true of studying: solitude helps. Even if it is not possible to have a whole room to yourself, having your own space in which to study can make it much easier for you to succeed. All your supplies will be in one place and handy.

In addition, by always studying in the same place you get your mind ready to work. Walking into your study area sends signals to your brain: "Brain, we're getting down to work here." That's because a study center helps you concentrate on your work and get into the habit of studying. Figure 2-4 shows you which places work well—and which ones don't.

Your study center should have good light, study tools (textbooks, reference books, paper, pens), and quiet. You can't study if music is blaring, if you're talking to friends, or if Fido is barking to be let out.

- Study in a calm, quiet place.
- If you don't have a whole room in which to study, consider converting part of a room for your own space. A small closet, part of an attic or basement, or the corner of a room can be converted to a quiet study area.
- Turn off the television and radio, and eliminate other distractions.
- Study at the same time so people know to leave you alone.

Quick Tip

In addition to formal study in your study center, try to use "wasted" time reviewing notes, learning math formulas and vocabulary, and so on.

Home Supplies	
________	Assignment pad
________	Binders or notebooks
________	Calculator
________	Dictionary
________	Paper
________	Pens
________	Pencils
________	Pencil sharpener
________	Ruler
________	Textbooks
________	Telephone numbers and e-mail addresses of several classmates who earn good grades (in case you miss assignments, etc.)
________	Watch or clock

Fig. 2-2 Here are the supplies you need for a home study center.

If you're fortunate enough to have your own computer, it should be a central part of your study center. Computers can help you prepare well-organized notes, make easy-to-read outlines, and write essays and reports.

If the computer is in another part of the house, set up a quiet time to use it for homework and studying. Find a time that is convenient for you and everyone else, too. For example, if the computer is in the family room, you might want to use it at 3:00 in the afternoon when your family members are in another part of the house. You wouldn't want to use it from 8:00 to 10:00 at night when everyone else is watching television in the same room.

Make an "appointment" to use the computer at the same time every day. Your family members will know that you're serious about working on the computer and respect your determination.

School Supplies	
__________	Assignment pad
__________	Binders or notebooks
__________	Calculator
__________	Dictionary
__________	Homework (completed)
__________	Paper
__________	Pens
__________	Pencils
__________	Textbooks
__________	Watch or clock

Fig. 2-3 Bring these items with you to every class.

Keep Up with Assignments

Many of my students are mature learners. As a result, they come to class with a heavy load of responsibilities, including family and job obligations. I hear this excuse often: "Because of family situations or job demands, I keep missing class. I never seem to know what's going on in class." And indeed they don't.

Attend All Classes

Clearly, the best policy is to attend every single class. Just as clearly, that's not always possible. However, many instructors will allow you to make up a class by attending the same class at a different time. For example, this semester I'm teaching Technical Writing on Mondays and Wednesdays from 9:30 to 11:00 and again from 2:00 to 3:15. I also teach the same class Thursday evenings from 6:00 to 8:45. I allow my students to attend whichever class suits their schedule. If you anticipate having to miss a class, ask whether your instructor offers the same class at a different time and will allow you to attend it as a makeup.

Great Study Areas	Poor Study Areas
In your room at a desk	In front of the television
In a calm corner of the house	In your room on the bed
In a quiet part of the school or public library	On the train, bus, or subway

Fig. 2-4 Set up a study center.

Contact the Instructor

Sometimes, however, you must miss a class and can't make it up. In these instances, you should try to contact the instructor by phone or e-mail. If you're absent from class, always try to contact the instructor first. That way, you are showing your commitment to class as well as getting the information directly from the source.

Consult the Syllabus

Other times, however, you won't be able to reach the instructor. In that case, you may be able to consult the syllabus. A *syllabus* is a listing of the following:

- Class activities
- Essay tests
- Exams
- Labs
- Quizzes
- Reading assignments
- Speeches

Instructors prepare their own syllabi and distribute them to the class at the first or second class meeting. A syllabus is a wonderful document because it helps you keep up with all the assignments. The syllabus lays out the class responsibilities, the instructor's expectations, and the general rules for the class. If you stay in the class, the instructor is going to assume that you agree to the rules and will complete all the work to the best of your ability. If you don't like or don't agree with something in the syllabus, discuss it with the instructor or transfer to another class. Never assume that an instructor will not do something printed in the syllabus. For example, if the syllabus requires you to give three speeches during the semester, don't assume that the instructor will make an exception for you because you are afraid of speaking in front of a class. Read your syllabus and understand what it says.

Instructors are not required to create and distribute a syllabus, although they are strongly encouraged to do so.

Arrange for a Study Partner

Remember, you're in the big leagues now. This means the instructor is not responsible for keeping you up-to-speed. *You* are. Therefore, consider getting a study partner as additional insurance against missing classwork or misunderstanding assignments.

Find one or more classmates and trade telephone numbers. When you must be absent from class, contact your study partner to get assignments you missed. You can contact your study partner to talk about assignments you don't understand, too. Finally, you can review material for tests with your study partner.

How can you select good study partners? Look for classmates who

- Take school seriously
- Earn higher grades than you do right now
- Understand the lectures and assignments
- Keep up with all the work
- Are trustworthy
- Are well organized
- Are rarely, if ever, absent

Even if the study partner you select is in all your classes, select at least two or three partners so you always have a backup person to contact.

✔ Maximize your achievement by adopting a positive attitude. Decide that you can succeed, and you will stand a far better chance of reaching your goals.

✔ Establish study goals. Be enthusiastic about learning. Be disciplined and determined. Prepare for the future and use your time wisely.

✔ Set up a study center in a quiet place. Stock it with the supplies you need to succeed, including a dictionary, a calculator, pens, and paper.

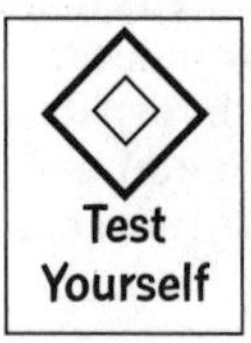

QUESTIONS

True-False Questions

1. The mind is a powerful force. If you talk yourself into failing, you probably will fail.
2. If you talk yourself into success, you have a good chance of doing well.

3. The connection between attitude and achievement has not yet been documented.
4. Cramming is an effective study technique, so it's not necessary to divide your workload into manageable chunks.
5. Use all your time. For example, use the hour between classes to review notes.
6. Be sure to build in study breaks. You'll study more effectively if you take brief breaks, about 15 minutes each.
7. You can skip classes and still do very well if you do all the reading and get the notes from a classmate.
8. It's not a good idea to ask questions in class because your instructor is likely to think that you're not very intelligent.
9. Good students set short-term goals but not long-term goals.
10. Studying in a quiet place—preferably the same place—every day helps you concentrate and learn more effectively.
11. Most people can concentrate remarkably well and learn a great deal when they study while watching television, listening to the radio, or talking on the telephone.
12. Find a study partner to help you keep up with assignments you missed and to clarify information you might have misread or misheard.

Completion Questions

1. Never skip any _________ near exam time—you may miss a review session and other crucial information covered by the instructor.
2. To stop setting up roadblocks in the classroom, start seeing school as a _________ force, not something deliberately designed to bring you down.
3. Studying brings short-term and long-term _________.
4. Your self-_________ will soar as people praise your achievements.
5. Be prepared in all your classes. Bring your ___________, ___________, and __________.
6. When you are in a class, always try to sit in the _________ of the room. This reduces distractions and shows the instructor that you are serious about learning.
7. Your _________ should have good light, your study tools (textbooks, reference books, paper, pens), and quiet.
8. Always try to study at the same _________ every day so people at home realize and respect your determination to succeed. For example, you might study at 7:00 in the morning, before you go to work, or at 7:00 in the evening, after dinner.
9. When you must be absent from class, consult your written _________ and contact the instructor to see what you missed.
10. Even if the study partner you select is in all your classes, select at least _________ study partners so you always have a backup person to contact.

Multiple-Choice Questions

1. You can improve your chances for success on tests by doing all of the following *except*
   (a) Being enthusiastic about learning
   (b) Having self-respect
   (c) Not worrying about the future
   (d) Having discipline and using your time wisely
2. When you know the answer in class, you should
   (a) Check with a friend to make sure that you have it right before you speak
   (b) Keep quiet so you don't seem like a show-off
   (c) Raise your hand
   (d) Look down at your desk
3. Long-term goals are set
   (a) An hour away
   (b) A day away
   (c) A week away
   (d) Years into the future
4. You must have all the following supplies in your at-home study center *except*
   (a) A computer
   (b) Pens, pencils, and paper
   (c) A calculator
   (d) A dictionary
5. Establishing your own study center helps you
   (a) Understand what was said in class
   (b) Concentrate on your work and get into the habit of studying
   (c) Work more effectively with your instructor
   (d) Make up for classes you might have missed
6. Which of the following is the *best* study area?
   (a) On the train, bus, or subway
   (b) In your room on the bed
   (c) In front of the television
   (d) In a quiet part of the school or public library
7. Work with one or more study partners to
   (a) Help you keep up with work you might have missed
   (b) Have more fun in class
   (c) Get out of going to so many classes
   (d) Impress the instructor with your determination

8. When you choose study partners, look for classmates who
   (a) Know how to have a good time
   (b) Are on your level academically
   (c) Take class seriously and keep up with the work
   (d) Are slightly below your level academically
9. A listing of all class assignments is called a
   (a) Roster
   (b) Syllabub
   (c) Syllabus
   (d) Study system
10. If you must miss a class, you should
   (a) Talk to your study partner first
   (b) Let it slide until the next class
   (c) Figure everything out on your own to show that you are independent
   (d) Contact the instructor, consult the syllabus, and talk to your study partner

ANSWER KEY

True-False Questions

1. T 2. T 3. F 4. F 5. T 6. T 7. F 8. F 9. F 10. T 11. F 12. T

Completion Questions

1. Classes 2. Positive 3. Rewards 4. Self-confidence 5. Books, notebooks, and homework 6. Front 7. Study center 8. Time 9. Syllabus 10. Two

Multiple-Choice Questions

1. c 2. c 3. d 4. a 5. b 6. d 7. a 8. c 9. c 10. d

PART 2

Study Smarter, Not Harder

CHAPTER 3

Effective Time Management Skills

You should read this chapter if you need to review or learn about

- Polishing your time management skills
- Setting a study schedule
- Dealing with procrastination

Get Started

In this chapter, you will learn easy and effective time management skills that will serve you well now, in your studies, and later in life. The emphasis here is on study success, so we zero in on making sure you study enough to get the grades you need—and deserve.

How Much Time Should You Study?

In 1999, the University of California at Los Angeles surveyed over 364,000 students. Researchers discovered that in their senior year of high school, students were studying far less than they had in the past. Figure 3-1 illustrates the difference in study time.

Year	Weekly Study	Time Percentage
1999	6 hours or more	31.5%
1987	6 hours or more	43.7%

Fig. 3-1 Study time has declined.

Nearly 20 percent of the students surveyed admitted that they studied less than an hour *a week*. No wonder they're not earning the grades they want or acquiring the skills they need. This leads to great frustration for everyone: graduates realize they aren't fully prepared, and employers bemoan the poorly educated incoming labor.

In general, you should figure on studying two hours *a day* for every hour of class time, as shown in Figure 3-2.

Class Time	Daily Study Time
1 hour	2 hours
90 minutes	3 hours
2 hours	4 hours

Fig. 3-2 The minimum amount of time you need to master the material.

It's not going to come as a shock, then, to learn that a significant number of students who insist they know the material thoroughly are astonished when they fail their first tests. The first hint for studying smart is an easy one: put in the time. Recognize that your studies must be your priority. Set aside the time to study. As Figure 3.2 shows, you should study at least twice the amount of time you spend in class.

Time Flies

When it comes to study success, the secret isn't lack of time—it's making the best use of your time. Doing well in your studies has surprisingly little to do with your raw intelligence. Brilliant students can flunk out if they waste their time, and average students can ace their classes by using their time wisely.

Quick Tip

In the chaotic whirlwind of attending classes, don't forget to enjoy what you're doing and the people you meet while you're there. You can make lifelong friends out of people you meet in classes.

Why do you feel so rushed and stressed since you've started classes? Why is it you don't have enough time to study? Many activities make your life demanding, and there's always something to distract busy people from their studies. Before you can plan your time, you must understand how you are spending your time now. Where does all that time go? Take the inventory in Figure 3-3 to find out.

Your grand total is the number of hours you have left for studying after you've done everything you need to do and everything you want to do. Here's a sample, figured on the high side:

Sleep	7 hours × 7 days	= 49 hours
Grooming	1 hour × 7 days	= 7 hours
Eating	1 hour × 7 days	= 7 hours
Commuting	1 hour × 7 days	= 7 hours
Errands	1 hour × 7 days	= 7 hours
Family responsibilities	1 hour × 7 days	= 7 hours
Job	8 hours × 5 days	= 40 hours
Social life	1 hour × 7 days	= 7 hours
E-mail/phone	15 min × 7 days	= 2 hours
Classes	3 hours × 4 days	= 12 hours
	Total hours:	145 hours
	168 – 145	= 23 hours
	Grand total	= 23 hours left

You have 23 hours left if you work 40 hours a week; if you don't have a job, you've got a whopping 63 hours a week left to study. In either case, that's a lot of hours left to devote to studying. However, if you still don't have enough hours to get your studying done, you have these options:

- Choice 1: Cut your nonessential activities.
- Choice 2: Cut your essential activities.
- Choice 3: Use your time more wisely.

Time Worksheet

		Hours per Week
1. On average, how many hours do you sleep each night?	______ × 7 =	______
2. On average, how many hours a day do you spend showering, dressing, and grooming?	______ × 7 =	______
3. On average, how many hours a day do you spend eating? (Include cooking, serving, and cleaning up if you cook for yourself.)	______ × 7 =	______
4. On average, how many hours a day do you spend getting to class? (Include the time it takes to walk across campus or to commute.)	______ × 7 =	______
5. On average, how many hours a day do you spend doing errands such as laundry and cleaning?	______ × 7 =	______
6. On average, how many hours a day do you spend on activities such as clubs, sports, exercise, religious services, and so on?	______ × 7 =	______
7. On average, how many hours a day do you work at a job?	______ × 7 =	______
8. On average, how many hours a day do you spend with friends, family, housework, home repairs, going out, watching TV, golfing, community work,and so on?	______ × 7 =	______
9. On average, how many hours a day do you spend on e-mail or on the phone?	______ × 7 =	______
10. How many hours a day do you spend in class?	______ × 7 =	______
	Total hours:	______
	Subtract from 168 (number of hours in a week)	______
	Grand total:	______

Fig. 3-3 Complete this time management worksheet.

Clearly, choice 2 is unrealistic. Essential activities are things you have to do: going to work, taking care of your home, and attending class. That leaves choices 1 and 3. Let's look at them now.

Make the Most of Your Time

It may seem as if there aren't enough hours in the week to get everything done, but I've just tossed that excuse out the window. The time is there—it's up to you to use it as efficiently as possible.

Take a look at what you've written. Can you see some major time wasters on your list? Maybe you spend nine hours a week watching television, playing video games, and styling your hair. This cuts into family life, class time, and study time.

What happens if you don't have any real time wasters? Perhaps you're using your time very efficiently, but you still don't have enough study time to pass your classes. For example, you might be working 40 hours a week and truly do not have the time to get your studying done. If that's the case, you might be able to work part-time for a semester or even a year and push ahead to finish your classes and your degree.

Study the list and see what adjustments you can make in the way you spend your time. Then learn how to use your time wisely.

Quick Tip

Only *you* can decide how to spend your time. Don't let spouses, relatives, friends, classmates, and neighbors bully you into taking on more responsibilities than you can reasonably handle.

Set Priorities

Learning time management skills is a matter of setting priorities. Start by recognizing that everyone is an individual: what works for one person may not work for another. Your classmate may decide to spend nights in a drunken stupor, cut class, and cram like mad. The lucky puppy may be able to pull his tail out of the fire this way, but this may not work for you. People like your classmate ruin it for the rest of us because they make time management seem like a snap. It's not. Follow the five easy steps below to learn to use your time well:

1. *Understand your personal style.* Some people can stay up until 2:00 A.M. studying; others must hit the pillow by 10:00 P.M. or be useless the next day. Some students work great under pressure; others crumble in a panic. For example, my son can stay up very late, but he must eat regular meals or he becomes crabby. My daughter, in contrast, needs a solid eight

hours of sleep, but she can skip meals and still be a sweetheart. Think about the conditions that help you succeed and make them a priority in your life. This will help you succeed in your studies and classwork.

2. *Recognize your limitations.* We all have limits: learn yours. Know when you've had enough studying and need to take a break. Know when you're not getting the material in class and need to seek extra help. Know which classes are hardest for you and will require extra effort. Know when you must hit the books or risk failing.

Spend a few days recording exactly how you spend your time. Write down everything, and be honest. Remember, you're only doing this for yourself. When you've completed your list, see how you spend your time. Look for overall balance. Make sure you are sleeping enough, because no amount of study will make up for too little sleep. Also check that you have time set aside for meals, for fun, and for yourself.

3. *Achieve a balance.* One of the hardest things about planning your time is finding the right balance between doing what you *have* to do and doing what you *want* to do. Setting priorities is the key: Planning your time offers you the best chance of being able to fit everything you want and need to do into your educational life—especially time for studying.

Make a Study Schedule

Time has a sneaky way of slipping away. Fortunately, you can get a handle on your time by making a study schedule. A study schedule helps you set goals as well as get your work done. A study schedule also helps you . . .

- Break down tasks into manageable parts
- Keep up with assignments
- Get into a study routine
- Make the most of your time

Making a schedule can help you accomplish all your activities so you can achieve your goals. A computer spreadsheet program is great for this, but the old-fashioned paper-and-pencil format works fine, too. List the days across the top and the time (in one-hour or half-hour increments, whichever suits you best) down the left-hand side.

1. Start by writing down essential activities, including sleeping, eating, attending classes, and study time.
2. Then fill in chores such as food shopping, laundry, and housecleaning, because even though chores must be done eventually, they can be put off for a while if necessary. Also fill in job time and commuting time, if these apply. These may or may not be able to be adjusted if you decide to make studying a priority.
3. Add socializing, clubs, sports, and other fun activities.
4. Adjust the schedule as needed. For example, add more study time during the week before midterms, finals, and other crucial exams.

Figure 3-4 shows a sample study schedule that a student I know made. She works as a teacher and is studying to earn her master's degree. She must get the degree to earn her permanent teacher's certification and so keep her job.

Time	Mon.	Tues.	Wed.	Thurs.	Fri.	Weekends
	Job	Job	Job	Job	Job	Big assignments
4:00 P.M.	Study	Study	Study	Study	Gym	Big assignments
5:00 P.M.	Study	Study	Study	Study	Study	Chores
6:00 P.M.	Dinner	Dinner	Dinner	Dinner	Gym	Socializing
7:00 P.M.	Class	Class	Class	Class	Chores	Socializing
8:00 P.M.	Class	Class	Class	Class	Chores	Socializing
9:00 P.M.	Study	Study	Study	Study	Chores	Socializing
10:00 P.M.	Study/prepare for the next day			→	→	Socializing
11:00 P.M.	Sleep	Sleep	Sleep	Sleep	Sleep	

Fig. 3-4 Sample study schedule.

Notice that my friend studies before class as well as after. Before class, she can review notes so she can actively participate in class; after class, she can go over what was said to help remember it. There's also some extra time built in on weekends to take into account major assignments such as labs, papers, and tests.

My friend gets ready for work and school the night before to avoid early-morning panic. She penciled in some social time on weekends, so she can unwind and relax with friends and family.

Quick Tip

It's not enough to make a study schedule; you also have to follow it!

Use the blank form in Figure 3-5 for your own study schedule. Tailor the schedule to fit your individual needs. Make photocopies of the schedule and post them in your room to help you become master of your fate. Don't back yourself into a corner and become a stress puppy.

A schedule is a waste of time if you don't use it. But be kind to yourself. If you skip an hour of studying this week to attend a party, don't beat yourself up. Instead, cut an hour from somewhere else in your schedule (eat a little faster, leave a meeting early) and make up the time. With a little bit of flexibility and a nip and tuck here and there, you'll soon have a schedule that will help you use your time wisely and fit in enough studying.

Time	Mon.	Tues.	Wed.	Thurs.	Fri.	Weekends
3:00 P.M.						
4:00 P.M.						
5:00 P.M.						
6:00 P.M.						
7:00 P.M.						
8:00 P.M.						
9:00 P.M.						

Fig. 3-5 Make your own study schedule.

Study Hints

The following hints can make it easier for you to get the most from your study time:

1. *Use your free time during the school day.* The hours between classes are perhaps your most valuable study time, but they're often ignored. If you have a break—even a short one—use it to review the material and edit the notes you just took.

2. *Study before and after class.* You'll get the most bang for your study buck by reviewing your notes immediately before and after the class.

3. *Space study periods.* Figure on spending 50 to 90 minutes of study at a time. More than that and you'll start to burn out; study for less, and you won't have a chance to work up a head of steam. It's more efficient to study hard for a clear-cut period of time and take a break rather than studying until you're frazzled.

For People Who *Can't* Keep to a Study Schedule . . .

Sticking to a strict schedule is difficult for some students and downright impossible for a small (but significant) minority. If you suspect that a strict schedule will make you break out in hives, not to worry. You can still succeed by managing your time in the following way.

1. *Take the long view.* Make a long-term schedule by writing down only your fixed commitments. These include the obligations you are required to meet every week, such as classes and job hours. Use a pocket calendar for this purpose.

2. *Focus on immediate events.* Now make a short list of *major events* and *amount of work* you have to accomplish in each subject this week. This may include nonstudy activities. If you wish, put a star next to the tasks that are most important. Figure 3-6 shows a sample schedule. (I starred the economics test because it counts 25 percent of the grade.) Because these responsibilities change weekly, you'll have to make a new list each week. Revise your list during the week to take into account new information you get. For instance, you may learn that a test has been postponed, a paper moved up, or an extra reading added.

Weekly Schedule Arranged by Day	
Monday:	Write English essay; due Wednesday (2–3 hours writing time) Finish 40 pages in Psychology 203 by Friday
Tuesday:	* Study for economics test (2 hours) Read 150 pages for history class by Friday
Wednesday:	* Study for economics test (2 hours)
Thursday:	* Economics test
Friday:	Begin math project (due in one week)

Fig. 3-6 Alternate study schedule.

3. *Set your daily goals.* Every morning, write your daily schedule on a note card. Jot down exactly what you want to get done that day. You can use an assignment pad, a Day-Timer, or just a plain old index card. (Figure 3-7 shows a sample on an index card.) You can carry this card with you and cross out each item as you accomplish it. Listing your activities helps you keep track of what you have to do each day.

Take Care of Yourself

I've stressed the importance of throwing spontaneity to the wind and getting yourself on a schedule. That said, never endanger your health to achieve your goals. I mentioned this briefly already, but it's worth emphasizing. To maximize your chances of study success, keep yourself in tip-top health. Here are a few of my most successful tips. (I use all of them myself,

Monday	
4:00–4:15	Skim notes before class
4:30–5:30	Class: unit test on terms
5:45–6:00	Eat dinner; proofread essay
6:00–7:00	Class; hand in paper
7:30–8:30	Gym
9:00–	Pick up milk and eggs on way home; study math afterward

Fig. 3-7 Daily study schedule.

and I earned a B.A., M.A., Ph.D. and a Certificate in Technical Writing, the last three degrees while working full-time and raising a family.)

- Get a flu shot and a pneumonia shot. There are no side effects to either shot, and they are an easy way to prevent a miserable week in bed—or months of debilitating illness.
- Eat right. You know the drill: Eat six servings of fruit and vegetables; avoid fad diets; and go light on junk food.
- Eat regular meals. Eat all three: breakfast, lunch, and dinner. Skipping meals runs you down fast.
- Get regular exercise. Not only is exercise good for your body, but it's great for your brain. It helps relieve stress so you can concentrate more fully. Daily exercise breaks during high-stress times such as midterms and finals are especially important.
- Get enough sleep. It's tempting to get the extra time you need by sleeping less, but try hard to resist skimping on sleep. Instead, take power naps on the train or bus and study in spare moments while you're on phone hold or waiting at the dentist's office.
- See the doctor when you first get sick. Catching a minor illness early helps prevent it from developing into a major problem. Every semester, I lose half a dozen students due to bronchitis, pneumonia, strep throat, and other serious illnesses that could have been cured fast had they been attended to at first symptoms. See the dentist every year, too.
- Dress for the seasons. Wear layers of clothing so you're never too warm or too cold. Wear a raincoat or use an umbrella when it rains.
- Attend to cuts and bruises so they don't get infected.
- Watch your mental health. If you feel yourself going over the edge, slow down. You may wish to speak to your professor about taking an incomplete in a class and finishing it when you're not so stressed.

Quick Tip

Students tend to abuse caffeine, especially around exam time. Many people guzzle mug after mug of coffee in an attempt to stay awake to study. However, too much caffeine can lead to forgetfulness, so drinking too much coffee, cola, or tea while studying is counterproductive.

Tomorrow Is Another Day

Well, yes, Scarlett, but not always when it comes to studying. You shouldn't beat yourself up about slipping from your study schedule here and there, but neither should you take refuge in these old excuses:

- "I'll get it done tomorrow."
- "I'll study better tomorrow [morning, afternoon, evening]—anything but today."
- "What do you expect? I've always been a procrastinator."

You're in school to get an education. To do so, you have to attend class, pay attention, get your work done, and study. If you tend to procrastinate, now is the time to break the habit.

Two of the biggest time wasters are the Internet and the telephone. Don't spend more than one hour a day on e-mail or surfing the web—even for research. If you love to chat on the phone (and I sure do!), get a portable telephone and multitask. Empty the dishwasher, put in a load of laundry, and pack your lunch while you chat.

✔ Track where your time is going, understand your personal style, recognize your limitations, and achieve a balance in your life.

✔ Set a study schedule and keep it. You can set both short-term and long-term goals.

✔ Deal with procrastination by limiting e-mail and telephone chat time and resolving to buckle down and study.

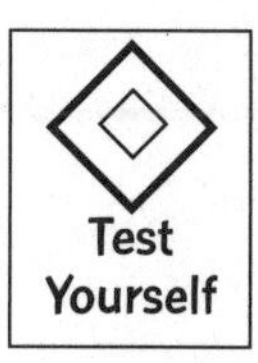

QUESTIONS

True-False Questions

1. In general, students today are studying far more than students did in the past decade.

2. If you are taking a two-hour class, it is reasonable for the instructor to expect you to study four hours for that class.
3. When it comes to study success, the secret isn't lack of time—it's making the best use of your time.
4. When it comes to effective study skills, one size *does* fit all. What works for one person will work for another.
5. As you figure out how to use your time well, start by understanding your personal style.
6. Don't bother recording exactly how you spend your time. Writing down everything is just a waste of time.
7. The hours between classes are perhaps your most valuable study time, but they're often ignored.
8. It's more efficient to cram until you've learned everything you have to know than to study for a clear-cut period of time and take a break.
9. If you suspect that a strict schedule will make you break out in hives, you are doomed to academic failure.
10. To maximize your chances of study success, keep yourself in good health.

Completion Questions

1. If you are taking a 90-minute class, you should set aside _________ hour(s) to study.
2. Doing well in your studies has surprisingly little to do with your _________.
3. Only _________ can decide how to spend your time.
4. Learning time management skills is a matter of _________.
5. We all have _________: learn yours. Know when you've had enough studying and need to take a break.
6. One of the hardest things about planning your time is finding the right balance between doing what you *have* to do and doing what you _________ to do.
7. Get ready for work and school the night before to avoid early-morning _________.
8. It's not enough to make a study schedule; you also have to _________ it!
9. Figure on spending _________ minutes of study at a time.
10. Never endanger your mental or physical _________ to achieve your goals.

Multiple-Choice Questions

1. In general, figure on studying _________ for every hour of class time.
   (a) Two hours a day
   (b) One hour a day

   (c) 30 minutes a day
   (d) 15 minutes a day

2. If you work a 40-hour week, you should still have about how much time left over to devote to studying?
   (a) About 5 hours
   (b) About 7 hours
   (c) About 10 hours
   (d) About 20 hours
3. If you do not work at all, about how much time should you have left over to study after you have completed all your regular chores and fulfilled your normal responsibilities?
   (a) About 2 hours
   (b) About 10 hours
   (c) About 20 hours
   (d) About 60 hours
4. If you still don't have enough hours to get your studying done, you have all the following reasonable options *except*
   (a) Cutting your nonessential activities
   (b) Cutting your essential activities
   (c) Not studying
   (d) Using your time more wisely
5. To succeed in your studies and classwork, think about the
   (a) Conditions that help you succeed and make them a priority in your life
   (b) What goals other people have set for you
   (c) How you are similar to all other people
   (d) How difficult it will be for you to succeed
6. Recognizing your limitations involves all of the following *except*
   (a) Trying your hardest to succeed and believing in yourself
   (b) Understanding when you're not getting the material in class and need to seek extra help
   (c) Knowing which classes are hardest for you and will require extra effort
   (d) Seeing when you must hit the books or risk failing
7. A study schedule helps you achieve all of the following goals *except*
   (a) Making the most of your time
   (b) Getting into a study routine
   (c) Failing your classes
   (d) Keeping up with assignments
8. You'll get the most bang for your study buck by reviewing your notes immediately—

(a) During class
(b) Before and after the class
(c) Before class
(d) After class

9. To keep yourself healthy,
(a) Get regular exercise
(b) Eat a lot, but don't worry about achieving a food balance
(c) Don't get too much sleep because it will make you groggy
(d) Avoid seeing the doctor because there are too many germs in the office

10. For people in school or taking classes, two of the biggest time wasters are
(a) Sleeping and eating
(b) Studying and asking questions in class
(c) Reading and writing
(d) E-mail and the telephone

ANSWER KEY

True-False Questions

1. F 2. T 3. T 4. F 5. T 6. F 7. T 8. F 9. T 10. T

Completion Questions

1. Three 2. Intelligence 3. You 4. Setting priorities 5. Limits 6. Want
7. Panic 8. Follow or use 9. 50 to 90 10. Health

Multiple-Choice Questions

1. a 2. d 3. d 4. c 5. a 6. a 7. c 8. b 9. a 10. d

CHAPTER 4

Work to Your Strengths

You should read this chapter if you need to review or learn about

- The seven different types of intelligence
- Effective listening skills
- Study techniques for the learning disabled

In Chapter 3, we covered ways that you can make the most of your study time. In this chapter, we discuss different types of intelligence to determine how you learn best. We explore effective techniques to improve your listening skills, too. Finally, this chapter explores specific ways that learning disabled students can study more efficiently and effectively.

Get Started

We are all unique. We have different strengths, weaknesses, abilities, and needs. Therefore, it should be no surprise that we all learn in different ways. Identify your learning style(s) to make the most of your strengths and talents.

Understand the Seven Styles of Learning

- It seems like Iman is always humming, singing, and chanting. She can learn anything if she applies it to a tune. Otherwise, the information takes her much longer to retain. Information she learned by singing, however, goes in without any effort and seems to stay in her memory forever.
- Tracey is the class mediator, the one who resolves conflicts and makes friends with the new kid in class. But Tracey wonders if she would do better in class if she were less involved in relationships and more interested in her work.
- Jovita is a genuinely nice person, but she doesn't get along well with others. As a result, she finds it impossible to work in a group.
- Chanthay keeps up with a demanding schedule of two varsity sports and still makes time to be with his friends. He finds it much easier to study when he paces back and forth; in fact, he feels acutely uncomfortable when he's forced to sit for even short periods of time.
- Liz learned the alphabet when she was just a toddler and was reading by the time she was three. Liz is rarely without a book, but she just can't pass math—no matter how much she studies.
- Ryan loves math, puzzles, and sports. He finds it difficult to pay attention to other subjects, however. They bore him to tears.
- Chang-sun has always been curious. As a toddler, he loved looking for bugs, twigs, and unusual rocks. He's always taking things apart and putting them back to together. Unfortunately for his grades, it's like torture for him to complete worksheets and take-home tests.

Which one of these descriptions sounds like you? Perhaps more than one? If so, you're not alone!

In 1983, Howard Gardner wrote *Frames of Mind: The Theory of Multiple Intelligences,* questioning the traditional view of intelligence. Gardner postulated that intelligence is more than the math and verbal skills measured on IQ tests. Gardner described seven different types of intelligence:

- Auditory-musical learning
- Interpersonal learning

- Intrapersonal learning
- Kinesthetic learning
- Linguistic learning
- Logical-mathematical learning
- Spatial learning

Refer to Figure 4-1. Which style best describe your unique personality?

Research indicates that each type of intelligence is located in a different part of the brain. Because the different parts of the brain cooperate with each other, scientists believe that the seven types of learning interact with each other as well.

Most people have a combination of different "intelligences," often with one that is dominant. You may have noticed this dominance from your early school years. Perhaps you have seen your learning style emerge over time. Different environments encourage the development of specific intelligences. However, because of the emphasis on formal testing, schools tend to favor students who are strong in linguistic and logical-mathematical intelligences.

However, all learners have different learning styles as well as different abilities, and one size does *not* fit all. The same teaching method and study method are not effective with all students. Student performance improves markedly when learning styles are accommodated.

Learning Style	Characteristics
Auditory-musical	Is sensitive to music and nonverbal sounds; responds to rhythm and music; enjoys listening to music; likes to play music
Interpersonal	Understands other people and easily interprets their feelings and moods; organizes well; communicates easily and comfortably; socializes with skill and enjoyment; able to put people at ease
Intrapersonal	Prefers working alone to working in groups; intuitive; independent; private; self-motivated
Kinesthetic	Processes knowledge through bodily sensations; has excellent fine-motor coordination; communicates through body language more than words
Linguistic	Is verbal; thinks in words; has highly developed auditory skills; likes to read and write
Logical-mathematical	Thinks conceptually; capable of highly abstract thinking, logic, and reasoning
Spatial	Thinks in visual images and pictures; enjoys drawing, designing, building, inventing, daydreaming

Fig. 4-1 Characteristics of the seven learning styles.

Quick Tip

If you study in a group, try to study with people who *do not* share your learning styles. This will help you process the information in different ways.

Gardner's theories are now commonly used in many schools and textbooks. For example, if you were educated a decade or so ago, you may have been taught through a combination of lectures and blackboard work, now often called "chalk and talk." Today, however, students may be asked to act out a famous historical incident (tapping the strengths of kinesthetic learner), plot a graph of historical events (appealing to spatial learners), or lead a project team (designed for interpersonal learners.)

Tap *Your* Best Learning Style

In most college classes and professional certificate courses, little attempt is made to integrate different learning styles. Instead, most information is presented in lecture form. This is intentional. After all, lectures *are* the fastest way to get information across. Unfortunately, lectures are not the most effective teaching technique for students whose strength is not linguistic learning.

Everyone has at least two, and often even more, intelligences. You'll learn more quickly and easily if you follow these steps:

1. Identify your strongest intelligences. One intelligence is usually dominant, but not always. (About 60 percent of the population identify themselves as linguistic learners, but that's self-identification, so the actual number may be lower or higher.)
2. Find the learning techniques that match your strongest intelligences.
3. Experiment with different techniques until you find the ones that work best for you.
4. Be flexible. The learning techniques that work best in math may not work best in language classes, for example.

You can use Gardner's research to help you learn more effectively. Study Figure 4-2 to see which techniques work best for you.

Quick Tip

Be aware of the environment in which you learn best. Auditory-musical learners often retain more when they play music softly in the background; kinesthetic learners may remember more when they move around as they study. Pay attention to such factors as lighting, time of day, and physical setting to make the most of your study time.

If you are . . .	You will learn more easily by . . .
An auditory-musical learner	Setting information to music, tunes, and jingles Linking information to the mood of a musical piece Repeating the material as you study Tape-recording material and listening to it Having someone read to you Discussing facts with other people in a study group Studying with quiet music in the background Working in groups
An interpersonal learner	Studying with a partner Studying in a group
An intrapersonal learner	Studying alone Using any of the preceding techniques that work for you
A kinesthetic learner	Working with manipulatives such as models Moving around as you study Acting out concepts as you read and review them Pacing/walking as you study
A linguistic learner	Reading information as well as listening to it Restating/rewriting information in your own words Using color-coded notes and highlighted notes Using flash cards and other visual aids
A logical-mathematical learner	Reading the entire chapter first to get the overview Re-solving mathematical problems as you study Trying new ways of solving problems Looking at new ways of interpreting material Dividing processes into their steps or components Breaking big tasks into smaller steps
A spatial learner	Building models Sketching abstract concepts to make them specific Reading books that contain pictures, illustrations, charts, and diagrams Preparing your own concept maps from your notes Linking information on the same topic with the same-color highlighter

Fig. 4-2 Learn more by using your own specific learning styles.

Master Listening Skills

Once you have identified your specific intelligence(s), you can focus on adapting your learning environment and study skills to your strengths and on beefing up your other intelligences. However, no matter which intelligences you have, all learning and comprehension can be increased by good listening skills.

Just as there are different intelligences, so there are different kinds of listening: informational listening, evaluative listening, and empathic listening.

1. *Informational listening.* This is the type of listening you do in class when you're listening to a lecture or a group presentation or being asked questions. It's the primary kind of classroom listening. With this kind of listening, you gather as many facts as possible, focusing on accuracy of perception. Informational listening demands that you focus on specific details, distinguish between different pieces of information, and organize the information into a meaningful whole.

2. *Evaluative listening.* Here's where you weigh what has been said to see whether you agree with it. Start the process with informational listening to make sure that you have all the facts. When you are fairly sure that you understand the issues, you can then evaluate them and make decisions based on the facts, evidence, and speaker's credibility. This type of listening is most helpful when you are weighing information from a variety of different speakers. For example, you'll use evaluative listening when you listen to two speakers on the same topic who disagree with each other. It is a crucial listening skill for critical thinking, the essence of high-order thinking skills.

3. *Empathic listening.* This type of listening is to provide the speaker with emotional support to help him or her come to a decision, solve a problem, or resolve a situation. As a result, this type of listening focuses more on emotions than on reason or ethics. As an empathic listener, you can restate the issues, ask questions, and critically analyze the issues. Your intention here is not to make a decision for the speaker, however. Rather, it is to support the speaker in his or her own independent decision-making process. This type of listening occurs when you're offering support to a group member, for instance.

Banish Poor Listening Habits

Being able to listen well is an invaluable skill for students. Each of us has bad listening habits that can be overcome with training and practice. Here are three of the most common bad listening habits:

- *Selective listening* happens when we listen only to those parts of a message that directly concern us. For instance, during a class you may let your mind drift away until you hear your name, information about the homework, or facts about an upcoming test. You will be a better student if you listen to the entire message.
- *Pseudolistening* occurs when you only go through the motions of listening. You look as though you're listening, but your mind is miles away. When I see my students engage in

pseudolistening, I usually say: "Earth to student! Earth to student! Come back to this planet, please!" Correct pseudolistening by really focusing on what the speaker is saying so you know what is on the test and when it is being given.

- *Self-centered listening* means that you mentally rehearse your answer while another person is still speaking. It is focusing on your own response rather than on the speaker's words. This often happens in class when you're waiting for the teacher to finish talking so you can respond. As you wait, you tune out the teacher so you can concentrate on your response. Correct self-centered listening by letting the other person finish speaking before you begin to frame your answer.

Identify Learning Disabilities

If you have experienced prolonged difficulty in learning and retaining information, you may be suffering from a learning disorder. Here are some situations to consider.

Do you have problems . . .

- Stating something in an organized way?
- Following directions, particularly long sequences?
- Catching inferences and subtleties?
- Understanding jokes or sarcasm?
- Understanding abstract words or words with multiple meanings?
- Telling a story in sequence?

These are all common *language* problems for students with learning disabilities.

Do you have problems . . .

- Confusing *b* and *d* (such as reading *bog* for *dog*)?
- With the order of letters in words (such as reading *was* for *saw*)?
- Keeping your place on a page when reading, sometimes getting lost in the middle of a line or at the end of the line?
- Remembering common words taught from one day to the next (knowing them one day but not the next)?
- Trying to figure out a word you don't know?
- With reading in general?

These are all common *reading* problems for students with learning disabilities.

Do you have problems . . .

- Memorizing multiplication facts?
- Reversing two-place numbers (53 becomes 35, for example)?

- Understanding place value?
- Solving problems without counting on your fingers?
- Working problems in written symbolic form with paper and pencil?
- Solving math problems in daily life, such as figuring the percentage of a discount?
- Remembering the sequence of steps required to multiply or divide?
- Switching from one process to another, such as dividing and subtracting in long division?
- Solving problems in the right direction?

These are all common *math* problems for students with learning disabilities.

Students with certain kinds of learning disabilities may have problems organizing facts and concepts, predicting the consequences of their actions, categorizing objects, and transferring learning from one lesson to another.

Figure 4-3 shows the most common learning disorders. If you suspect that you have such a disorder, you should consider consulting a professional trained in diagnosing learning disorders. Most schools and colleges have psychologists on staff or can refer you to the appropriate professional for testing, assessment, and diagnosis.

Learning Disability	Definition
Attention-deficit/hyperactivity disorder	A sustained inability to focus on a subject. People with this ADHD find it very difficult to concentrate on the subject they're studying.
Aphasia	Inability to understand or express written or spoken language.
Distractibility	Being easily distracted and thrown off track.
Dyscalculia	Problems adding, subtracting, multiplying, etc.
Dysgraphia	Inability to express ideas in writing
Dyslexia	Partial or complete inability to read or to understand what you read silently or aloud.
Dysnomia	Difficulty finding the appropriate word for the situation.
Hyperactivity	Inappropriate increased activity.
Hypoactivity	Decreased activity.
Imperception	Inability of the central nervous system to organize sensory information.

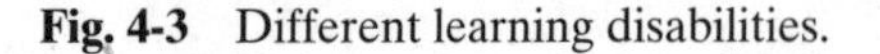

Fig. 4-3 Different learning disabilities.

Quick Tip

If you *do* have a learning disability, you're in distinguished company! The following people have been reported in the media as having learning disabilities. (There are no tests that accurately indicate their disabilities.)

Harry Belafonte	Julius Caesar	Cher
Winston Churchill	Tom Cruise	Leonardo da Vinci
Charles Darwin	Walt Disney	Thomas A. Edison
Albert Einstein	Whoopi Goldberg	Michelangelo
Napoleon	Pablo Picasso	Franklin D. Roosevelt
Anwar Sadat	Vincent van Gogh	George Washington

Strategies for Dealing with Learning Disabilities

The Americans with Disabilities Act (ADA) of 1990 guarantees persons with a disability fair and equal access to all public services, including education As a result, all high schools, colleges, and universities that receive federal funding are required to make accommodations and modifications based on diagnosed disabilities. *If you are learning disabled, you must actively seek the help that you are due by law.* No one will seek you out. Follow these steps:

1. Present yourself to the appropriate campus official. Every qualifying campus has one. The official will not look for you; you have to find him or her.
2. Present documentation of a disability. In some cases, it will be your testing and reports along with the Individualized Educational Plan (IEP) from high school. In other cases you have a private diagnosis. These reports must recommend the necessary accommodations/modifications needed to achieve class success.

The college or university is under no obligation to make modifications if you do not identify yourself. If you aren't certain what to do, seek a trained advocate.

Here are some modifications that can be arranged to help learning disabled students:

- Use of tape recorder, calculator, word processor, and dictionary in class
- Photocopies of professor's notes, a student volunteer note taker, enlarged print for worksheets/assignments
- Reduced number of items required in assignments/quizzes as long as the student has learned the objective

- Testing modifications (extended time, testing away from distractions, oral rather than written responses, alternative testing methods, additional directions)

The following general suggestions can help people with learning disabilities function more effectively in the classroom. These techniques can be used whether you're studying on your own or in a group.

- Sit up front and close to the instructor. Don't sit near a window. This will help reduce distractions so you can focus more easily.
- Use an assignment book to keep track of your work. Keep the book with you at all times and use it to track your assignments and homework.
- Use an expanding file folder instead of individual loose folders to keep loose papers, such as handouts.
- Enroll in a keyboarding/typing class. This will help you produce legible assignments as well as avail yourself of the online spellchecker and thesaurus.
- If you have access to a computer and you can work faster on a computer, ask your instructors if you can hand in all work printed out from a computer. This strategy is especially helpful for anyone with a written-language disability or who takes longer to write by hand.
- Use small electronic reminder devices to remember really important assignments or ideas.
- Tape your ideas onto a tape recorder, then type up, review, and edit.
- Use Post-its to jot down notes. Leave the notes sticking out of a book so you can find them again easily.
- Study during the day rather than at night.
- Ask your teachers for help when you need it. Go to the resource room, tutoring center, learning center, or writing center, for example.

Quick Tip

All the techniques for learning disabled students are effective for other students, as well. You may find these strategies especially useful if you are learning English as a second language, for example.

- ✔ There are seven different intelligences. Identify your specific intelligences so you can tailor your study techniques to your strength.
- ✔ Brush up on your listening skills.
- ✔ If you know that you have a learning disability or suspect that you do, get the help that you're entitled to by federal law. Adapt your study techniques as described in this chapter.

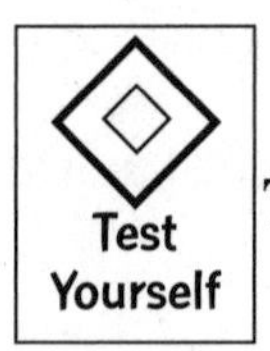

Questions

True-False Questions

1. No matter what our strengths, weaknesses, abilities, and needs, we all learn in basically the same way.
2. Identify your learning style(s) to make the most of your strengths and talents.
3. In 1983, Howard Gardner wrote *Frames of Mind: The Theory of Multiple Intelligences,* questioning the traditional view of intelligence.
4. Gardner described three different intelligences, including strengths in verbal and spatial skills.
5. If you think conceptually, Gardner would classify you as a logical-mathematical learner.
6. Most people have only one intelligence, because the different intelligences do not work together.
7. If you study in a group, try to study with people who *do not* share your learning styles.
8. Be flexible. The learning techniques that work best in math may not work best in language classes, for example.
9. If you are an intrapersonal learner, you are probably most comfortable studying in large groups.
10. Empathic listening is the type of listening you do in class when you're listening to a lecture or a group presentation or are being asked questions

Completion Questions

1. Gardner classified people who understand others and easily interprets their feelings and moods as _________ learners.
2. Linguistic learners study best through _________.
3. According to Gardner, _________ learners enjoy drawing, designing, building, inventing, and daydreaming.
4. _________ is the type of listening you do when you weigh what has been said to see whether you agree with it.
5. _________ demands that you focus on specific details, distinguish between different pieces of information, and organize the information into a meaningful whole.
6. _________ occurs when you only go through the motions of listening. You look like you're listening, but your mind is miles away.
7. Correct problems with _________ listening by letting the other person speak before you begin to frame your answer.
8. _________ is a type of learning disability characterized by a sustained inability to focus on a subject.

9. A law called _________ guarantees persons with a disability fair and equal access to all public services, including education.
10. If you are learning disabled, use an _________ to keep track of your work. Use it to track your assignments and homework.

Multiple-Choice Questions

1. Gardner postulated that intelligence is
   (a) One signal skill that everyone has
   (b) Easily tested and improved
   (c) More than the math and verbal skills that are measured on IQ tests
   (d) Never changing and unable to be improved or developed
2. Gardner described all the following types of intelligences *except*
   (a) Intrapersonal learning
   (b) Auditory-musical learning
   (c) Interpersonal learning
   (d) External-internal learning
3. Kinesthetic learners absorb knowledge most effectively when they
   (a) Study by themselves
   (b) Work with manipulatives such as models
   (c) Read and write
   (d) Sing softly to themselves
4. Because of the emphasis on formal testing, schools tend to favor students who are strong in
   (a) Kinesthetic intelligence
   (b) Interpersonal intelligence
   (c) Linguistic and logical-mathematical intelligences
   (d) Intrapersonal intelligence
5. All of the following are types of listening *except*
   (a) Sub-rosa listening
   (b) Informational listening
   (c) Evaluative listening
   (d) Empathic listening
6. What type of poor listening occurs when you listen only to those parts of a message that directly concern you?
   (a) Cautious listening
   (b) Self-centered listening
   (c) Pseudolistening
   (d) Selective listening

7. Students with certain kinds of learning disabilities may have problems with all of the following study situations *except*
   (a) Earning high scores on tests
   (b) Organizing facts and concepts
   (c) Predicting the consequences of their actions
   (d) Categorizing objects
8. Distractibility is a type of learning disability characterized by
   (a) Problems adding, subtracting, and multiplying
   (b) Inability to express ideas in writing
   (c) Being easily distracted and thrown off track
   (d) Inappropriate increased activity
9. If you are learning disabled and seeking testing modifications, you should
   (a) Seek out the help yourself by speaking with the appropriate campus official
   (b) Wait until you are contacted
   (c) First speak with your professor
   (d) Do nothing
10. If you are learning disabled, try to
    (a) Sit in the back of the room
    (b) Sit near a window
    (c) Never take notes; absorb as much information as you can from listening
    (d) Sit up front and close to the instructor

ANSWER KEY

True-False Questions

1. F 2. T 3. T 4. F 5. T 6. F 7. T 8. T 9. F 10. F

Completion Questions

1. Interpersonal 2. Reading and writing 3. Spatial 4. Evaluative listening 5. Informational listening 6. Pseudolistening 7. Self-centered 8. Attention-deficit/hyperactivity disorder 9. The Americans with Disabilities Act 10. Assignment book

Multiple-Choice Questions

1. c 2. d 3. b 4. c 5. a 6. d 7. a 8. c 9. a 10. d

CHAPTER 5

Notes from the Underground

You should read this chapter if you need to review or learn about

- Taking notes as direct quotations, summaries, and paraphrases
- Different note-taking techniques
- Making useful study outlines

In Chapter 4, you learned all about the seven types of intelligence to determine how you learn best. Now you will find out how to take complete and useful study notes. You will first learn all about copying information verbatim, summarizing, and paraphrasing. Then you will explore different note-taking layouts to find the ones that are best for you.

Get Started

There are different ways to take notes. Discover the formats and structures that work best for each subject, your level of expertise, and your personal learning style.

The Three Big Rules for Great Notes

No one can remember all the material they read or hear during a lecture. That's why you need to take notes. Taking good notes helps you remember what you read and reinforces what you learned. Good notes also serve as a study guide to help you get top grades on tests.

There are three main ways to take notes: *writing direct quotations, summarizing,* and *paraphrasing.* Each is explained in detail in this chapter. Regardless of the methods you use, the overall techniques remain the same.

Here are the three basic guidelines.

1. Keep your notes short. If you write too much, you'll be right back where you started—trying to separate essential from nonessential information. Try these methods:

- Write sentence fragments rather than complete sentences.
- Use abbreviations to save space and time. For example,

  + or & = and
  b/c = because
  w/ = with

- Use sketches, charts, and lists to separate the important facts from the minor details.

2. Be sure to mark direct quotes with quotation marks. This can help you distinguish between your own words and the writer's or instructor's words.

3. Check and double-check your notes. Be sure that you have spelled all names correctly and copied dates correctly. Check that you have spelled the easy words correctly, too; many errors creep in because writers overlook the obvious words.

Noting Direct Quotations

A *direct quotation* is word-for-word copying, exactly as the material appears in the source. If there is an error in the source, you even copy that, writing [*sic*] next to the mistake. Show that a note is a direct quotation by surrounding it with quotation marks (" ")

What should you quote?

- Quote key points—passages that sum up the main idea in a pithy way.
- Quote subtle ideas. Look for passages whose meaning would be watered down or lost if you summarized or paraphrased them.
- Quote powerful writing. If the passage is memorable or famous, it will give your test paper authority.

Here's a sample to use as a model:

Quick Tip

In general, quote briefly when you take notes. Remember that long quotations are difficult to remember and memorize.

Topic: Nez Percé surrender

"It is cold, and we have no blankets; the little children are freezing to death. My people, some of them, have run away to the hills, and have no blankets, no food. No one knows where they are—perhaps freezing to death. I want to have time to look for my children, to see how many of them I can find. Maybe I shall find them among the dead. Hear me, my chiefs! I am tired; my heart is sick and sad. From where the sun now stands I will fight no more forever."

Comments: Very moving, emotional speech. Shows tragic consequences of displacement of Native Americans.

Lend Me Your Ears: Great Speeches in History, p. 108.

Summarizing

A *summary* is a smaller version of the original, reducing the passage to its essential meaning. Be sure to summarize carefully to avoid distorting the meaning of the original passage. What should you summarize?

- Background information
- Commentaries
- Explanations
- Evaluations
- A writer's or speaker's line of thinking or argument

When you summarize, write only the key information. Look for the following elements:

- The main idea
- Important names, dates, numbers
- Key details
- Any questions you have about the material

To find the key information, listen or read for word clues, such as *the most important reason, the main point,* or *this will be on the test.* Instructors and writers often repeat vital facts in different ways, so watch for repetition. Pay special attention at the very beginning and end of a lecture, when an instructor often introduces and summarizes the main points. The same is true in a reading. Here's a sample summary to use as a model:

Original

Topic: Clarence Darrow against capital punishment

"Now, why am I opposed to capital punishment? It is too horrible a thing for the state to undertake. We are told by my friend, 'Oh, the killer does it; why shouldn't the state?' I would hate to live in a state that I didn't think was better than a murderer.

But I told you the real reason. The people of a state kill a man because he killed someone else—that is all—without the slightest logic, without the slightest application to life, simply from anger, nothing else!

I am against it because I believe it is inhuman, because I believe that as the hearts of men have softened they have gradually gotten rid of brutal punishment, because I believe it will only be a few years until it will be banished forever from every civilized country—even New York—because I believe that it has no effect whatever to stop murder."

Lend Me Your Ears: Great Speeches in History, p. 108.

Summary

Topic: Clarence Darrow against capital punishment

Rage and a desire for retribution are not sufficient justification for capital punishment. It is a cruel, inhuman, and uncivilized form of punishment. Further, capital punishment does nothing to deter crime. For these reasons, he believes capital punishment will soon be eliminated, even in NY.

Comments: Original speech has an ironic, sarcastic tone.

Lend Me Your Ears: Great Speeches in History, p. 108.

Paraphrasing

A *paraphrase* is a restatement of the writer's original words. It often includes examples and explanations from the original source. A paraphrase may be longer than the original, shorter than the original, or the same length as the original. You may paraphrase information that is important but too long to write in the original form.

Here's a sample to use as a model:

Original

Topic: Social responsibility (JFK inauguration speech)

"In the long history of the world, only a few generations have been granted the role of defending freedom in its hour of maximum danger. I do not shrink from that responsibility—I welcome it. I do not believe that any of us would exchange places with any other people or any other generation. The energy, the faith, the devotion which we bring to this endeavor will light our country and all who serve it—and the glow from that fire can truly light the world.

And so, my fellow Americans, ask not what your country can do for you—ask what you can do for your country."

Lend Me Your Ears: Great Speeches in History, p. 811.

Paraphrase

Topic: social responsibility (JFK inauguration speech)

America faces great peril. As a result, America is now faced with the challenge of standing up for liberty. Not many countries have ever been in this position. Kennedy welcomes this challenge because he believes his actions (and America's valiant response) can stand as a beacon for the rest of the world to follow.

"And so, my fellow Americans, ask not what your country can do for you—ask what you can do for your country."

Comments: A very famous and stirring speech. Famous quote.

Lend Me Your Ears: Great Speeches in History, p. 811.

How Much Is Enough?

Taking effective notes is a delicate balance between writing too much and writing too little. This isn't as crucial when it comes to taking notes from a reading, because you can always return to the text and correct any problems with your notes. In these instances, you add what you missed and cross out what you repeated.

However, when it comes to a classroom lecture, it's important that you get it right the first time because there's no second act. If the instructor agrees, you can always bring a tape recorder to class and tape the lecture. *Always* get the instructor's permission before you tape a lecture. I'm not a fan of tape-recording lectures because I find that my students tend to zone out and not pay attention when they're recording. Then they find it very tedious to listen to the entire lecture again, so they usually don't. They feel as if they're doing the same work twice—and they are. That said, if you think taping lectures would be helpful, get permission and go for it. In any event, you are still going to have to take notes.

Following is an example of a lecture on the human skeleton and effective notes on it. Read the margin notes to see the justification for each note.

Lecture

Important numbers

As babies we start off with about 300 bones in our skeleton, but some bones join together as we grow. There are 206 separate bones in an adult's body.

Main idea

Key detail

Have you ever wondered why we need a skeleton? One important reason concerns our muscles and internal organs. They are very soft and need protection. Some organs need more protection than others. For instance, our brain and spinal cord are protected by the skull and spine.

Key detail	The heart, liver, lungs, and intestines are all easily damaged, so they are protected by ribs, hip bones, and our spine.
Main idea	Skeletons also help us stand up. Without a skeleton, we would slump into a heap. Our muscles are strong, but without a skeleton we wouldn't have anything to pull against and we would be unable to stand up or move.

Notes

Skeleton	*300 bones in child, 206 bones in adult because bones fuse.* *—Protects muscles and internal organs* *—Enables us to stand and move* *—Skull and spine protect brain and spinal cord* *—Ribs, hip bones, and spine protect heart, liver, lungs, intestines*

Top Five Note-Taking Techniques

There are different ways that you can take notes. As we have discussed, the method you select depends on the subject, how much you know about it, and your personal style. For example, spatial learners often find it very helpful to take notes as charts, graphs, and other visuals. Try each of the following methods to see which ones work for you.

1. *Divided-page format.* Fold your paper in half vertically to create a narrow column and a wide one. The left column should be about an inch and a half wide; the right column, seven inches wide. Write your notes in the wide right column. Write key words and ideas in the narrow left column. You can add additional material to the narrow left column as you review and study your notes. This method makes it easier to call out important facts and ideas.

2. *Webbing.* As you read a text or listen to a lecture, isolate the key idea. Write it in the middle of a sheet of paper. Add lines radiating out from the circle. At the end of each line, draw a circle and fill it in with a subtopic. Figure 5-1 shows a sample web based on a lecture about the Congressional Medal of Honor.

When you create webs, be sure to leave yourself enough room. Write only key words. Webs are great ways to take notes because they help you to write only the essential information. This makes it much easier to study later.

Quick Tip

The web method of note taking works best with well-written textbooks and speakers whose lectures are well organized. This method won't work as well when the lecturer is poorly organized because it will be much more difficult to find the main idea and supporting details.

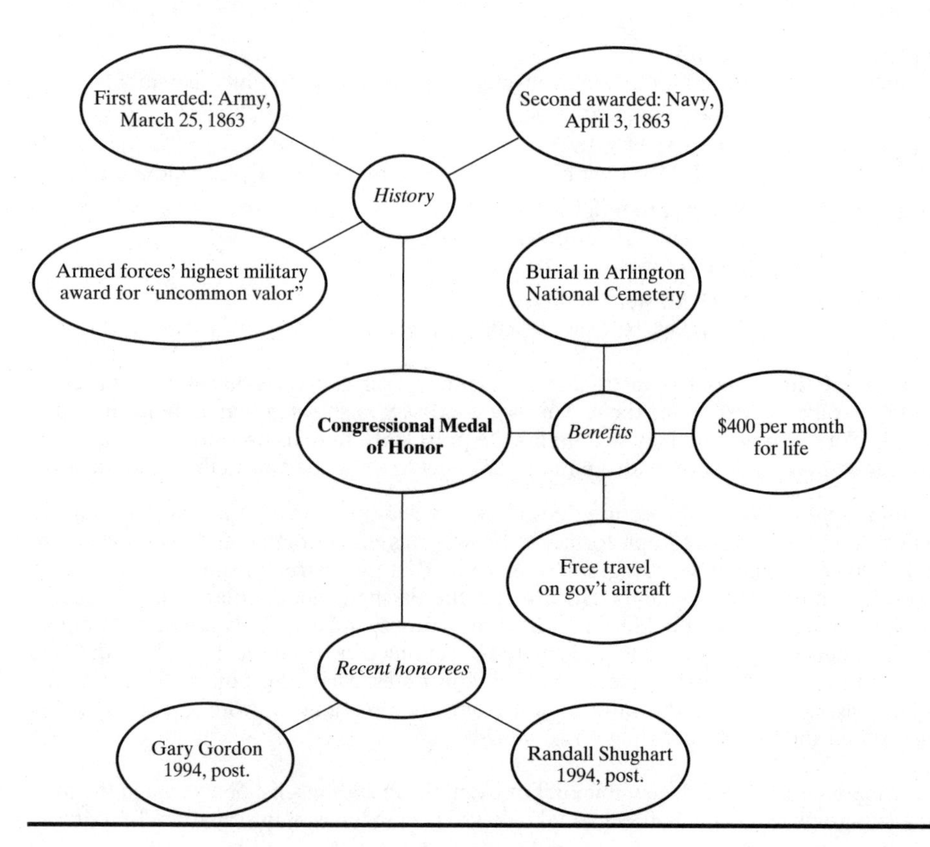

Fig. 5-1 Example of webbing method of note taking.

3. *Visuals.* Webs aren't the only graphic organizers you can use to take notes. Create pictures and diagrams to show the relationship between ideas, as well. Draw any illustrations that help make the process clear. For example, you can use arrows to create a flowchart that illustrates the process of language acquisition, as follows:

Pidgin →	pidgin speakers have children →	a creole
(makeshift jargon)	(consistent word order, affixes, tenses, complex sentence structures)	

You might arrange your notes in chart form, as the following chart on the topic of the Congressional Medal of Honor shows:

Subtopics	**Details**
Significance	Given for actions above and beyond the call of duty in combat
History	Army: March 25, 1863 Navy: April 3, 1863 April 1991: First black soldier honored (Army Cpl. Freddie Stowers)
Benefits	$400 per month for life Burial in Arlington National Cemetery Free travel on gov't aircraft
Recent honorees	1994: Master Sgt. Gary Gordon 1994: Sgt. 1st Class Randall Shughart

4. *Lists.* If the textbook or instructor is presenting a series of facts that all have the same importance, you may wish to list them. This is a good way of showing that all items have the same rank. For example, you may wish to list the presidents, famous inventors, or a series of math theories. Start each entry with a number or bullet to set it apart from the other entries.

5. *Paragraphs.* When the lecture doesn't have a clear method of organization, consider arranging your notes in paragraph form. Try to write as many fragments (incomplete sentences) as you can to keep the paragraphs easy to read. If the instructor speaks very quickly, you'll be forced to write fragments. However, if the pacing is good, you can include some complete sentences for exact definitions, direct quotations, and especially important points.

Skip lines between paragraphs to indicate the beginning of a new topic. If you get confused or lose the thread of the lecture, leave space in your notes. That way, you can return to the confusing passage and add the information from your reading or from speaking to the instructor after the lecture or during office hours.

These methods can easily be combined. For example, including a list or a visual in the middle of a paragraph can make it easier to take down specific types of information. In a similar way, adding a quick drawing can help you illustrate a key point.

Quick Tip

If you keyboard faster than you handwrite (and many of us do!), consider bringing a laptop to class and using it as you take notes. Of course, you can always keyboard notes you take from a reading. Keyboarding also has the advantage of making your notes easier to read.

Outline and Highlight

Outlining is such a useful method of note taking that it deserves its own discussion. Many students find it especially effective to take notes in outline form because it helps them arrange and categorize information.

When you make an outline, you're not just blankly recording facts; rather, you're actively thinking about the message that you're hearing or reading. Therefore, outlining can be an invaluable way of fixing the information in your mind because it forces you to engage with the content.

After you create the outline, go back over it and highlight the most important information. Here is a general outline format you can use as you take notes.

Title: ______________________________

I. First main idea ______________________

____

A. Detail ______________________

1. Reason or example ______________

a. Detail ______________

b. Detail ______________

2. Reason or example ______________

a. Detail ______________

b. Detail ______________

B. Detail ______________________

1. Reason or example ______________

a. Detail ______________

b. Detail ______________

2. Reason or example ______________

a. Detail ______________

b. Detail ______________

II. Second main idea ______________________

____

A. Detail ______________________

1. Reason or example ______________

a. Detail ______________

b. Detail ______________

2. Reason or example ______________________________
    a. Detail ______________________________
    b. Detail ______________________________

B. Detail ______________________________
1. Reason or example ______________________________
    a. Detail ______________________________
    b. Detail ______________________________
2. Reason or example ______________________________
    a. Detail ______________________________
    b. Detail ______________________________

Regardless of the note-taking methods you use, consider the following ways to make your notes easier to read:

Quick Tip

Your notes will be useless unless you can read them! Be sure to write or print clearly.

- *Use different colors.* Consider setting off important information in a different color. For example, when you are taking notes from a book, you may wish to write all headings in red and the rest of the page in blue or black. This makes the headings stand out.
- *Highlight key sections.* Go back over your notes with a yellow or green highlighter and set off key points. This makes them pop right off the page. Just the act of highlighting helps fix the information in your mind, but when you go back over your notes later, you'll know which information is most important to study. If you find that highlighting works well for you, take notes on only one side of the page, as the highlighter has a tendency to bleed through to the back of the page.
- *Add graphic signals.* Use arrows, stars, and underlining to indicate important points in your notes. You can add these while you're taking notes or during a review session.

Tips for Students with Learning Disabilities

The following suggestions will work for all students, but they are likely to be especially helpful for students who have learning disabilities. If you fall into this category, try each of these techniques to see which ones prove most effective for you.

- When you take notes, divide your paper in half and write "Topics" on left side and "Details" on right side. This helps you categorize and arrange information logically.

Quick Tip

Always copy down everything an instructor writes on the board. If it's on the board, you can assume it's important.

- Use a piece of carbon paper between pages so you always have a second copy of the notes you've taken. Notes have a way of getting misplaced.
- Ask if you can use a tape recorder to record the instructor's lecture. That way, if you find your attention wandering, you will still be able to review the complete material later.
- Create note cards out of index cards. Write a heading and then write details. The small space on note cards helps you limit what you write, forcing you to find the key information.
- Write down all words in bold print on note cards and their definitions. Review several note cards daily to fix the information in your mind.
- Ask your instructors for help when you need it. Don't be a stranger.

✔ There are many ways to take good notes. Select the methods that work best for your specific learning styles, the subject matter, and your degree of familiarity with it.

✔ You can take notes by writing down direct quotations, by summarizing, or by paraphrasing.

Try taking notes in the divided-page format, webbing, visuals, lists, paragraphs, and outlines.

Regardless of the note-taking methods you use, use different colors, highlighting, and graphic signals to make your notes easier to read.

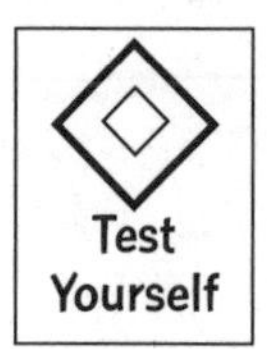

QUESTIONS

True-False Questions

1. There is basically only one way to take good notes.
2. People need to take notes because nobody can remember all the material they read or hear during a lecture. Taking notes also helps you focus in on the key information you need.
3. When you take notes, write sentence fragments rather than complete sentences.
4. If you are taking notes and a direct quotation contains an error, correct the error. That way, you will not have an error in your notes.

5. Be sure to summarize carefully so you don't distort the meaning of the original passage.
6. Paraphrase information that is important but too short to write in the original form.
7. Taking effective notes is a delicate balance between writing too much and writing too little.
8. Webs are great ways to take notes because they help you to write only the essential information.
9. When the lecture doesn't have a clear method of organization, consider arranging your notes in web form.
10. If you get confused or lose the thread of the lecture, just keep writing. Do not leave space in your notes.

Completion Questions

1. Good notes also serve as a _________ that helps you get top grades on tests.
2. There are three main ways to take notes: writing direct quotations, summarizing, and _________.
3. Keep your notes _________. If you write too much, you'll be right back where you started—trying to separate essential from the nonessential information.
4. Use _________ to save space and time. For example, use + or & instead of *and.*
5. A _________ is word-for-word copying, exactly as the material appears in the source.
6. A _________ is a smaller version of the original, reducing the passage to its essential meaning.
7. To find the key information, listen or read for _________ such as *the most important reason, the main point,* or *this will be on the test.*
8. A _________ is a restatement of the writer's original words. It often includes examples and explanations from the original source.
9. The web method of note taking works best with well-written textbooks and speakers whose lectures are _________.
10. Create pictures and diagrams to show the relationship between _________.

Multiple-Choice Questions

1. Select the note-taking techniques you use based on all the following *except*
   (a) The subject
   (b) Your level of expertise in it
   (c) Your personal learning style
   (d) What the instructor prefers

2. Quote all of the following information *except*
   (a) Key points
   (b) Long passages
   (c) Subtle ideas
   (d) Examples of powerful writing
3. When should you pay special attention during a lecture to catch key points?
   (a) In the beginning
   (b) In the end
   (c) In the middle
   (d) At the beginning and end
4. A paraphrase is always
   (a) Shorter than the original source
   (b) Longer than the original source
   (c) The length that best suits the material
   (d) The same length as the original source
5. Before you tape record a lecture,
   (a) You don't have to do anything special
   (b) Reread the textbook
   (c) Always get the instructor's permission
   (d) Speak to a classmate to review the material
6. Visual notes include all the following *except*
   (a) Pictures
   (b) Paragraphs
   (c) Webs
   (d) Diagrams
7. To show that all items in your notes are the same rank, you should
   (a) Write them verbatim
   (b) Directly quote them
   (c) Write them in a paragraph
   (d) List them
8. When you make an outline, you are
   (a) Actively thinking about the information you are hearing or reading
   (b) Simply recording facts
   (c) Writing as much as you can
   (d) Arranging the information from most to least important
9. You can make your notes easier to read by
   (a) Writing them early in the day

(b) Writing them quickly
(c) Using different colors and highlighting important passages
(d) Handwriting them rather than keyboarding them

10. If you have a learning disability,
(a) Tape-record all lectures rather than trying to take notes
(b) Have someone else take notes for you
(c) Stick to only one method of note taking
(d) Try special techniques to find the ones that work best for you

ANSWER KEY

True-False Questions

1. F 2. T 3. T 4. F 5. T 6. F 7. T 8. T 9. F 10. F

Completion Questions

1. Study guide 2. Paraphrasing 3. Short or brief 4. Abbreviations 5. Direct quotation 6. Summary 7. Word clues 8. Paraphrase 9. Well-organized 10. Ideas

Multiple-Choice Questions

1. a 2. b 3. d 4. c 5. c 6. b 7. d 8. a 9. c 10. d

CHAPTER 6

Improve Your Memory

You should read this chapter if you need to review or learn about

- How memory works
- Ways to improve your memory so you recall what you studied
- Using mnemonics as a memory aid

In Chapter 5, you learned how to take useful notes and make good outlines. Now you will learn how to sharpen your memory so you remember what you studied.

Get Started

Many people find they can't remember information they need for tests. However, even students with good memories can benefit from learning how to remember more of what they studied. A good memory is an invaluable tool for study and test success.

How Memory Works

Have any of the following memory glitches ever happened to you?

- You try to memorize information but find your mind wandering. You spend hours staring at the book, but few facts stick.
- You memorize information but garble it on the test.
- You can remember some types of information but not other types.
- You study something, think you've got it down pat, but go blank when you take the test.
- You learn what you need for the test, but you forget it right after the test. Then you have to memorize it all over again for the midterm or final exam.

If so, you're not alone! Memorization is a vital part of the study process. Every successful student has figured out ways to retain more of what they learn. "Not me," you say. "I have always had a bad memory." There's nothing wrong with your memory! A memory is not a physical trait like flatfeet or weak ankles. Memorization is a skill, like hitting a home run or riding a bicycle. You can improve your memory, just as you can improve any other skill. Start by learning about memory.

The memory process has three steps:

1. Learning
2. Storing
3. Recalling

Most people find that their memories work this way:

Easiest to remember	Pictures
↓	Words
Most difficult to remember	Numbers

To remember a fact, it's not enough to learn it; you must be able to store it in your brain so that you can recall it at will. You have to be able to retrieve the memory when you need it for a test or other assessment.

There are two basic types of memory:

- *Short-term memory,* which lasts about half a minute
- *Long-term memory,* which lasts for a long period of time, as long as decades

New information automatically goes into the short-term memory buffer without any effort on your part. For example, if you decide to take four items out of the refrigerator, you'll remember what you need just until the chore is done. Then the memory gets erased because you no longer need it. Your brain has made a conscious choice to dump the information.

When you study, however, you want to lock information into your long-term memory. To do so, you have to make a deliberate effort to remember it. That's where memory techniques come into play.

Psych Yourself into Success

Just as you can psych yourself into failure, you can psych yourself into success. It's especially important to take a positive attitude when it comes to memory. *Believe* that you have an excellent memory and that you can succeed by using the memory techniques explained in the rest of this chapter.

Because most so-called memory problems are a result of distraction, lack of interest, lack of attention, and poor organization, follow these steps to improve your retention immediately:

- *Minimize distraction.* Memorize material in a quiet place, such as your bedroom, an unused corner of the house, or a very quiet section of the library. Close the door. Turn off the stereo and the television. Switch off your beeper. Don't answer the phone. You may be able to study while listening to music, but it is far more difficult to memorize in a noisy setting.
- *Get interested in the text.* Many things you have to memorize are boring. That's the truth. Don't lie to yourself, but don't fight it. You know that you have to memorize the material even if it is boring. Focus on some aspect that you find interesting and let yourself enjoy it. The more you fight the material, the harder it will be to memorize and retain.
- *Stay focused on the text.* The average adult has an attention span of 10 to 30 minutes; therefore, break the time you spend memorizing into chunks of no more than half an hour each. If you find sitting that long a chore, bribe yourself with little treats. For example, promise yourself a 10-minute break after each half hour of memorization.
- *Beef up your organizational skills.* Be sure that you have all the material you need to memorize the facts at hand: your textbooks, articles, printouts, and so forth. Set aside enough time to really memorize the facts you need so you're not trying to cram in a lot of information at the last minute. Cramming while you memorize is a recipe for disaster.

Memorize the most difficult or most important information during your "prime" time. For example, if you are a morning person, tackle memorization right after breakfast (always eat breakfast!). If you find your attention span is longer and sharper at night, save memorization for then. If you're not sure when you're at your peak, spread your reading and memorizing throughout the day. No matter when you are most alert, you are always better off breaking your memorizing into short periods to increase your recall.

Six Simple Steps to a Better Memory

The true art of memory is the art of attention.
—Samuel Johnson

You've just learned that good memory skills require a desire to improve. Now we'll turn to proven memory tactics. You won't be able to use every strategy in this chapter, but you don't have to. Instead, discover which strategies you like and understand. Use these strategies as often as possible. When it comes to memory, practice *does* make perfect.

Quick Tip

The two biggest inhibitors of memory are stress and attitude, so minimize physical and mental stress as much as possible. You've already learned the importance of adopting a positive attitude.

Following are my six simple steps to a better memory. I'll introduce the steps here and explain them in subsequent sections.

1. Understand it.
2. Associate it.
3. Visualize it.
4. Use mnemonics.
5. Review it.
6. Use it or lose it.

Understand What You're Memorizing

Don't confuse *memorizing* information with *learning* it. Study these equations:

Memorizing information ≠ understanding information

Understanding information = remembering information + knowing what it means + knowing how to use it

You can memorize great piles of information and not have a clue how it applies in context. Obviously, this isn't going to do you any good when test time comes. Merely spouting back reams of facts isn't going to get you the grade you want. Nor will it help you understand what you are supposed to be learning.

There is a common fallacy that memory is a mechanical process. It's often called *rote learning,* or learning by heart. But fixing something firmly in your mind is only one part of memory. Memory is also recalling and connecting meaningful ideas in a meaningful way. When you memorize, you remember material that you understand and have thought about. You can never memorize a lesson that you don't truly understand.

Always begin by understanding the material. To get the most understanding from a text, follow these three steps:

1. *Organize the material in a logical way.* Information that is arranged in a sensible way is *always* easier to memorize than material that is disorganized. Never assume that a text is

clear or that a teacher has given well-organized notes. Even if you're lucky and the material is already logically arranged, you can rearrange it in another format that makes more sense to you. Always be sure that you have retained the original meaning, however. Here are some logical ways to organize material:

- Alphabetical order
- Cause and effect
- Grouping similar items
- Least to most important
- Most to least important
- Numerical order
- Order of importance
- Problem-solution format
- Time order

Select the method that makes the most sense to you and best fits the context. For example, if you're memorizing information about the Vietnam War, consider time order; if you're memorizing math theorems, try the problem-solution format.

2. *Restate what you read in your own words.* Paraphrase or summarize it. Say your paraphrase or summary aloud or write it down.

3. *Get help.* Clarify any problems instead of soldiering on. Check a reference text such as an encyclopedia, almanac, or dictionary. Contact a classmate for an explanation. Ask the teacher or professor for further information.

Quick Tip

Always memorize information in small pieces, because your brain can retain only about a half dozen pieces of information at one time. If you try to learn more than seven pieces of information at a time, some will get forgotten before you can lock it in your long-term memory.

Associate Information to Memorize It

Tying new information to what you already know can help you make information stick. You can do this using *association.*

Association helps you link something you are trying to remember to an image or situation you already know and can easily picture. You make associations all the time without thinking about them. For example, the locker combination 369 is easy to remember because you associate it with multiples of 3. By connecting new ideas to what you already know, you're giving your brain a way to retain the information. For example, if you know that *either* is spelled *ei* rather than *ie,* you can use this to learn that *neither* follows the same pattern.

Objects can be associated in many different ways. Here are some examples:

- Having the same smell, shape, or feeling
- Having a similar smell, shape, or feeling
- Being placed on top of each other
- Crashing into each other
- Merging together
- Wrapping around each other
- Rotating around each other or dancing together

For instance, children are taught new letters and words by linking them with information they already know. The teacher shows children an A and an apple. The children associate the two, which helps them remember that *apple* begins with the letter *a.*

Quick Tip

What happens if you can't come up with a logical association? Don't worry. Any association at all will work. In fact, the more absurd an association, the easier it usually is to remember.

There are several different ways to associate objects and ideas to improve your memory. Here are two of the most useful techniques built on association.

1. *The peg system.* This method is best used for remembering ordered lists of terms. To use this technique, peg, or associate, a new idea with a word. Then link the pegged words together in a chain of events to help you remember the items in the list.

For example, say you have to memorize the following list of countries: Afghanistan-Cuba-China-Argentina. To memorize them, you might imagine an afghan (Afghanistan) on the bed that Castro (Cuba) naps on; then Castro picks up a china plate (China) and sings a song from *Evita* (Argentina). Associating these ideas can help you remember the new information.

2. *The room system.* Also known as the loci (Latin for "place") method, the room system was developed by Roman orators who needed to memorize long speeches. These toastmasters would select a familiar building or forum and set aside a number of spots, or loci, to remind them of parts of their speech. These speakers realized that people tend to remember more when they can key the study context (the physical location) to the text.

Say that you have to remember quotes from a Shakespearean play. You are going to be asked not only to explain the quotes but also to identify the act in which they appear. To remember the information in each act of a play, read each act in a different room, or just imagine that you are doing so. For example, read act 1 in the cafeteria, act 2 on the bus, act 3 in the kitchen, act 4 in the park, and act 5 in the common room. On the exam, when you see each quote, you'll remember where you were sitting when you first read it. This will help you remember in which act each quote appears.

Use Visualization to Improve Your Memory

As you memorize new information, form a mental picture of a person, place, thing, or idea. Do this by imagining how it looks, smells, sounds, tastes, or feels. The more vividly you can create that mental image and the more personal you make it, the more likely you will be to recall what you need to know.

Preparing for a standardized test, for example, you might need to remember as many word definitions as possible. To remember that *phobia* means "fear of," you might visualize Frankenstein. Add an association to this: the *F* in *Frankenstein* links to the *f* sound in *phobia.*

Create pictures, maps, diagrams, cartoons, and charts. Draw pictures or cartoon characters, graphs, tables, charts, timelines, and so on to aid memory. Even simple stick figures and drawings are useful if you are a visual learner. Pay attention to pictures and charts in textbooks.

As you visualize, use all your senses. Use your body, too. You'll remember 90 percent of what you do, 75 percent of what you see, and 20 percent of what you hear if you tap kinesthetic memory. Make it physical. Adding a physical activity such as pacing, jumping, throwing a ball, or writing enhances the specific memory for many people. Singing works great, too. Songs stick in our minds because of their strong rhythm. Set important facts such as state capitals, presidents, and science facts to songs to help fix them in your mind.

Quick Tip

Are there any shortcuts to a good memory? Some people claim that the herbal extract Ginkgo biloba is a memory booster. Others claim that bananas and vitamins E, C, and choline can increase your memory. I suggest sticking with the tried-and-true memory-boosting techniques in this chapter rather than relying on unproven shortcuts.

Improve Your Memory with Mnemonics

Mnemonics (neh-*mon*-iks) are memory tricks that help you by using cues that are visual, linear, or auditory. It's a big word but an easy and effective concept. Mnemonics are little devices that jog your mind, including the following:

- Acronyms
- Acrostics
- Jingles
- Mind maps
- Sayings
- Songs

You're already using mnemonics in your daily life. To adjust your clock for daylight saving time, you use the mnemonic "spring ahead, fall back" to remember to set the clock ahead an hour in the spring and back an hour in the fall. To remember how to identify poison ivy, you use this mnemonic: "Leaves of three, let it be; berries white, take flight!" To remember how many days in each month, you repeat this mnemonic: "Thirty days hath September, April, June, and November. All the rest have 31 (except for February which has 28)." And everyone knows this famous mnemonic used to spell words that contain *ie* and *ei:*

> *I* before *E,* except after *C*
> or when sounded like *A*
> as in *neighbor* and *weigh*

Figure 6-1 lists some common and useful words that fit this rule.

I* before *e	**Except after *c***	**Sounded as *a***
Achieve	Ceiling	Freight
Believe	Conceit	Neighbor
Chief	Conceive	Reign
Fierce	Deceit	Sleigh
Fiend	Deceive	Vein
Grief	Perceive	Weigh
Piece	Receipt	Weight
Relief	Receive	
Siege		
Shriek		

Fig. 6-1 Words that contain *ie* and *ei.*

Now let's explore the different types of mnemonics in greater detail. Study Figure 6-2.

As you memorize information, choose and create the mnemonics that best stick in your mind. Here are some factors to consider as you use mnemonics:

- *The specific information you are memorizing.* Some information lends itself better to certain types of mnemonics. For example, consider using acronyms for only a few facts (such

<table>
<tr><th>Mnemonic</th><th>Definition</th><th>Example</th></tr>
<tr><td>Acronyms</td><td>Each letter in the word represents the first letter of a fact you need to memorize</td><td>FACE
(spaces on the musical scale: FACE)</td></tr>
<tr><td>Acrostics</td><td>Create a sentence using the first letter of each word</td><td>Every Good Boy Does Fine (lines on the musical scale: EGBDF)</td></tr>
<tr><td>Jingles</td><td>Set information to a quick song</td><td>In 1492, Columbus sailed the ocean blue</td></tr>
<tr><td>Mind maps</td><td>Visuals such as webs or diagrams</td><td>Rosetta stone's languages
| | |
Demotic→Greek→hieroglyphics</td></tr>
<tr><td>Sayings</td><td>Create a saying or adapt an existing one</td><td>"What's up, DOC?" denotes the order of the phases of the moon by the shape of the letters:
D Waxing half-moon with the curve on the right
O Full moon
C Waning crescent moon with the curve on the left, heading toward a new moon</td></tr>
<tr><td>Songs</td><td>Set information to a tune</td><td>"The Alphabet Song"</td></tr>
</table>

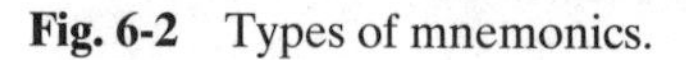

Fig. 6-2 Types of mnemonics.

as the continents or the Great Lakes), but use songs for a great deal of information (such as all the kings and queens of England).

- *Your level of prior knowledge.* The more you know, the easier the mnemonic can be, since it will be easier for you to link the information with what you already know.

Figures 6-3 and 6-4 list additional academic mnemonics. See how many of these common, useful academic mnemonics you know.

Quick Tip

Pluto is technically slightly closer to the sun than Neptune, but for 238 years of Pluto's 248-year orbit, little Pluto is the ninth planet.

Mnemonic	Stands For
Please Excuse My Dear Aunt Sally	Order of operations in solving a math equation: parentheses, exponents, multiplication, division, addition, subtraction
Sohcahtoa	Order in which to divide the legs of triangles: soh = sine cah = cosine toa = tangent
Lucy Can't Drink Milk	Roman numerals: LCDM (50, 100, 500, 1000)
Toronto Girls Can Flirt And Only Quit To Chase Dwarves	Hardness scale for minerals: talc, gypsum, calcite, flurite, appetite, orthoclase, quartz, topaz, corumdum, diamond
Camels Often Sit Down Carefully; Perhaps Their Joints Creak; Persistent Early Oiling Might Prevent Permanent Rheumatism	Geological time periods, oldest to present: Cambrian, Ordovician, Silurian, Devonian, Carboniferous, Permian, Triassic, Jurassic, Cretaceous, Paleocene, Eocene, Oligocene, Miocene, Pliocene, Pleistocene, and Recent
King David Come Out For God's Sake	The taxonomic hierarchy in botany: kingdom, division, class, order, family, genus, species
My Very Educated Mother Just Served Us Nine Pizzas	Order of the Planets: Mercury, Venus, Earth, Mars, Jupiter, Saturn, Uranus, Neptune, Pluto
Roy G. Biv	The order of colors in the spectrum: red, orange, yellow, green, blue, indigo, violet

Fig. 6-3 Science and math mnemonics.

Acronyms, or acrostics, use the first letter of each word you're trying to remember to build a mnemonic. Some acronyms have become common words themselves. How many of these acronyms do you use to remember common devices?

- Laser (light amplification by stimulated emission of radiation)
- Radar (radio detecting and ranging)
- Scuba (self-contained underwater breathing apparatus)
- Snafu (situation normal, all fouled up)

As you memorize new information, create your own mnemonics. These can be rhymes, jingles, acronyms, or any other memory pegs. For example, remember a checklist of things to bring to work each day by putting the items in an order that has a beat to it: *briefcase, keys, train ticket, newspaper, lunch money.* Say it as you leave your home each day, and you'll be prepared.

Mnemonic	Stands For
I Am A Person	The oceans: Indian, Arctic, Atlantic, Pacific
Eat An Aspirin After A Nighttime Snack	The continents: Europe, Antarctica, Asia Africa, Australia, North America, South America (the second letter in the first three *A* words helps you to remember the A continents)
HOMES	The Great Lakes: Huron, Ontario, Michigan, Erie, Superior
Sam's Horse Must Eat Oats	The Great Lakes, in order from west to east
See Mr. Huron Eating Oranges	The Great Lakes in order of size: Superior, Michigan, Huron, Erie, Ontario
Divorced, Beheaded, Died; Divorced, Beheaded, Survived	The fate of Henry VIII's wives

Fig. 6-4 History and geography mnemonics.

Review Information to Memorize It

- The average adult cannot remember 50 percent of what he or she has just read.
- A day later, recall drops to 20 percent.

Quick and constant review can help you fix the facts in your memory. It takes 15 to 25 minutes of practice over several days to memorize and retain information successfully. Figure on spending about 40 percent of your learning time reviewing new information that you are trying to memorize. Follow the timetable shown in Figure 6-5.

Time to Review	Reason
Directly after class	To reinforce short-term memory
Right before going to sleep	To use the subconscious to continue processing information
Within 24 hours	To help fix long-term memory
Each day, for about 10 minutes	To help fix long-term memory
In a month	To help fix long-term memory

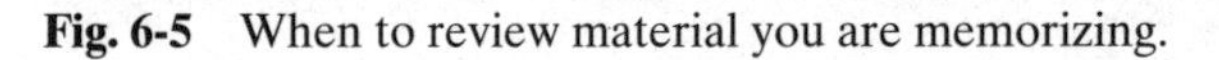

Fig. 6-5 When to review material you are memorizing.

- To make the most of your review, recite facts aloud or write them down. You might have used this technique by writing spelling words over and over to help memorize them. Try it now with these tricky spelling words: *chocolate, laboratory, February, spaghetti, forty.*
- Because verbal rehearsal is such an effective memory tool, study with someone or use a tape recorder to say aloud what needs to be memorized.
- Write information that you have memorized on index cards. Use these flash cards often to help you remember historic dates, definitions, foreign language vocabulary, math formulas, and other facts and ideas.
- Finally, typing or rewriting notes is a very effective memory device if you learn best kinesthetically, by using your body.

Use It or Lose It

To retain what you memorize, use it. But using it doesn't mean repeating it like a mantra. To fix a memory in your mind, follow these suggestions:

- Review the information every day. This is especially helpful with important information that you've memorized for midterms, finals, standardized assessments, licensing exams, entrance exams, and certification tests.
- Think about what you memorized. Apply the facts to new situations and link them to new facts that you must memorize. Make them a part of your life.
- A few days after your memorize new facts, quiz yourself on what you memorized. (Don't quiz yourself immediately after you memorize the information because that tests only short-term recall, not long-term memory.) The quiz can be oral or written, as long as it helps you use the information.

Don't get upset if it takes you a few seconds to recall the information. If you hit a blank, think back to your associations, visualizations, or mnemonics. Wait a few seconds for the information to be retrieved. If it still doesn't come to mind, try a new approach. For example, if you associated it the first time, try creating a new mnemonic.

- ✔ Memorization is a skill. You can improve your memory, just as you can improve any other skill.
- ✔ The memory process has three steps: learning, storing, and recalling.
- ✔ There are two basic types of memory: *short-term memory,* lasts about half a minute, and *long-term memory,* which lasts for a long period of time.

- ✔ Improve your memory by minimizing distraction, getting interested in the text, staying focused on the text, and beefing up your organizational skills.
- ✔ Follow these six steps to memorize more effectively: *understand it, associate it, visualize it, use mnemonics, repeat it,* and *use it.*

Test Yourself

Questions

True-False Questions

1. Memorization is a vital part of the study process.
2. People are born with a good memory; a good memory is not something you can develop much beyond your natural capacity.
3. The memory process has three steps: learning, storing, memorizing.
4. Nearly all people find it easier to remember pictures than words and numbers.
5. There are two basic types of memory: short-term memory and long-term memory.
6. To improve your memory, study with music in the background. This helps reduce distractions and thus helps you concentrate.
7. Memorizing information is not the same as learning it.
8. To get the most understanding from a text, organize the material in a logical way.
9. *Mnemonics* is the technique of using mechanical devices to help you memorize more effectively.
10. The average adult cannot remember 50 percent of what he or she has just read. A day later, recall drops to 20 percent.

Completion Questions

1. Short term memory lasts about _________.
2. The two biggest inhibitors of memory are _________ and _________.
3. The average person can memorize no more than _________ pieces of information at a time.
4. Tying new information to what you already know can help you make information stick. You can do this by using _________.
5. When you form a mental picture of a piece of information, you are using _______ to remember the information.
6. Memory techniques that help you by using cues that are visual, linear, or auditory are called _________.
7. To make the most of your review, _________.

8. To keep the information that you memorized, it is important to _________ it.
9. A few days after your memorize new facts, _________ yourself on what you memorized.
10. If you can't remember something using one memory technique, you should _________.

Multiple-Choice Questions

1. Without any effort on your part, new information automatically goes into your
   (a) General memory zone
   (b) Long-term memory
   (c) Short-term memory
   (d) Memory buffer
2. When you study, however, you want to lock the information into
   (a) The test center of your brain
   (b) The memory buffer
   (c) Your short-term memory
   (d) Your long-term memory
3. Most so-called memory problems are a result of all of the following *except*
   (a) A poor memory that you were born with
   (b) Distractions
   (c) Lack of attention
   (d) Poor organization
4. Memorize the most difficult or most important information
   (a) In the morning
   (b) At your "prime" time
   (c) In the evening
   (d) In the afternoon
5. Always begin memorizing new information by
   (a) Repeating the material several times
   (b) Understanding the material
   (c) Doing something to distract yourself
   (d) Writing the information over and over
6. Two of the most useful association methods for improving memory are
   (a) Visualization and recall
   (b) Sleep and mnemonics
   (c) Memorization and rest
   (d) The peg system and the room system

7. All of the following are types of mnemonics *except*
   (a) Writing the information over and over
   (b) Acronyms and sayings
   (c) Acrostics and jingles
   (d) Mind maps and songs
8. It takes _________ minutes of practice over several days to successfully memorize and retain information.
   (a) 1 to 5
   (b) 5 to 10
   (c) 15 to 25
   (d) 30 to 75
9. To fix a memory in your mind,
   (a) Let the information sit undisturbed for a few weeks
   (b) Don't think about it
   (c) Review the information every day
   (d) Avoid quizzing yourself so you don't displace the memory
10. Memorizing new information _________ you heard or read it will improve your memory significantly.
    (a) A day after
    (b) The same day
    (c) A week after
    (d) A month after

ANSWER KEY

True-False Questions

1. T 2. F 3. F 4. T 5. T 6. F 7. T 8. T 9. F 10. T

Completion Questions

1. half a minute 2. stress and attitude 3. seven 4. association 5. visualization 6. mnemonics 7. recite facts aloud or write them down 8. use 9. quiz or test 10. try another technique

Multiple-Choice Questions

1. c 2. d 3. a 4. b 5. b 6. d 7. a 8. c 9. c 10. b

CHAPTER 7

Pump Up Your Vocabulary

You should read this chapter if you need to review or learn about

- Pronouncing words correctly
- Using a dictionary, word cards, and mnemonics
- Defining words through context clues
- Multiple-meaning words
- Word origins
- A word's connotation and denotation

In Chapter 7, you explored different ways to sharpen your memory to help you remember what you study. Now discover how to improve your vocabulary. Having a wide vocabulary makes it easier for you to understand what you read and hear in class. Having a good vocabulary can also give you the confidence to participate in class discussions, often an important factor in your final grade.

Get Started

A rich vocabulary is a key to academic success. Build your vocabulary by learning to pronounce words correctly; by using a dictionary, word cards, and mnemonics; and through context clues.

Pronounce Words Correctly to Improve Your Vocabulary

Knowing the meaning of a word is only half the battle; you also have to know how to pronounce it. It's astonishing how many words are misunderstood and misused simply because they are mispronounced. Here are the four most common reasons for mispronouncing words:

1. *Letters are dropped.* Often, speakers drop letters from words. For instance, the food poisoning known as *salmonella* is correctly pronounced sal-muh-*nel*-uh. Dropping the first *l* results in sam-uh-*nel*-uh. Unstressed vowels are often dropped, even on relatively common words. *Interesting* (*in*-ter-s-ting) becomes *intresting* (*in*-trehs-ting), *miniature* (*min*-ee-ay-toor) becomes *minature* (*min*-ah-toor), and *veterinarian* (vet-er-eh-*nayr*-ee-an) becomes *vet-ernarian* (vet-er-*nayr*-ee-an). Consonants also get lost in the shuffle. The first *r* in February is a case in point. How often have you heard *February* pronounced *Feb*-oo-ehr-ee or even *Feb*-ree instead of *Feb*-roo-ehr-ee?

2. *Letters are added.* In addition, speakers often insert an extra letter or two when they say a word. Unfortunately, this can make the word confusing or even unrecognizable. For instance, *ambidextrous* (able to use either hand) has four syllables and is correctly pronounced am-bi-*deks*-trus. But sometimes speakers add an extra syllable to get am-bi-*deks*-tree-us or am-bi-*deks*-tru-us. *Chimney* has two syllables: *chim*-nee. However, people often add a syllable to pronounce the word incorrectly as *chim*-ah-nee. *Wondrous,* correctly pronounced *wun*-drus, becomes *wun*-der-us. *Lightning* is correctly pronounced as *lite*-ning but often gets this added bonus: *lite*-en-ning.

3. *Letters are switched.* For example, *abhor* (hate) becomes uh-*bor* rather than ab-*hor.* This is an understandable mistake, as are many other mispronunciations involving switched letters. Unfortunately, these mistakes get in the way of comprehension.

4. *Sounds are garbled.* *Library* is correctly pronounced *lie*-brer-ee. I often hear the word pronounced *lie*-berry. Even the relatively simple word *picture* can become *pitcher.* The pronunciation problem is especially acute with words that can function as more than one part of speech. The word *ally* is a case in point. As a noun, it's pronounced *al*-eye. As a verb, it's pronounced uh-*ly*.

Quick Tip

Careless pronunciation often results in careless spelling. As a result, people are unwilling to write even some common words for fear of misspelling them. The following words are often misspelled because a letter is omitted: *Arctic, candidate, diphtheria, eighth, government, probably, quantity, recognize, representative, surprise, symptom.* Conversely, the following words are usually misspelled because a letter is added: *athletics, burglar, disastrous, encumbrance, forty, hindrance, jewelry, mischievous, pronunciation, remembrance, schedule, umbrella.*

Use a Dictionary

A dictionary improves your vocabulary by providing definitions, word histories, and parts of speech, too. It's the best source for the words you need inside and outside the classroom.

All dictionaries are *not* the same. Different types of dictionaries fit different needs. For example, some dictionaries have been written mainly for scholars and people who research the history of language. The most famous scholarly dictionary is *The Oxford English Dictionary* (OED), an unabridged dictionary that contains more than 500,000 entries. The most recent OED contains about 60 million words in 20 volumes. If shelf space is an issue and you simply can't live without an OED, however, online and CD-ROM versions are available.

Some dictionaries have been created mainly for adults, college students, high school students, and elementary school students. The best-selling general dictionaries include the following:

- *The American Heritage Dictionary of the English Language*
- *Merriam-Webster's Collegiate Dictionary*
- *Merriam-Webster's Pocket Dictionary*
- *The New Shorter Oxford English Dictionary*
- *The Random House College Dictionary*
- *Webster's Third New International Dictionary*

These dictionaries, and others like them, are available in electronic versions as well.

Which dictionary should you purchase and use? With more than 30,000 dictionaries currently offered for sale online, you've got some shopping to do. Here's what you need:

1. A dictionary containing all the words that you are likely to encounter in your school, personal, and professional life.
2. Words explained in terms that you can understand.

3. A size that fits your needs. You might wish to buy a hardbound dictionary for home and a smaller paperback for school.
4. An online dictionary can't fulfill all your needs, unless you like to tote around your PowerBook and fire it up all the time. Always keep a printed dictionary on hand, even though you may have an online dictionary as well.

When you're trying to find a word in the dictionary, begin by making an educated guess about its spelling. The odds are in your favor. However, the more spelling patterns you know for a given sound, the better your chances for finding the word fast. You can find a pronunciation chart at the beginning of any dictionary. Once you've narrowed down your search and you're flipping through the pages, use the *guide words* located on the upper corners of the pages to guide your search. Then follow strict alphabetical order.

Quick Tip

A *thesaurus* is a reference book that contains synonyms and antonyms. A thesaurus is especially helpful when you're trying to express an idea but you don't know how to phrase it. It is also a helpful reference book when you are trying to find a better word than the one you've been using. This helps you state exact shades of meaning rather than approximations. As a result, your vocabulary increases by heaps and heaps of words.

Make Word Cards

As you hear and read new words, write each new vocabulary word on the front of an index card, one word per card. Then write the definition and pronunciation on the back, as shown in Figure 7-1. Study the cards every chance you get. Take them with you on the bus, train, and plane; hide them in your lap and sneak a peek during dull dates, meetings, and meals. Rotate the cards so you remember many different words.

Use Mnemonics

As you learned in the previous chapter, *mnemonics* (ni-*mon*-iks) are memory tricks that help you remember things. Use them to help you remember new words and to help you distinguish between confusing words.

For example, to remember that station*a*ry means st*a*nding still, stress the *a,* contained in both words. To remember that *stationery* refers to writing paper, associate the *er* in station*er*y with the *er* in lett*er*s. *Desert* and *dessert* become easier to define and use when you remember that *dessert* has a double *s,* as in *s*trawberry *s*hortcake. Create your own mnemonics to help you remember new words as well as the easily confused words that you use every day.

[Front of card]

caprice

[Back of card]

sudden, unpredictable change of mind, a whim (kah-preece)

Fig. 7-1 Example of word card.

Use Context Clues

When you use *context clues,* you interpret a word's specific meaning by examining its relationship to other words in the sentence. To improve your vocabulary, you must understand how a word interacts with other words. Although context can sometimes be as unreliable as your boss or the weather, it can also come through in impressive ways.

Context clues come in different forms. The most common types of context clues include these four:

- Restatement context clues
- Definitions after colons and transitions
- Inferential context clues
- Contrast context clues

Restatement Context Clues

Speakers and writers want their words to be understood so their messages go through. As a result, they will often define a difficult word where it first appears in the text. Study this example:

> The Army Corps of Engineers distributed 26 million plastic bags throughout the region. Volunteers filled each bag with 35 pounds of sand and then stacked them to create *levees,* makeshift barriers against the floodwaters.

Directly after the word *levee,* readers get the definition: "makeshift barriers against the floodwaters."

Definitions After Colons and Transitions

Speakers and writers often provide context clues in the form of definitions after colons and transitions. For example,

> The media trumpets our obsession with appearance, claiming that Americans are more fit than ever before. However, just the opposite is true. In fact, at least one-third of the American population is classified as *obese:* being more than 20 percent over a person's ideal body weight.

Directly after the colon, the writer defines *obese:* "being more than 20 percent over a person's ideal body weight."

Inferential Context Clues

Sometimes you will have to *infer* the meaning from what you already know and details you have heard or read. When you *make an inference,* you combine what you already know with spoken or textual clues to discover the unstated information. As you read the following passage, use context clues to infer what *forerunner* means:

> In 1862, in order to support the Civil War effort, Congress enacted the nation's first income tax law. It was a *forerunner* of our modern income tax in that it was based on the principles of graduated, or progressive taxation and of withholding income at the source.

Context clue	+	what I know	=	inference
The *forerunner* was the "nation's first income tax law."	+	*fore* means "before"	=	forerunner means "before or precede"

Contrast Context Clues

You can also figure out an unknown word when an opposite or contrast is presented. When you do this, you're making an inference. For example, you can define *literal* by finding its contrast in the sentence:

It is hard to use *literal* language when talking about nature because people tend to talk about nature using figurative language.

Literal language must be the opposite of *figurative language.* If you know that figurative language means words and expressions not meant to be taken at face value, you can infer that *literal* must mean "the strict or exact meaning." Other synonyms would include *verbatim* or *word-for-word.*

Distinguish Between Multiple-Meaning Words

Building your vocabulary means more than simply learning new words. It also means telling the difference between words that you already know. The word *favor,* for example, has many different meanings. Here are six of them: "a kind act," "friendly regard," "being approved," "a gift," "to support," "to resemble."

Here are some additional examples of multiple-meaning words:

Word	Example	Meaning	Example	Meaning
Address	Home *address*	Residence	Graduation *address*	Speech
Game	Play a *game*	Sport	Have a *game* leg	Injured
Rash	Have a *rash*	Skin problem	*Rash* action	Hasty

When you read, you often come across a word that you think you know but that doesn't make sense in the sentence you're reading, which is your clue that the word has more than one meaning. In this case, you must choose the meaning that fits the context.

To do so, follow these three simple steps:

1. Read the sentence and find the word with multiple meanings.
2. Look for context clues that tell you which meaning of the word fits.
3. Substitute a synonym for the word to see whether it makes sense. If not, try another meaning for the word. Continue until you find the right meaning.

Learn Word Origins

Many words have entered English from other languages. How many? Three out of every four English words are foreign-born! For example, *bon mot* (clever saying) came from French, *patio* (courtyard) came from Spanish, and *duet* (musical piece for two) came from Italian.

One of the most effective ways to stretch your vocabulary is to learn a word's origins. This helps you link related words to figure out the meaning and usage of many other commonly used words that have entered English from around the world. Knowing a word's origin can also help you pronounce and use it correctly.

You can find the origin of a word in the dictionary. Many words have very interesting stories. Here are several:

- *Mentor* means "trusted teacher or guide." In the *Odyssey,* Mentor is Odysseus's friend. He also tutors Odysseus's son Telemachus. The word developed from Mentor's name.
- *Mesmerize* means "hypnotize" or "fascinate." In 1775, an Austrian doctor named Friedrich Mesmer first demonstrated the technique of hypnotism. The word was created from his name.
- *Quisling* means "traitor, someone who betrays his or her country." The word comes from the name of Vidkun Quisling (1887–1945), a Norwegian army officer who collaborated with the Nazis during World War II.

Quick Tip

Learning prefixes, suffixes, and roots can also help you decode many unfamiliar words. Memorize just a few of these to unlock scores of new words.

Distinguish Connotation and Denotation

Every word has a *denotation,* its dictionary meaning. In addition, many words have *connotations,* emotional overtones. Two words may have similar denotations but very different connotations. For example, *sobbing* and *blubbering* have the same denotation, "crying." However, *sobbing* suggests pitiful crying, whereas *blubbering* suggests foolish, overwrought crying. Being able to distinguish connotations is crucial because it helps you understand the speaker's or writer's point. It enables you to understand fine shades of meaning, too.

Here are some additional examples of connotation and denotation:

Word Denotation	Positive Connotation	Negative Connotation
Confused	Puzzled	Flustered
Without a friend	Friendless	Reclusive
Raw	Unrefined	Crude
Inexperienced	Trusting	Naive

✔ Knowing the meaning of a word is only half the battle; you also have to know how to pronounce it.

✔ A dictionary helps you improve your vocabulary by providing definitions, word histories, and parts of speech, too. Carry a pocket dictionary with you and use it.

✔ Use word cards and mnemonics to help you remember new words.

- Try to define unfamiliar words by using context clues, a word's relationship to other words in the sentence. Distinguish between multiple-meaning words by using context clues.

- Learn word origins to stretch your vocabulary.
- Distinguish between *denotation* (a word's dictionary meaning) and *connotation* (its emotional overtones). This will help you understand a speaker's message and express yourself more clearly.

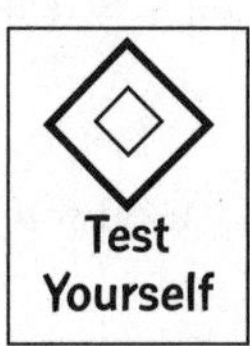

QUESTIONS

True-False Questions

1. Fatty deposits on artery walls combine with calcium compounds to cause *arteriosclerosis,* hardening of the arteries. *Arteriosclerosis* means "hardening of the arteries."
2. The upper left part of the heart, the left *atrium,* receives blood returning from circulation. *Atrium* means "the upper left part of the heart."
3. *Reckless* has a positive connotation.
4. *Paunchy* has a positive connotation.
5. *Inferior* has a more positive connotation than *trivial* or *petty.*
6. In the following sentence, the author uses a context clue to define *lethargy:* "One symptom of this condition is lethargy—for example, a feeling of passivity and inactivity."
7. Unusually *reticent,* Marco said very little about his family life. *Reticent* means "reserved."
8. Sports should be fun, but some people make it *onerous.* As used in this sentence, *onerous* means "melancholy."
9. Tornadoes are *perilous* storms because they can pick up a house and drop it hundreds of feet away. As used in this sentence, *perilous* means "shielded."
10. Most shark meat is processed for *consumption*—for example, the Chinese use shark fins in soup, and the Italians eat about 10 million pounds of shark a year. As used in this sentence, *consumption* means "eaten."

Completion Questions

1. In many Native American tribes, the *shaman,* or medicine man, acted as a ceremonial priest. *Shaman* means __________.
2. I believe that life is short so we should enjoy what we eat. As a result, I consume mass quantities of *confectioneries,* delicious candies. *Confectioneries* means __________.

3. Born in 1833, John Styth Pemberton was a *pharmacist,* a drugstore owner, who moved to Atlanta, Georgia, in 1869. *Pharmacist* means _________.
4. To make a living, he created *patent medicines,* homemade medicines that were sold without a prescription. *Patent medicines* means _________.
5. On the slide, the scientists saw that a drop of water contained *bacteria,* one-celled organisms that are too small to be seen by the naked eye. *Bacteria* means _________.
6. She jumped into the *fray* and enjoyed every minute of the fight. *Fray* means _________.
7. As with all electric *currents* or discharges, lightning will follow the *path of least resistance.* This means that it will take the route that is easiest for it to travel on. *Current* means _________.
8. In the previous sentence, *the path of least resistance* means _________.
9. Many settlers on the vast American plains in the late nineteenth century used *sod,* or earth, as a building material for their houses. *Sod* means _________.
10. Then arrange a handful of *mulch,* dead leaves, on the top of the soil. *Mulch* means _________.

Multiple-Choice Questions

1. Luis was *resigned* to working overtime on Friday night. *Resigned* means
   (a) Quitting a job
   (b) Giving in unhappily but without resistance
   (c) Delighted about
   (d) Furious with
2. Her heart kept pumping blood to the surface of her body and to all of the extremities. You can use context clues to define *extremities* as
   (a) Arteries
   (b) Fingers and toes
   (c) Veins
   (d) Muscles
3. The plumber used a *snake* to clear the drain. As used in this sentence, *snake* means
   (a) Legless reptile
   (b) Long, bendable metal tool
   (c) Sneaky, disloyal person
   (d) Twist
4. My uncle is a tall, *spare* man, as thin as a stick. As used in this sentence, *spare* means
   (a) Small in amount, not quite enough
   (b) Treat with mercy

(c) Extra, not in regular use
(d) Lean and slender

5. The *furrows* of the old wagon trail were clearly visible, but snow covered the marks of the last wheels. *Furrows* most nearly means
   (a) Tracks
   (b) Fold
   (c) Splinters
   (d) Remains
6. Select the word with a neutral connotation.
   (a) Warped
   (b) Gnarled
   (c) Bent
   (d) Contorted
7. The *return* on their investment was 10 percent annually. As used here, *return* means
   (a) Profit from an investment
   (b) Homecoming
   (c) Results
   (d) Recovery
8. Choose the word with the most positive connotation.
   (a) Fawning
   (b) Obsequious
   (c) Groveling
   (d) Polite
9. The nearly frozen prospectors *threshed* their arms back and forth, beating their hands with all their might. What context clue does the author use to define *threshed?*
   (a) Prospectors
   (b) Arms
   (c) Beating their hands with all their might
   (d) Nearly frozen
10. The cat stretched out close enough to the fire for warmth but far enough away to avoid being *singed. Singed* most nearly means
    (a) Caught
    (b) Burned
    (c) Chased away
    (d) Terrified
11. He was *petrified* at the sight of the huge lion. As used in this sentence, *petrified* means
    (a) Astonished
    (b) Turned into stone

(c) Surprised
(d) Paralyzed with fear

12. The *petrified* tree has been standing in the forest for thousands of years. As used in this sentence, *petrified* means
    (a) Turned into stone
    (b) Paralyzed with fear
    (c) Huge
    (d) Worshipped

ANSWER KEY

True-False Questions

1. T 2. T 3. F 4. F 5. F 6. T 7. T 8. F 9. F 10. T

Completion Questions

1. Medicine man 2. Candies 3. Drugstore owner 4. Homemade medicines that were sold without a prescription 5. One-celled organisms that are too small to be seen by the naked eye 6. Fight 7. Discharges 8. The route on which it is easiest to travel 9. Earth 10. Dead leaves

Multiple-Choice Questions

1. b 2. b 3. b 4. d 5. a 6. c 7. a 8. d 9. c 10. b 11. d 12. a

PART 3

CHAPTER 8

Be an Active Reader

You should read this chapter if you need to review or learn about

- Previewing a text and making predictions
- Setting a purpose for reading
- Tapping prior knowledge
- Asking and answering questions

Does this sound like you?

- "My mind wanders when I'm reading. I don't seem to understand what I'm reading, and I can't remember any of it."
- "I can't find the important material in the textbook."
- "I can't keep up with my reading assignments, so I cram the night before a test."

It's no secret that being a good reader makes every part of your classwork easier—especially studying and taking tests.

In Chapter 7, you explored different ways to improve your vocabulary. Now discover how to read with greater comprehension.

Get Started

Being an active reader can help you understand more of what you read and remember it longer. To be an active reader, preview a text, set a purpose for reading, build on what you already know, and dialogue with the text.

Preview a Text

Before you read or study, determine whether you're reading *fiction* (a made-up story) or *nonfiction* (a real-life account of a person, place, thing, or idea.) You'll probably read fiction quickly because you'll be swept along with the plot, characters, and setting. You'll probably read nonfiction more slowly because you will concentrate on the ideas. You will reread important and difficult parts of the text, too.

Then *preview* the reading by examining the different parts of the text. Active readers (like you!) preview a text to help them know what they will discover as they read.

Preview these parts of any book:

- The cover
- The title
- The table of contents and subtitles
- Pictures, illustrations, photographs, charts, or maps
- The captions

1. *Preview the cover.* Bet you've heard the old saying "You can't judge a book by its cover." Actually, you *can!* Looking at a book's cover can tell you a lot about what's inside. Before you start to read any book, examine the front and back covers. As you study the cover, ask yourself these questions:

   - What clues about the story do I get from the pictures on the front and back covers?
   - Who wrote the book? Have I read any other books by this author?
   - Did any famous people comment about the book on the back cover? If so, what do their comments tell me about the book?
   - Inside the jacket flaps (if any), how is the story described?

2. *Preview the title.* Now read the book's title. See what it tells you about the contents. For example, you can ask yourself the following questions if you're reading a novel:

   - What does the title mean? Does it have more than one meaning?
   - What reasons could the writer have for choosing this title?
   - Based on the title, what do I predict will happen in the story?

3. *Preview the table of contents and subtitles.* Open the book and scan the table of contents. If you're reading an article or chapter, flip the pages, read the subtitles, and ask questions. For example, if you're reading a nonfiction book such as this one, you could ask yourself these questions:

- What will this book teach me?
- What main topics does this book cover?
- How are the topics arranged? What will I read first, second, and so on?

4. *Preview any pictures, illustrations, photographs, charts, or maps.* When you look at the pictures inside the book, ask yourself these questions:

- What different types of pictures, photographs, and maps are included?
- What do these visuals show?
- Why did the writer include these illustrations? What purpose do they serve?
- Based on the pictures, what do I think this book is about?

5. *Preview the captions.* Most pictures, photographs, and other illustrations have captions. These sentences, usually placed under the pictures, describe what is shown in the pictures and may offer additional information. As you preview the captions, ask yourself these questions:

- What facts do I get from the captions?
- Based on the captions, what does this book describe?

Make Predictions

As you read, your brain is always trying to figure out what is coming next in the story. Make, revise, and confirm your predictions to increase your reading comprehension. Follow these steps:

1. *Make predictions.* When you make predictions, you make educated guesses about what's to come in a text. The process looks like this:

What I know + story clues = prediction

Make predictions by looking at the title, subtitles, headings, illustrations, and captions. From these story clues and what you already know, you can predict what will happen in the story. For example, if you previewed a passage called "Leaders of the Pack," you might predict that the story would be about presidents, kings, or even dogs.

2. *Revise predictions.* As you read, adjust your predictions to take into account any new information you gather from your reading or from outside sources. Ask yourself questions like these:

- What new information did I find?
- How does this information affect my predictions?
- How should I change my predictions to make them more accurate?

3. *Confirm predictions.* Finally, read on until you find the information you need to verify your predictions. See how accurate your predictions were. If you were off the mark, find out why. Did you overlook some crucial details? Did you misunderstand a subheading? Use this information as you set new predictions for the rest of the reading. Ask yourself these questions:

- How accurate were my predictions?
- What new predictions can I make using the facts I just read?

Now let's try an exercise with the following reading. Follow these steps:

1. Preview the passage.
2. Make predictions.
3. Read the passage to confirm or change your predictions.

Property

And so the reliance on property, including the reliance on governments which protect it, is the want of self-reliance. Men have looked away from themselves and at things so long that they have come to esteem the religious, learned and civil institutions as guards of property, and they deprecate assaults on these, because they feel them to be assaults on property. They measure their esteem of each other by what each has, and not by what each is. But a cultivated man becomes ashamed of his property, out of new respect for his nature. Especially he hates what he has if he sees that it is accidental—came to him by inheritance, or gift, or crime; then he feels that it is not having; it does not belong to him, has no root in him and merely lies there because no revolution or no robber takes it away. But that which a man is, does always by necessity acquire; and what the man acquires, is living property, which does not wait the beck of rulers, or mobs, or revolutions, or fire, or storm, or bankruptcies, but perpetually renews itself wherever the man breathes. "Thy lot or portion of life," said the Caliph Ali, "is seeking after thee; therefore be at rest from seeking after it." Our dependence on these foreign goods leads us to our slavish respect for numbers. The political parties meet in numerous conventions; the greater the concourse and with each new uproar of announcement, The delegation from Essex! The Democrats from New Hampshire! The Whigs of Maine! The young patriot feels himself stronger than before by a new thousand of eyes and arms. In like manner the reformers summon conventions and vote and resolve in multitude. Not so, O friends! Will the God deign to enter and inhabit you, but by a method precisely the reverse. It is only as a man puts off all foreign support and stands alone that I see him to be strong and to prevail. He is weaker by every recruit to his banner. Is not a man better than a town? He who knows that power is inborn, that he is weak because he has looked for good out of him and elsewhere, and, so perceiving, throws himself unhesitatingly on his thought, instantly fights himself, stands in the erect position, commands his limbs, works miracles; just as a man who stands on his feet is stronger than a man who stands on his head.

—*Ralph Waldo Emerson*

Set a Purpose for Reading

Why are you reading this book? Are you reading this book for the same reason you read an e-mail from your friend? Of course not. That's because you read for different reasons. Your reason for reading is your *purpose* for reading.

After you preview and predict, it's time to set a purpose for reading. Here are some of the main purposes you have for reading:

- To confirm a belief
- To discover opinions
- To get facts
- To get instructions
- To have fun
- To learn new information
- To learn new vocabulary
- To review notes

Your purpose for reading shapes the way you read. For example, when you study, you read slowly so you understand and remember the material. You don't want to miss any facts or details that could be important. You also take notes to record key words, dates, and facts. If you are reading to be entertained, however, you read more quickly. You might even skim some of the description in your haste to see how the story turns out.

Setting a purpose saves time. If you know why you're reading, you can go straight to the book or article that has the information you need. You won't waste time reading material that you don't need at that time.

Setting a purpose improves understanding. By setting a purpose for reading, you'll be sure to get the most out of what you read. Knowing what you want to find out helps you concentrate on that information and remember it better.

Tap Prior Knowledge

Use what you know to make your reading easier and more productive. Connecting new facts with your prior knowledge helps you remember new information when you study it.

After you preview, predict, and set a purpose for reading, take a few minutes to jot down notes about what you already know about the passage. Ask yourself, "What do I know about this subject?" Decide what you want to find out. After you finish reading, you can complete your chart by writing down what you learned.

You can arrange your ideas on a chart like this:

What I know	What I want to find out	What I learned
___________	___________	___________
___________	___________	___________
___________	___________	___________
___________	___________	___________

Read the following passage. On a separate piece of paper, fill out your chart.

Men are like plants; the goodness and flavor of the fruit proceeds from the peculiar soil and exposition in which they grow. We are nothing but what we derive from the air we breathe, the climate we inhabit, the government we obey, the system of religion we profess, and the nature of our employment. Here you will find but few crimes; these have acquired as yet no root among us. I wish I were able to trace all my ideas; if my ignorance prevents me from describing them properly, I hope I shall be able to delineate a few of the outlines; which is all I propose.

Those who live near the sea feed more on fish than on flesh and often encounter that boisterous element. This renders them more bold and enterprising; this leads them to neglect the confined occupations of the land. They see and converse with a variety of people; their intercourse with mankind becomes extensive. The sea inspires them with a love of traffic, a desire of transporting produce from one place to another, and leads them to a variety of resources which supply the place of labor. Those who inhabit the middle settlement, by far the most numerous, must be very different; the simple cultivation of the earth purifies them, but the indulgences of the government, the soft remonstrances of religion, the rank of independent freeholders, must necessarily inspire them with sentiments, very little known in Europe among a people of the same class of freemen, religious indifference, are their characteristics.

Exclusive of those general characteristics, each province has its own, founded on the government, climate, mode of husbandry, customs, and peculiarity of circumstances. Europeans submit insensibly to these great powers and become, in the course of a few generations, not only Americans in general, but either Pennsylvanians, Virginians, or provincials under some other name. Whoever traverses the continent must easily observe those strong differences, which will grow more evident in time. The inhabitants of Canada, Massachusetts, the middle provinces, the southern ones, will be as different as their climates; their only points of unity will be those of religion and language.

Ask and Answer Questions

Ask yourself questions to define unfamiliar words, clarify confusing passages, or locate the main idea. You can also ask yourself questions to isolate the text organization; the author's purpose; or to make, revise, or confirm predictions. Answer the questions based on the information you find by rereading or reading on.

Here are some sample questions you can ask yourself as you read:

- What does this unfamiliar word mean? How can I use context clues to define the word?
- Am I confused because the word has multiple meanings? If so, which meaning is being used here?
- What point is the author making in this passage? Where is the topic sentence or main idea?
- What is the author's purpose? Is it to tell a story? To explain or inform? To persuade? To describe?
- How is this passage organized?
- How is the text organization linked to the author's purpose?

Practice Makes Perfect

Stick with it. If you've been a passive reader for many years, it's going to take some time to develop an active role in your learning.

To speed the process along, in addition to reading required material such as textbooks, read for pleasure as well. Consider reading best-sellers, classic works of fiction and nonfiction, newspapers, and magazines. However, reading *anything* is better than not reading at all. Even reading trashy novels will help boost your reading skills.

That said, here are some classic novels and plays, both traditional and new, that you can read to get started:

The Adventures of Huckleberry Finn
The Age of Innocence
All My Sons
All the Pretty Horses
Anna Karenina
Antigone
As I Lay Dying
The Awakening
The Birthday Party
Beloved
Billy Budd
Bless Me, Ultima
Candide
Catch-22
Ceremony
The Color Purple
Clockwork Orange
Crime and Punishment
The Crucible
Cry, the Beloved Country
Delta Wedding
David Copperfield (or any novel by Dickens)
Dinner at the Homesick Restaurant
A Doll's House (or any play by Ibsen)
Dr. Faustus
Emma
An Enemy of the People
Equus
A Farewell to Arms
The Glass Menagerie
The Great Gatsby
Gulliver's Travels
Hamlet
Heart of Darkness
The Iceman Cometh
Invisible Man
Jane Eyre
Jasmine
The Joy Luck Club
Jude the Obscure (or any novel by Hardy)

King Lear (or any play by Shakespeare)
A Lesson Before Dying
Lord Jim
The Mayor of Casterbridge
A Member of the Wedding
Moby Dick
Mrs. Dalloway
Native Son
The Oresteia (or any Greek tragedy)
Our Town
The Piano Lesson
A Portrait of the Artist as a Young Man
The Portrait of a Lady
Praisesong for the Widow
Pride and Prejudice
Pnin
A Raisin in the Sun
Saint Joan (or any play by Shaw)
The Scarlet Letter
The Shipping News
Song of Solomon
Sons and Lovers
The Sound and the Fury
The Stone Angel
Sula
Their Eyes Were Watching God
Things Fall Apart
The Turn of the Screw
Waiting for Godot
The Warden
Wuthering Heights
1984

Also consider the following suggestions to help you become a better reader.

- Practice these reading techniques 15 to 20 minutes a day. Follow the schedule and you'll see progress.
- Try reading at the same time every day, in the same place, so you get into a reading routine.
- Keep a "reading diary," listing all the different things you have read. You'll feel good looking back at all the reading you've done.
- Don't give up! Learning any skill takes time and effort, but it's really worth it.

✔ Be an active reader by previewing a text and making predictions before you start reading.

✔ Set a purpose for reading. Your purpose might be to find out information or discover the author's point of view on an issue, for example.

Bring what you already know to the table: combine your prior knowledge with the new information you discover in the text.

Clarify confusing passages and ideas by asking yourself questions as you read. Read on to find the answers in the text.

Practice makes perfect. The more you read, the better a reader you will become.

Questions

True-False Questions

1. You should always preview nonfiction (such as textbooks), but it's not necessary to preview fiction (such as novels and short stories).
2. When you preview a book, if any famous people commented about the book on the back cover, you should decide what their comments tell you about the book.
3. If you're reading a nonfiction book such as this one, make predictions about the characters, plot, setting, and theme.
4. Making predictions is basically a form of making inferences, because you are combining what you already know with story clues to read between the lines.
5. When you study, read slowly so you understand and remember the material. You don't want to miss any facts or details that could be important.
6. Setting a purpose for reading takes extra time, but it's well worth it.
7. When you ask yourself questions, you are in effect carrying on a dialogue with the text.
8. Even the slowest reader can improve very quickly by following these suggestions because reading is fundamentally a passive process.
9. You should read only classic novels to improve your reading speed and comprehension; it's a waste of time to read newspapers, magazines, and trashy novels.
10. Practice makes perfect. The more you read, the better a reader you will become—and the more you will enjoy it.

Completion Questions

1. Before you read a text in depth, __________ the text to find out what types of information it contains.
2. As you preview the __________ of a book, decide how many different meanings it might have and why the author chose it for the text.
3. Most pictures, photographs, and other illustrations have __________, which sentences, usually placed under the pictures, that describe what is shown and may add additional information.
4. When you __________, you make educated guesses about what's to come in a text.
5. As you read, __________ your predictions to take into account any new information you gather from your reading or from outside sources.
6. Your reason for reading is your __________ for reading.
7. When you use __________, you are using what you already know to make your reading easier and more productive.
8. Ask yourself __________ to define unfamiliar words, clarify confusing passages, or locate the main idea in a text.

9. To become a better reader, in addition to reading what's required, consider reading for __________ as well.
10. Keep a "__________," listing all the different things you have read. You'll feel good looking back at all the reading you've done.

Multiple-Choice Questions

1. Reading predictions are
   (a) Educated guesses about upcoming events in a text
   (b) The author's purpose
   (c) A way the author organizes the text
   (d) Based on denotation and connotation
2. Good readers make, revise, and confirm their predictions for all of the following reasons *except*
   (a) To understand what they read in greater detail
   (b) To enjoy reading more
   (c) To decrease reading time sharply
   (d) To appreciate the writer's craft
3. Preview all of the following parts of any text *except*
   (a) The title
   (b) The table of contents and subtitles
   (c) What your friends say about the book
   (d) Pictures, illustrations, photographs, charts, or maps
4. After you preview and predict, read on until you find the information you need to
   (a) Set new predictions
   (b) Verify your predictions
   (c) Enjoy the text
   (d) Write about the text
5. Powerful readers follow these three steps when they read:
   (a) Preview, confirm predictions, set new predictions
   (b) Confirm predictions, predict, preview
   (c) Predict, review, reread
   (d) Preview, predict, confirm predictions
6. Readers may read for all of the following purposes for reading *except*
   (a) To confirm a belief or to discover opinions
   (b) To learn new information
   (c) To get facts and instructions
   (d) To set predictions

7. By setting a purpose for reading, you'll accomplish all of the following *except*
   (a) Earn a very high grade on the class test
   (b) Get the most out of what you read
   (c) Enjoy the reading more
   (d) Understand the author's reason for writing
8. You can also ask yourself questions to accomplish all of the following *except*
   (a) Isolate the text organization
   (b) Discover the author's purpose
   (c) Make predictions
   (d) Make, revise, or confirm predictions
9. All of the following books are considered classics because of their high quality *except*
   (a) *Desire and Desire*
   (b) *The Adventures of Huckleberry Finn*
   (c) *A Doll's House*
   (d) *Moby Dick*
10. Good readers
   (a) Are born, not made
   (b) Are made, not born
   (c) Approach a text passively
   (d) Have relatively poor vocabulary

ANSWER KEY

True-False Questions

1. F 2. T 3. F 4. T 5. T 6. F 7. T 8. F 9. F 10. T

Completion Questions

1. Preview 2. Title 3. Captions 4. Make predictions 5. Adjust or revise 6. Purpose 7. Prior knowledge 8. Questions 9. Fun or pleasure 10. Reading diary

Multiple-Choice Questions

1. a 2. d 3. c 4. b 5. d 6. d 7. a 8. c 9. a 10. b

CHAPTER 9

Use Proven Reading Techniques

You should read this chapter if you need to review or learn about

- Skimming, scanning, and summarizing a text
- Effective ways to improve your reading comprehension
- Monitoring your reading comprehension

Happily, reading doesn't have to be a chore. In this chapter, you will build on what you learned in Chapter 8 to make reading easier and more time-effective. Try each of the methods and decide which ones work best for you.

Get Started

There are a number of excellent ways to get more from your reading. These include *skimming, scanning, summarizing, questioning, reciting,* and *reviewing.* With practice, these techniques become second nature. As you increase your reading speed and boost understanding, class reading and studying become far less difficult.

Skim and Scan

When you want to get a general idea about a text, you skim it. *Skimming* is a very fast method of reading that lets you glance at a passage to get its main idea or to find a key point. Skimming boosts comprehension because it helps you focus on the important parts of the text. If you go back and read the text in detail, you can zero in on the parts you need. You won't spend time lost in detail.

Follow these steps as you skim a text:

1. Preview the text by looking at the title, subheadings, pictures, and captions.
2. Make predictions and set a purpose for reading, just as you learned in Chapter 8.
3. Start skimming by running your eyes across the page. Try to read as fast as you can.
4. Focus on the key words. These will be nouns and verbs.
5. Look for the facts you need. These will often be in the first and last sentences. Read these facts more slowly.
6. Pause at the end of every page or passage to restate the meaning in your own words.

Quick Tip

Skimming isn't a substitute for a complete reading. Skim *before* you read the text . . . not *instead* of reading it.

Skim the following passage to get a general idea of its meaning. The text was written in 1645, and so contains some words and sentence structure characteristic of the era. I selected this particular passage because it very clearly typifies the level of readability and content that you can expect to encounter in a college or professional class (diction notwithstanding).

April 13, 1645. Mr. Hopkins, the governor of Hartford upon Connecticut, came to Boston, and brought his wife with him (a godly young woman, and of special parts) who was fallen into a sad infirmity, the loss of her understanding and reason, which had been growing on her diverse years, by occasion of her giving herself wholly to reading and writing, and had written many books. Her husband, being very loving and tender of her, was loath to grieve her; but he saw his error, when it was too late. For if she had attended to her household affairs, and such things as belong to women, and not gone out her way and calling to meddle in such things as are proper for men, whose minds are stronger, etc., she had kept her wits, and might have improved them usefully and honorably. He brought her to Boston, and left her with her brother, one Mr. Yale, a merchant, to try what means might be had here for her. But no help could be had.

Here's one way to state the general idea: "In the seventeenth century, some people believed that women were too delicate to take much learning; rather, they were fit only for household duties. Too much learning drove this woman mad."

Summarize to Increase Comprehension

To *summarize,* find the most important information and restate it in your own words. Summarize every time you study to help you understand and remember what you read. To ensure that you have included all the important details in your summary, it should answer the questions *who, what, when, where, why,* and *how.*

To summarize a passage:

1. Preview the passage, set predictions, and read the passage.
2. Find the main idea and important details.
3. Explain them in your own words.
4. Skim the passage again to make sure you have included all the important points.
5. Begin your summary by stating the main idea. Then summarize the key details.

Quick Tip

A summary is shorter than the original passage. You can remember this because both *summary* and *shorter* start with *s.*

At first, you might stop to summarize after every paragraph or two. With practice, however, you should be able to summarize a page or two at a time. Try it now by summarizing the following passage from a speech delivered by Sojourner Truth at the women's rights convention in Akron, Ohio, in 1851.

Well, children, where there is so much racket there must be something out of kilter. I think that 'twixt the Negroes of the South and the women at the North, all talking about rights, the white men will be in a fix pretty soon. But what's all this here talking about?

That man over there says that women need to be helped into carriages, and lifted over ditches, and to have the best place everywhere. Nobody ever helps me into carriages, or over mud-puddles, or gives me any best place! And ain't I a woman? Look at me! Look at my arm! I have ploughed and planted, and gathered into barns, and no man could head me! And ain't I a woman? I could work as much and eat as much as a man—when I could get it—and bear the lash as well! And ain't I a woman? I have borne thirteen children, and see them all sold off to slavery, and when I cried out with my mother's grief, none but Jesus heard me! And ain't I a woman?

Then they talk about this thing in the head; what's that they call it? ["Intellect" someone whispers.] That's it, honey. What's that got to do with women's rights or Negro's rights? If my cup won't hold but a pint, and yours holds a quart, wouldn't you be mean not to let me have my little half-measure full? . . .

If the first woman God ever made was strong enough to turn the world upside down all alone, these women together ought to be able to turn it back, and get it right side up again! And now they is asking to do it, the men better let them.

Obliged to you for hearing me, and now old Sojourner ain't got nothing more to say.

Here is a sample summary:

African Americans in the South are agitating for emancipation while white women in the North are agitating for suffrage. Some men claim that women are weak creatures, but I'm stronger than any man! No one ever helped me, either. I've felt more anguish, too, but no one ever gave me a break. No matter how intelligent someone claims to be, it doesn't matter. Women are strong and the men blocking their way better let them have their rights.

Skim, Question, Read, Recite, Review (SQ3R)

The SQ3R method is a great way to get the most out of your reading. It works especially well with material you have to study, such as textbooks. To use SQ3R, follow these steps:

1. *Survey.* Preview the text by reading the title, headings, illustrations, and captions. Based on your survey, make predictions about the contents. Then skim the passage to get its overall meaning.

2. *Question.* As you survey and skim, ask questions about the material and what you find. Start by turning the title into a question. For example, look ahead at the passage "Literature." Turn this title into a question such as "What will this author say about literature?" or "How does the author define literature?" As you read, look for the answer to this question.

3. *Read.* Read the passage and continue making and revising predictions. Try to find the main idea by looking at the topic sentence and details in each paragraph.

4. *Recite.* After you finish reading, look back over the passage. Focus on the title, headings, and topic sentences. Summarize the material in your head, reducing what you read to a few sentences. Then recite your summary aloud.

5. *Review.* Review by looking back to your predictions. Were they on target? If so, find the details you used to make them. If not, figure out where and why you guessed incorrectly.

Try SQ3R with the following passage, in which English essayist Thomas De Quincey (1785–1859) discusses the literature of knowledge and the literature of power.

Literature

What is it that we mean by *literature?* Popularly, and amongst the thoughtless, it is held to include everything that is printed in a book. Little logic is required to disturb *that* definition. The most thoughtless person is easily made aware that in the idea of *literature* one essential element is some relation to a general and common interest of man—so that what applies only to a local, or professional, or merely personal interest, even though presenting itself in the shape of a book will not belong to Literature. So far the definition is easily narrowed; and it is easily expanded. For not only is much that takes a station in books not literature; but inversely, much that really *is* literature never reaches a station in books. The weekly sermons of Christendom, that vast pulpit of literature which acts so extensively upon the popular mind—to warn, to uphold, to renew, to comfort, to alarm—does not attain the sanctuary of libraries in the ten-thousandth part of its extent. The Drama again—as, for instance, the finest of Shakespeare's plays in England, and all leading Athenian plays in the noontide of the Attic stage—operated as literature on the public mind, and were (according to the strictest letter of that term) *published* through the audiences that witnessed their representation some time before they were published as things to be read; and they were published in this scenic mode of publication with much more effect than they could have had as books during ages of costly copying or of costly printing. . . .

But a far more important correction, applicable to the common vague idea of literature, is to be sought not so much in a better definition of literature as in a sharper distinction of the two functions which it fulfills. In that great social organ which, collectively, we call literature, there may be distinguished two separate offices. . . . There is, first, the literature of *knowledge;* and secondly, the literature of *power.* The function of the first is—to *teach;* the function of the second is—to *move:* the first is a rudder; the second, a sail. The first speaks to the *mere* discursive [ordered in a logical way] understanding; the second speaks ultimately, to the higher understanding or reason, but always *through* affections of pleasure and sympathy.

Here's how one reader used SQ3R with this passage:

- *Survey.* "Based on reading the title and heading, I predict that this paragraph will tell about literature."
- *Question.* "I'll turn the title into this question: What is this writer going to say about literature?"
- *Read.* "I've read about halfway. I now predict that the author will continue to narrow his definition of literature by talking about what literature *is* and what it *is not.*"
- *Recite.* "Here's my summary: Some people think that *literature* is anything printed in a book, but a lot of what is printed in a book is not literature at all. On the other hand, much of what never gets printed *is* literature, such as sermons and the plays of Shakespeare and the Greeks. They became 'published' by being spread through the pulpit and the stage. Literature has two purposes: to teach and to empower."

- *Review.* "I guessed correctly: the author continues to narrow his definition of literature and provide examples."

Skim, Mark, Read, Review (SMRR)

As with SQ3R, SMRR combines many powerful reading techniques to give you a study boost. SMRR is especially good when you are studying a text, because you highlight important details. However, try both SQ3R and SMRR to decide which one works better for you. Here's how to use SMRR:

- *Skim.* Preview the passage by scanning the title, heading, art, and captions. Then read the passage as quickly as you can.
- *Mark.* Using a highlighter, pencil, or pen, mark the topic sentence and key details. Of course, never mark a text that doesn't belong to you!
- *Read.* Read the text slowly and carefully, checking that you correctly identified the main idea and important points.
- *Reread.* Go back over the text, checking that you understood the main idea.

Quick Tip

Photocopy an important text that you don't own so you can annotate it. Highlighters don't work well on photocopy paper, so use a pencil or a pen.

The following passage is from Winston Churchill's first speech as prime minister, delivered on May 19, 1940. As you read the passage, practice using SMRR.

> I speak to you for the first time as Prime Minister in a solemn hour for the life of our country, of our Empire, of our Allies, and, above all, of the cause of Freedom. A tremendous battle is raging in France and Flanders. The Germans, by a remarkable combination of air bombing and heavily armored tanks, have broken through the French defenses north of the Maginot Line, and strong columns of their armored vehicles are ravaging the open country, which for the first day or two was without defenders. They have penetrated deeply and spread alarm and confusion in their track. Behind them there are now appearing infantry in lorries, and behind them again, the large masses are moving forward. The regroupment of the French armies to make head against, and also to strike at, this intruding wedge has been proceeding for several days, largely assisted by the magnificent forces of the Royal Air Force.
>
> We must not allow ourselves to be intimidated by the presence of these armored vehicles in unexpected places behind our lines. If they are behind our Front, the French are also at many points fighting actively behind theirs. Both sides are therefore in an extremely dangerous position. And if the French Army, and our own Army, are well handled, as I believe they will be, if the French retain that genius for recovery and

counter-attack for which they have so long been famous, and if the British Army shows the dogged endurance and solid fighting power of which there have been so many examples in the past—then a sudden transformation of the scene might spring into being.

It would be foolish, however, to disguise the gravity of the hour. It would be still more foolish to lose heart and courage or to suppose that well-trained, well-equipped armies numbering three or four million men can be overcome in the space of a few weeks, or even a few months, by a scoop, or raid of mechanized vehicles, however formidable. We may look with confidence to the stabilization of the Front in France, and to the general engagement of the masses, which will enable the qualities of the French and British soldiers to be matched squarely against those of their adversaries. For myself, I have invincible confidence in the French Army and its leaders. Only a very small part of that splendid army has yet been heavily engaged; and only a very small part of France has yet been invaded. There is good evidence to show that practically the whole of the specialized and mechanized forces of the enemy have already been thrown into the battle; and we know that very heavy losses have been inflicted upon them. No officer or man, no brigade or division, which grapples at close quarters with the enemy, wherever encountered, can fail to make a worthy contribution to the general result. The Armies must cast away the idea of resisting behind concrete lines or natural obstacles, and must realize that mastery can only be regained by furious and unrelenting assault. . . .

Our task is not only to win the battle—but to win the War. After this battle on France abates, there will come the battle for our island—for all that Britain is, and all that Britain means. That will be the struggle. In that supreme emergency we shall not hesitate to take every step, even the most drastic, to call forth from our people the last ounce and the last inch of effort of which they are capable. The interests of property, the hours of labor, are nothing compared with the struggle for life and honor, for right and freedom, to which we have vowed ourselves. . . .

Today is Trinity Sunday. Centuries ago words were written to be a call and a spur to the faithful servants of Truth and Justice: "Arm yourselves, and be ye men of valor, and be in readiness for the conflict; for it is better for us to perish in battle than to look upon the outrage of our nation and our altar. And the Will of God is in Heaven, even so let it be."

Monitor Comprehension

As you read, check on your understanding. It's especially important to pause and regroup if you get confused. Ask yourself, "What am I having trouble understanding?" Once you know, try some of the following strategies to get back on track.

Strategy Checklist

- Read more slowly.
- Reread any parts that confuse you.
- Look back at the pictures, charts, illustrations, and photographs.
- Use the details to visualize or imagine the scene you're reading.
- Restate what you've read in your own words.
- Ask yourself, "What is the main idea?" Reread the text for details and clues.

- Get some help. Use a reference book such as a dictionary to help you define words you don't know. Ask a professor or classmate to help you interpret a passage.

You can also change your reading rate to accommodate the text. Vary your reading rate in the following ways:

Skim the text when . . .

- You want to preview text to decide whether to read it
- You need only a general idea of the contents of the text

Scan the text when . . .

- You need to find a specific fact in the text
- You are looking for names or dates
- You need only some of the information from the text

Read slowly and carefully when . . .

- You're confused about the content or stuck on a specific point
- You've lost the author's main idea
- You're studying for a test
- You want to make sure you understand all of the author's points
- The information contains a lot of difficult or new words
- The information contains a lot of new concepts or ideas

Read at a comfortable rate when . . .

- You're reading for enjoyment
- The text seems fairly easy to read

Quick Tip

Practice is the best way to boost your critical reading comprehension skills, so read every minute you can. "I don't have the time to read," you say. Think about little parcels of time that are otherwise wasted. Use the time you spend standing in line at the bus stop, sitting in the dentist's office, or tapping your heels waiting for a late appointment. You can use all of these "lost minutes" to read.

- ✔ Get an overview of a text by skimming and scanning it.
- ✔ Summarize a text by restating the content in your own words.
- ✔ Boost your reading comprehension by using the proven reading strategies of SQ3R (skim, question, read, recite, review) and SMRR (skim, mark, read, review).

✔ If you lose the thread of the text, stop and reread. You can also look back at the pictures, restate and summarize the content, and check with an outside source for clarification.

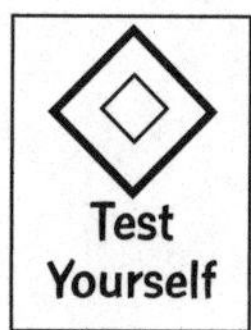

QUESTIONS

True-False Questions

1. When you want to get a general idea about a text and you don't have much time, your best bet is reading the text slowly and carefully.
2. Skimming is a good substitute for a complete reading.
3. Skim *before* you read the text . . . not *instead* of reading it.
4. Summarize every time you study to help you understand and remember what you read.
5. A summary is usually far longer than the original passage.
6. Always preview the text by reading the title, headings, illustrations, and captions
7. SMRR is especially good when you're studying a text, because you highlight important details.
8. As you read, don't pause and regroup if you get confused. It's more important to press on because all confusing passages will be clarified by the end.
9. Read at a comfortable rate when you need only some of the information from the text.
10. Practice is the best way to boost your critical reading comprehension skills, so read every minute you can.

Completion Questions

1. _________ is a very fast method of reading that lets you glance at a passage to identify its main idea or to find a key point.
2. To _________, find the most important information and restate it in your own words.
3. To ensure that you have included all the important _________ in your summary, your summary should answer the questions *who, what, when, where, why,* and *how.*
4. Based on your survey, make _________ about the contents of a passage.
5. As you survey and skim, ask questions about the material and what you find. Start by turning the title into a _________.
6. Summarize the material in your head, reducing what you read to a few sentences. Then _________ your summary aloud.
7. You can also change your _________ to accommodate the difficulty of the text.

8. _________ the text when you need only a general idea of the contents of the text.
9. Read _________ when you're studying for a test.
10. To read every minute you can, why not use the _________ you spend waiting in line at the bus stop, sitting in the dentist's office, or tapping your heels waiting for a late appointment.

Multiple-Choice Questions

1. Follow these steps as you skim a text:
   (a) Skim, preview, and pause to restate the meaning
   (b) Make predictions, skim, preview, and pause to restate the meaning
   (c) Preview, make predictions, skim, and pause to restate the meaning
   (d) Make predictions, skim, preview, and pause to restate the meaning
2. To summarize a passage,
   (a) Preview, find the main idea and key details, and restate them in your own words
   (b) Preview the passage, set predictions, and read the passage
   (c) Summarize the key details and then state the main idea
   (d) Read the passage, preview, and summarize by restating the main idea in your own words
3. SQ3R stands for
   (a) Skim, question, read, recite, review
   (b) Scan, question, recite, review, read
   (c) Skim, question, review, reread, recite
   (d) Scan, question, read, review, reread
4. As you read a passage, try to find the main idea by looking
   (a) At the author's name
   (b) At the illustrations
   (c) Ahead to the ending
   (d) At the topic sentence and details in each paragraph
5. After you read, review the text by
   (a) Setting new predictions
   (b) Looking back to your prediction
   (c) Surveying the text
   (d) Once again studying the graphics and visuals
6. SMRR stands for
   (a) Summarize, mark, reread, review
   (b) Survey, mark, recite, reread

   (c) Scan, mark, review, revise
   (d) Skim, mark, read, review

7. If you become confused while you're reading, try all of the following techniques *except*
   (a) Stop reading and try a different text
   (b) Reread any parts that confuse you
   (c) Restate what you've read in your own words
   (d) Use the details to visualize or imagine the scene you're reading
8. Skim the text when
   (a) You've lost the author's main idea
   (b) You're studying for a test
   (c) You want to preview text to decide whether to read it
   (d) You want to make sure you understand all of the author's points
9. Read slowly and carefully when
   (a) The information contains a lot of difficult or new words
   (b) You need to find a specific fact in the text
   (c) You are looking for names or dates
   (d) You need only some of the information from the text
10. Read at a comfortable rate when . . .
   (a) You want to preview text to decide whether to read it
   (b) You're reading for enjoyment
   (c) You need to find a specific fact in the text
   (d) You are looking for names or dates

ANSWER KEY

True-False Questions

1. F 2. F 3. T 4. T 5. F 6. T 7. T 8. F 9. F 10. T

Completion Questions

1. Skimming 2. Summarize 3. Details 4. Predictions 5. Question
6. Recite 7. Reading rate 8. Skim 9. Slowly or carefully 10. Time

Multiple-Choice Questions

1. c 2. a 3. a 4. d 5. b 6. d 7. a 8. c 9. a 10. b

CHAPTER 10

Meaning Matters

You should read this chapter if you need to review or learn about

- Identifying key details in a reading
- Finding the stated main idea in a text
- Making inferences and drawing conclusions from a passage

Get Started

Good readers draw meaning from identifying the main idea and key details that support the main idea. They also read between the lines to find unstated information in a text.

Identify Key Details

I kept six honest serving men
They taught me all I knew
Their names are What and Where and When
And How and Why and Who

—Rudyard Kipling

Like the poet Rudyard Kipling, readers can learn what they need to know by asking the important questions *what, where, when, how, why, which,* and *who.* That's because good readers are like detectives: they look for clues to support their conclusions. Reading comprehension is a vital part of study success, so examine every passage to find the *details:* small pieces of information that support the main idea.

How can you recognize details in a passage? Details will fall into these six main categories:

1. Examples — *Examples* illustrate a writer's point. Examples help readers understand a general statement by giving specific information that represents one part of the whole concept.
2. Facts — *Facts* are statements that can be proven. For example, the statement "John F. Kennedy was the first Catholic president of the United States" is a fact. It can be verified, and there are no reasonable arguments against it.
3. Statistics — *Statistics* are numbers used to give additional information. Statistics can be presented in different ways, such as charts, graphs, lists, percentages, and decimals.
4. Reasons — *Reasons* are explanations that tell *why* something happened. Reasons may also explain the cause of someone's beliefs or actions.
5. Definitions — *Definitions* are statements that explain what something means.
6. Descriptions — *Descriptions* are words or phrases that tell *how* something looks, smells, tastes, sounds, or feels. Descriptions use sensory words to help readers visualize or get a mental picture of what they are reading.

To better understand how details back up main ideas, study this Figure 10-1.

Follow this three-step plan to find the details in a passage.

1. *Identify the topic.* The *topic* of a paragraph is its subject. It tells what the paragraph is all about in one or two words. Sample topics include *Renaissance painters, supply-side economics, the Supreme Court, checks and balances, abnormal psychology, airplane safety, underwriting policies.*
2. *Identify the main idea.* After you find the topic, look for the *main idea.* It is be stated in the *topic sentence,* the sentence that gives the most general information about the topic. The topic sentence can be located anywhere in a paragraph, but very often it is be placed first. You know that you have picked the correct sentence if it introduces the topic or indicates what the entire passage discusses.

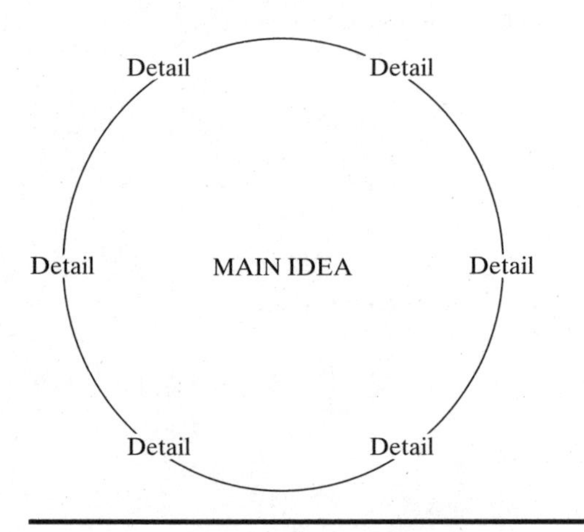

Fig. 10-1 Notice how the details support the main idea.

3. *Find details that back up the main idea.* Look for the details that directly back up the main idea. They are the fine points you can use to answer questions on your exams.

As you read the following passage, isolate the significant details. Then answer the questions.

The Highest Court in the Land

The federal system of courts in America is like a pyramid, with state courts on the bottom and federal courts in the middle. At the very top of the pyramid is the Supreme Court, the "court of last resort." The nine Supreme Court Justices have "original jurisdiction" (the power to try cases that have not been previously tried by a lower court) over very few types of cases. They may try disputes between two states, for example, or a case involving an ambassador. However these "original jurisdiction" cases are rare. Instead, most of the Supreme Court's time is spent reviewing decisions that have already been made in lower courts. Each year, the Supreme Court justices receive more than 5,000 petitions to review such decisions. They accept only the most important of these. The Supreme Court considers cases that demand a decision about the meaning of the Constitution, or a specific federal law. When the Supreme Court reaches a decision about a case, it's a final decision. The decisions of the Supreme Court result in laws that have an impact on us all.

1. According to the paragraph, how many justices serve on the Supreme Court?

   A. Six

   B. Nine

   C. Twelve

   D. 5000

2. Which types of cases do the Supreme Court justices review most often?

   A. Disputes between two states

   B. Cases involving ambassadors

   C. Cases about national monuments

   D. Decisions from lower courts

3. How many petitions a year are submitted to the Supreme Court?

   A. About nine

   B. At least 200

   C. Petitions are very rarely submitted to the Supreme Court

   D. More than 5000

4. The Supreme Court's decisions are special because

   A. They are final

   B. They can be reconsidered at a later date

   C. They are not very important

   D. They affect only some people in the nation

5. Based on these details, what do you think is the main idea of this paragraph?

   A. State courts are the lowest on the pyramid of the federal court system.

   B. The Supreme Court rarely tries "original jurisdiction" cases.

   C. The Supreme Court is the "court of last resort."

   D. The Supreme Court receives many petitions to review cases.

Answers

1. B 2. D 3. D 4. A 5. C

Try it again with the following passage. As you read, isolate the significant details. Then answer the questions.

Come One, Come All!

By the 1800s, several hundred medicine shows were traveling across America, giving a wide variety of shows. At one end of the scale were simple magic acts; at the other, complicated spectacles. From 1880 to 1910, one of the largest of these shows was "The King of the Road Shows," the Kickapoo Indian Medicine Company. Two experienced entertainers, Charles H. "Texas Charlie" Bigelow and John E. "Doc" Healy, had started the company more than two decades before. From their headquarters in New Haven, Connecticut, the partners sent as many as twenty-five shows at a time across America.

Texas Charlie managed the "medicine" end of the production, training the "Doctors" and "Professors" who gave the "Medical Lectures." Doc Healy was in charge of hiring the performers—from fiddlers to fire-eaters, including comedians, acrobats, singers, and jugglers. Both Indians and whites were hired. All the Indians, including Mohawks, Iroquois, Crees, Sioux, and Blackfeet, were billed as "pure-blooded Kickapoos," a completely fictional tribe.

All the entertainers wore outrageous costumes. The Native Americans were covered in feathers, colored beads, and crude weapons. The "Doctors" and "Professors" were equally glittery. Some wore fringed leather coats, silver-capped boots; others, fancy silk shirts, a type of tuxedo jacket called a "frock coat," and high silk hats. One of the most outlandish figures was the glib "Nevada Ned, the King of Gold." Born Ned T. Oliver, this entertainer wore a fancy suit studded with buttons made of gold. On his head he sported a huge sombrero dangling 100 gold coins.

During the summer, the Kickapoo shows were presented under enormous tents. When the weather turned chilly, the troupe moved into town halls and opera houses. Most often, the show was free. Occasionally, adults were charged a dime to get in. Where did the profits come from? The sale of "medicine." According to the show's advertisements, these wonder-working Kickapoo brews were "compounded according to secret ancient Kickapoo Indian tribal formulas." Among the ingredients were "blood root, feverwort, spirit gum, wild pokeberries, slippery elm, white oak bark, dock root, and other Natural Products." These "medicines" sold for fifty cents to a dollar a bottle, and were guaranteed to cure all the ills that afflict the human body.

1. According to paragraph 1, the Kickapoo Indian medicine show was started by

    A. Two men who did not have a lot of experience in the entertainment field

    B. Members of the Kickapoo Indian tribe

    C. Charles H. "Texas Charlie" Bigelow and John E. "Doc" Healy

    D. The King of the Road Shows

2. According to paragraph 2, the Kickapoo tribe was

    A. A group of Mohawks, Iroquois, Crees, Sioux, and Blackfeet

    B. A group of talented fiddlers, fire-eaters, comedians, acrobats, singers, and jugglers

    C. Pure-blooded Indians

    D. A made-up tribe

3. According to paragraph 3, which performers wore Western clothing such as leather jackets and fancy boots?

    A. The "Doctors" and "Professors"

    B. The Native Americans

    C. "Nevada Ned, the King of Gold"

    D. Everyone in the show at one time or another

4. According to paragraph 4, where did the Kickapoo entertainers perform when the weather was warm?

    A. In town halls

    B. Under huge tents

    C. In opera houses

    D. Out in the open air, under the stars

5. Based on these details, what do you think is the main idea of paragraph 3?

    A. The Native Americans wore the most beautiful costumes of all.

    B. One of the most far-out figures was the smooth-talking "Nevada Ned, the King of Gold."

    C. Everyone in the show wore wildly colorful outfits.

    D. The costumes cost a lot of money and were very difficult to make.

Answers
1. C 2. D 3. D 4. B 5. B

Find a Stated Main Idea

To find the stated main idea in a passage, follow these steps:

1. Find the *topic* or subject of the passage.
2. Look for a sentence that gives an overview of the topic. It will explain what the entire paragraph is about.
3. Check to see whether the sentence tells what the paragraph is about.

Although the stated main idea is often the first sentence, it can be in the middle or end of a paragraph as well. Following are some examples. The main idea in each one is underlined.

Main idea in the *beginning* of a passage

The Florida landscape boasts a wide variety of plant life—about thirty-five hundred different kinds. Almost half of all the different kinds of trees found in America grow in Florida. Some of Florida's woodlands are filled with majestic coniferous pines. Swamp maples, bald cypresses, bays, and oaks flourish in some of the state's forests. Still other wooded areas are a mix of different types and species of plant life. Dozens of different kinds of subtropical trees can be found in the Florida peninsula and the Keys. The warm climate in these areas nourishes the strangler fig, royal palm, and mangroves, for example.

Main idea in the *middle* of a passage

Businesspeople are dressed neatly—the women in suits or skirts and blouses and the men in jackets, ties, pressed pants, and stiffly starched shirts. Restaurant servers are polite to tourists and residents alike. Children stand quietly by their parents. Almost all aspects of life on the island are polite and civilized. People hold doors open for each other, wait to get into elevators until everyone has gotten off, and step aside to let those in a rush get by. At noon, the shops close and everyone goes home for a two-hour rest. But if you ask the shopkeepers to stay open a little longer, they will often gladly oblige.

Main idea in the *end* of a passage

The brown pelican, Florida's most popular bird, can often be seen perched on jetties, bridges, and piers. The state wetlands boast herons, egrets, wood ducks, and roseate spoonbills (often mistaken for flamingos). On the beach you can find sanderlings, plovers, and oystercatchers. The state bird, the mockingbird, likes living in suburban neighborhoods. Offshore, cormorants, black skimmers, and terns look for their dinner. Florida's forests shelter quail, wild turkey, owls, and woodpeckers. In all, more than a hundred native species of birds have been found in Florida.

Find the stated main idea in the following passage.

Tsunamis

Tsunamis, or seismic sea-waves, are gravity waves set in motion by underwater disturbances associated with earthquakes. These waves are frequently called "tidal waves" although they have nothing to do with the tides. Tsunamis consist of a decaying train of waves and may be detectable on tide gauges for as long as a week. Near its origin, the first wave of a tsunami may be the largest; at greater distances, the largest is normally between the second and seventh wave.

You can find the stated main idea in the first sentence: Tsunamis, or seismic sea-waves, are gravity waves set in motion by underwater disturbances associated with earthquakes.

Deduce an Unstated Main Idea

Sometimes writers don't directly state the main idea of a passage. In these cases, you have to make *inferences* to find the main idea. When you *make an inference,* you combine what you already know with spoken or textual clues to discover the unstated information. You may have head this referred to as "reading between the lines" or "putting two and two together." When you make an inference, you are drawing a conclusion from facts and speculation. In graphical form, the process of making an inference looks like this:

Text clues + what I know = inference

To find the unstated main idea in a passage, follow these steps:

1. Find the topic or subject of the passage.
2. Look for details that relate to the topic.
3. Make an inference about the main idea from the details.

Follow the three steps to infer the unstated main idea in the following passage.

Egypt, Land of the Pyramids

Egypt, a long, narrow, fertile strip of land in northeastern Africa, is the only place in the world where pyramids were built. Back then, all the water for the land and its people came from the mighty Nile River. Natural barriers protected the land from invaders. Around 300 B.C., when kings and other high Egyptian officials authorized the building of the first pyramids, these natural barriers protected the land from invaders. There were deserts to the east and west that cut off Egypt from the rest of the world. There were dangerous rapids on the Nile to the south. Delta marshes lay to the north. This circle of isolation allowed the Egyptians to work in peace and security. In addition, great supplies of raw materials were needed to build the pyramids. Ancient Egypt had an abundance of limestone, sandstone, and granite. These rocks were quarried close to the banks of the Nile. But these rocks had to be brought from quarries to the building sites. Egypt's most precious resource—the great Nile River—provided the means for transportation.

1. Find the topic or subject of the passage: *The pyramids of Egypt.*
2. Look for details that relate to the topic.

- *Natural barriers protected the land from invaders.*
- *Ancient Egypt had the raw materials: limestone, sandstone, and granite.*
- *Workers transported the stone on the Nile River.*

3. Make an inference about the main idea from the details: *Ancient Egypt had a unique combination of factors necessary for building the pyramids.*

Quick Tip

If you find that you're having difficulty inferring the unstated main idea, reread the passage or use one of the reading techniques such as SQR3 or SMRR that you learned in Chapter 9.

Now identify the unstated main idea in the following passage.

Ancient savage tribes played a primitive kind of football. About 2,500 years ago there was a ball-kicking game played by the Athenians, Spartans, and Corinthians, which the Greeks called *Episkuros.* The Romans had a somewhat similar game called *Harpastum.* According to several historical sources, the Romans brought the game with them when they invaded the British Isles in the first century, A.D. The game today known as "football" in the United States can be traced directly back to the English game of rugby, although there have been many changes to the game. Football was played informally on university fields more than a hundred years ago. In 1840, a yearly series of informal "scrimmages" started at Yale University. It took more than twenty-five years, however, for the game to become part of college life. The first formal intercollegiate football game was held between Princeton and Rutgers teams on November 6, 1869. It was held on Rutgers's home field at New Brunswick, New Jersey, and Rutgers won.

Which of the following statements represents the main idea?

A. The Romans, Athenians, Spartans, and Corinthians all played a game like football.
B. Football is a very old game; its history stretches back to ancient days.
C. American football comes from a British game called *rugby.*
D. Football is a more popular game than baseball, even though baseball is called "America's pastime."

Answer: Choice B. Eliminate choices A and C because they give supporting details, not the main idea. Eliminate choice D because it contains information that is not included in the paragraph.

✔ To identify key details in a passage, look for information that answers the questions *who, what, when, where, why,* and *how.*

✔ Look for the main idea, the author's point in a passage. Identifying the main idea helps you understand what you are reading.

✔ You can find a stated main idea in the topic sentence. Often, this will be the first or last sentence in a passage.

To infer an unstated main idea, combine details from the text with what you already know to draw conclusions.

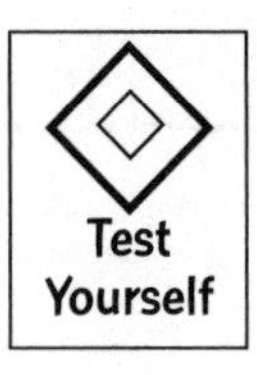

QUESTIONS

True-False Questions

1. Powerful readers are like detectives: they look for clues to support their conclusions about the author's point.
2. Details answer the questions *who, what, when, where, why,* and *how.*
3. Definitions are numbers used to give additional information.
4. A reason is a type of detail that can be verified, and there are no reasonable arguments against it.
5. Examples help readers understand a general statement by giving specific information that represents one part of the whole concept.
6. The topic sentence is usually located in the middle of a passage, with details above and below it.
7. When you make an inference, you are drawing a conclusion from what you already know and information in the text.
8. Finding a stated main idea can also be called "reading between the lines" or "putting two and two together."
9. Locating a stated main idea is easier than deducing an unstated main idea.
10. Good readers always look for the main idea in a passage to help them understand and recall the content.

Completion Questions

1. Reading comprehension is a vital part of study success, so you should examine every passage to find the _________, small pieces of information that support the main idea.
2. _________ are statements that can be proven.

3. _________ are statements that explain what something means. They often come from a dictionary.
4. Writers use details to help readers infer the _________ of a passage.
5. The *topic* of a paragraph is its _________.
6. The _________ is the sentence that gives the most general information about the topic.
7. When writers do not directly state the main idea of a passage, you have to make _________ to find the main idea.
8. Another term for making inferences is _________.
9. Every passage must contain a _________, the author's point.
10. If you can't find the main idea, you should _________ the passage and look for details.

Multiple-Choice Questions

1. Statistics can be presented in different ways, including all of the following *except*
   (a) Explanations that tell *why* something happened
   (b) Graphs
   (c) Decimals
   (d) Percentages
2. Descriptions are words or phrases that
   (a) Can be verified by outside sources
   (b) Explain why the author feels the way he or she does
   (c) Help readers visualize how something looks, smells, tastes, sounds, or feels
   (d) Involve numbers
3. To find the details in a passage, follow this process in the order stated:
   (a) Identify the topic, identify the main idea, find details that back up the main idea.
   (b) Skim the passage, identify the main idea, identify the topic.
   (c) Identify the main idea, find details that back up the main idea, identify the topic.
   (d) Identify the topic, find details that back up the main idea, reread the passage.
4. To find the stated main idea in a passage, follow this process in the order stated:
   (a) Look for a general statement, skim the passage, and draw conclusions about the content.
   (b) Find the topic, look for a general statement, and verify that the sentence summarizes the content.
   (c) Skim the passage, preview and predict, and find the topic sentence.
   (d) Locate the subject of the passage, "read between the lines," and verify the general statement.

5. The *topic* of a passage is also called its
   (a) Tone
   (b) Subject
   (c) Purpose
   (d) Audience
6. It's important to identify the main idea so that you
   (a) Study harder
   (b) Read more often
   (c) Read more quickly
   (d) Understand what you read
7. To find the unstated main idea in a passage, follow these steps:
   (a) Locate significant details, reread, draw a conclusion.
   (b) Draw a conclusion, find the topic, verify your inference by returning to the text.
   (c) Find the topic, look for relevant details, make an inference.
   (d) Make an inference, locate significant details, verify your conclusion by checking an outside source.

Read the following passage and answer the questions that follow:

What could be easier than grabbing a juicy cheeseburger, a creamy thick shake, and a bag of salty fries from a fast-food drive-in? It's fast and tastes great. These fast foods just seem to hit the spot that lettuce and bean sprouts can't. Unfortunately, in recent years Americans have discovered that many of their favorite fast foods are empty calories with no nutrition. Cheeseburgers, shakes, and fries are loaded with salt and fat; fried chicken has more cholesterol than motor oil. But what about people who just can't make it through a week without some fast food? Consider pizza. Although it is usually lumped together with all the other "fast foods"—burgers, fried chicken, hot dogs, and filet of fish, pizza is *not* the same as these foods. Pizza contains many of the vitamins and minerals that we need. This is especially true when the pizza is made with fresh ingredients. The crust provides us with carbohydrates, an excellent low-calorie source of energy. The cheese and meat provide our bodies with the building blocks of protein. The tomatoes, herbs, onions, and garlic supply us with vitamins and minerals.

8. What is the topic of this passage?
   (a) Pizza's relative nutritional value
   (b) The importance of good nutrition
   (c) Fast foods
   (d) The importance of eating well
9. What have many Americans learned recently?
   (a) Pizza tastes better than other fast foods.
   (b) Fast foods have a lot of salt and fat.

(c) Pizza costs less than other fast foods.
(d) Many fast foods taste great.

10. The implied main idea of this paragraph is
    (a) People should stay away from all junk food
    (b) Many fast foods are not good for you
    (c) Pizza is healthier for you than many people think
    (d) Pizza gives us carbohydrates for energy

ANSWER KEY

True-False Questions

1. T 2. T 3. F 4. F 5. T 6. F 7. T 8. F 9. T 10. T

Completion Questions

1. Details 2. Facts 3. Definitions 4. Main idea 5. Subject
6. Topic sentence 7. Inferences 8. Drawing conclusions or reading between the lines 9. Main idea 10. Reread

Multiple-Choice Questions

1. a 2. c 3. a 4. b 5. b 6. d 7. c 8. a 9. b 10. c

CHAPTER 11

Be a Power Reader

You should read this chapter if you need to review or learn about

- The relationship between reading and vocabulary
- Using genre structure clues to increase comprehension
- Pumping up your reading speed
- Understanding more of what you read

In Chapter 10, you learned how to identify key details in a text. Finding key pieces of information helps you to find the main idea in a text so you get the gist of what you're reading. In this chapter, you will learn techniques for reading faster and absorbing more.

Get Started

Boost your vocabulary, use textual structure clues, and learn speed-reading techniques to become a power reader. Faster reading + greater comprehension = test success.

Boost Your Vocabulary

When people say, "I can't read well," they often mean, "I get stuck on the difficult words." A bigger vocabulary and strong reading skills go hand in hand. The more words you know and understand, the more easily you will comprehend what you read. Because reading will be less of a chore, you'll enjoy it more, too. When you study words in this book as well as in other sources, mentally arrange them in these three categories:

1. *Words you know.* These are the words you can *define.* You should know secondary as well as primary definitions. You can comfortably use these words in a sentence, too. For example,

emollient uh *mawl* yunt adj., softening and soothing; n., something that softens or soothes

So you didn't know *emollient?* You do now!

2. *Words you* think *you know.* These are words that you have seen before and perhaps even used in conversation and speech. However, you're not exactly sure what they mean. As you read, you usually figure out these words by their *context,* the surrounding words and phrases.

- *Definition clues* have the definition right in the passage. The definition is a *synonym* (word that means the same). It may come before or after the unfamiliar word.
- *Contrast clues* tell you what something *isn't* rather than what it is. Often, you'll find contrast clues set off with *unlike, not,* or *instead of.*
- *Commonsense clues* encourage you to use what you already know to define the word.

3. *Words you've seen only once or never.* On nearly every test and in every professional document, you'll find words that are completely new to you. If you can't figure out these words through context clues and they are crucial to the meaning, it pays to stop reading and look them up in a dictionary. Keep a word journal, writing down all the new vocabulary you collect in this way. The simple act of writing the words can help fix them in your mind.

Use Structure Clues

Identifying the structure of a reading selection can also help you increase your comprehension. Fiction is structured according to *chronological* order, the order of time. Events are arranged from first to last, as on a timeline. Fiction writers often use dates to show the order of events. In addition, writers can use time-order words to show when events happen, word such as *after, at length, before, currently, during, eventually, first, second, third* (and so on) *finally, immediately, in the future, later, meanwhile, next, now, soon, subsequently, then, today.*

Nonfiction articles are often arranged in one of three ways: chronological order, cause-and-effect order, or comparison-and-contrast order.

- *Cause-and-effect order* shows the reason something happened (the cause) and the results (the effect). Signal words include *as a result, because, consequently, due to, for, for this* (*that*) *reason, if . . . then, nevertheless, since, so, so that, therefore, thus, this* (*that*) *is how.*
- *Comparison-and-contrast order* shows how two people, places, or things are the same (comparison) and different (contrast).

Determine Your Reading Speed and Comprehension

To determine your present *reading speed,* read the following selection, "Power to the People," for precisely one minute. Then note the line at which you stopped reading and multiply that number by 10 (the average number of words per line). This is your initial reading speed. See Figure 11-1 to determine your relative speed.

Reading Speed		
500–1500 words per minute	=	speed reader
250 words per minute	=	rate of average reader
150 words per minute	=	rate of average speaker

Fig. 11-1 Calculate your reading rate or speed.

Reading fast is useless if you don't understand what you read. To determine your present *level of comprehension,* allow yourself 15 minutes to read "Power to the People" and then answer the questions that follow. Score yourself by using the answer key to determine how well you understood the main idea. Compare your results to Figure 11-2.

Power to the People

1 America's electric utilities are finding that helping their customers use energy more efficiently can be a cost-effective and reliable alternative for meeting electricity demand growth. The opportunities for efficiency improvements are myriad and potential savings real, but customers and utilities have been slow to invest in the
5 most cost-effective energy-efficient technologies available.

Reading Comprehension		
Excellent comprehension	=	9–10 correct
Above-average comprehension	=	7–8 correct
Average comprehension	=	5–6 correct
Below-average comprehension	=	fewer than 4 correct

Fig. 11-2 Calculate your level of reading comprehension.

The energy efficiency of today's buildings and electric equipment and appliances falls far short of what is technically available. This efficiency gap has been attributed to a variety of market, institutional, technical, and behavioral constraints. Electric utility energy-efficiency programs have great potential to narrow this gap and
10 achieve significant energy savings.

Utilities' energy-efficiency programs promise savings for customers and utilities, profits for shareholders, improvements in industrial productivity, enhanced international competitiveness, and reduced environmental impact. But along with opportunities, greater reliance on energy efficiency as a resource to meet future electricity
15 needs also entails risks—that efficient technologies will not perform as well as promised, that anticipated savings will not be truly cost effective in practice, and that costs and benefits of energy-efficiency programs will not be shared equally among utility customers.

In 1992, utility power generation accounted for 36 percent of total primary energy
20 use in the United States, and electricity consumption is growing faster than overall use. Current growth forecasts range from 1 to 3.5 percent per year over the next decade. Meeting this new demand could require construction of the equivalent of 50 to 220 new 1,000-megawatt power plants over 10 years. The differences in estimated new capacity needs reflects hundreds of billions of dollars for utility rate payers. Of
25 course, prospective electricity demand growth rates are uncertain, adding to the risks that utilities face in planning and building for the future.

Energy-efficiency advocates have long maintained that it can be cheaper for rate payers and better for the environment and society to save energy rather than build new power plants. This view is now embraced by many utilities, regulators, share-
30 holders, and customers. With more than ten years of experience with utility energy-efficiency programs, initial results are promising, but many uncertainties remain.

Efforts to harness the utility sector to achieve greater energy efficiency have focused on three strategies:

Demand-side management programs—utility-led efforts intended to affect the
35 timing or amount of customer energy use. Examples include rebates, loans, energy audits, utility installation of efficiency equipment, and load-management programs.

Integrated resource planning—a technique used by utilities and regulators to develop flexible plans for providing reliable and economical electricity supply
40 through a process that explicitly compares supply- and demand-side resource options on a consistent basis and usually has opportunities for public participation.

Regulatory incentives—for investment in energy-saving technologies adopted to offset the bias against energy-efficiency investments in traditional rate-making methods. Typically, utility profits have been based on the total value of capital
45 invested and the amount of power sold—creating a strong financial disincentive against energy efficiency or other investments that could reduce power sales and utility revenues. Examples include mechanisms decoupling utility revenues from power sales, cost recovery or rate basing of efficiency program expenditures, and performance bonuses and penalties.

50 More than thirty states have adopted integrated resource planning and demand-side management programs, and programs are being developed rapidly in most of the remaining states.

1. It's plain that utilities have not helped their customers maximize savings because they
   (a) Have not invested in new technology
   (b) Are not willing to help customers
   (c) Are not aware of the new technologies available
   (d) Realize that power sources are already as efficient as they can be
2. According to this passage, what is the cause of the efficiency gap?
   (a) Technical problems
   (b) Potential savings
   (c) Customers' disinterest
   (d) At least four different reasons
3. Energy-efficiency programs can realize savings for
   (a) Customers
   (b) Utilities
   (c) Shareholders
   (d) All of the above
4. Among the risks the author cites for relying on greater energy efficiency are
   (a) Consumer distrust of new technologies
   (b) Concerns about equal distribution of profits
   (c) Fears that savings will not be real
   (d) Problems with the utility sector itself
5. What is the relationship of electricity consumption to overall energy use?
   (a) They are growing at the same rate.
   (b) Electricity consumption is growing more quickly.
   (c) Electricity consumption is growing more slowly.
   (d) There is no relationship at all.
6. How many more megawatts of power does the author estimate will be needed?
   (a) 1000
   (b) 50,000 to 220,000

   (c) 5000 to 22,000
   (d) In excess of 500,000
7. Who will pay for this new construction?
   (a) Utility companies
   (b) The federal government
   (c) Utility users
   (d) The state government
8. According to the article, more and more people are coming to believe that
   (a) New power plants are the wave of the future
   (b) The federal government should step in and regulate the energy industry
   (c) We should conserve energy rather than erect new power plants
   (d) Energy efficiency is an unworkable plan
9. Which of the following programs is most popular?
   (a) Regulatory incentives
   (b) Integrated resource planning and demand-side management programs
   (c) Integrated resource planning and regulatory incentives
   (d) Demand-side management programs and regulatory incentives
10. This passage was most likely written by
   (a) The speaker for a utility company
   (b) A company bidding on a new power plant
   (c) A disgruntled rate payer
   (d) An unbiased observer

Answers

1. a   2. d   3. d   4. c   5. b   6. c   7. c   8. a   9. b   10. d

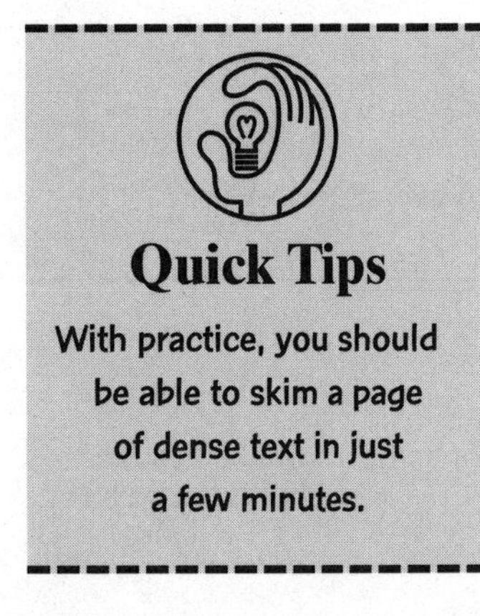

Skim a Passage to Pump Up Your Reading Speed

Francis Bacon once said, "Some books are to be tasted, others to be swallowed, and some to be chewed and digested." Consider this scenario: You have a real estate class in 15 minutes, but you haven't read the three chapters that will be discussed. Or how about these situations: You never got around to reading the article for your economics class, the material for your teacher certification class, or the briefs for LSAT review. What can you do? When you need a general idea of a text and you don't have the time to read in depth, *skimming* is the answer.

As you learned in previous chapters, skimming is a very fast way to read. Skimming allows you to glance at a passage to find specific information. This method is especially useful when there are only a few items of information that you want from a particular passage. It is not recommended as a substitute for studying a text in depth.

Here are two different ways that you can skim a passage.

Method 1: Straight down the middle

- Run your eyes down the middle of the page.
- Focus on the facts you need.

Method 2: Crisscross

- First scan from the top left corner to the bottom right corner.
- Then scan from the top right corner to the bottom left corner.

Skim either straight down the middle or crisscross with the following article. As you skim, look for the answers to these questions:

1. Where are the really interesting advances going to be made?
2. Why are huge databases useless?
3. What is the name of the Dow Jones News/Retrieval Service database retrieval service?
4. Why are these services important?
5. Who will be using such software in the future?

A Software Revolution

The really interesting advances are going to be in software development. Computers haven't made our lives simpler. In fact, they have made reality more complicated. These devices that were supposed to help us generate a great deal of information actually generated a great deal of data that has to be dealt with on a daily basis. Our customers have huge databases that they feel are the company's assets, but often there are so much data that they are virtually useless. Every single corporation is in that bind—or will be very shortly. They know that they have information about their clients, their suppliers, and their competitors, but they do not have a way to gather the data that can make it useful.

Dow Jones News/Retrieval Service has a DowQuest service. Here's how it works. Say that you have an article that you like. You can ask for more similar articles. That's an example of something that is terribly complicated that doesn't seem very complicated to people not familiar with how computers operate. It's a primitive version of what some leading-edge computer companies are already doing: making software that provides a simple way of looking at huge amounts of data. It's going to change the way that business operates.

The software will do what a very fast, very skilled, and very dedicated librarian could do. You can ask the computer a question in everyday language and the software will sift through your corporate database, find all the pertinent information, and throw out what is not useful. What will this accomplish? Fewer, not more, things will come across your desk. And you will get what you need.

Increasingly, you will see more business applications. For example, you will see an airline company using software to decide how much to charge for a seat or how many seats to allocate to each fare; a petrochemical company deciding how much of each product to manufacture given the kind of oil they have coming and the price they are paying for it. Business will make all these decisions more efficiently, thanks to the new software applications.

Answers

1. They will be in software development.
2. Their information cannot be easily accessed.
3. It is called DowQuest.
4. They will screen the information flooding in and you will get what you need.
5. Businesses will be using it.

Use Hand-Eye Techniques to Increase Reading Speed

Some people are able to read more quickly by using a marker, a pencil, or their fingers as they read. Running a marker across the page helps you focus on important words, details, and ideas. This helps you key into the most crucial facts and ignore extraneous details. Tracing your hand down the page automatically leads your eye down the type. This helps you move forward over the lines. Finally, moving your hand (or marker) down the page forces you to read faster than you speak. As a result, you don't mouth the words or read aloud, which always slows you down.

Here's how to use hand-eye techniques to pick up some reading speed:

1. Use an index card as a marker, hold a pencil eraser side down, or use your index finger.
2. Place your marker on the first word of the first line of type and focus your eyes *slightly* in front of your marker.
3. Move your marker from left to right across the line of type as you follow with your eyes.
4. When your eye reaches the right margin, move your marker slightly up and to the right to prevent abrupt stops.

Increase Your Comprehension by Reading on Three Levels

When you read, the full meaning of a text emerges on three levels: the *literal,* the *inferential,* and the *evaluative.* You will get more from a text if you learn to read on all three levels. Here's how to read for levels of meaning.

1. Look for the literal meaning.
   - Read exactly what the words say.
   - Find out what the author directly states in the text.
   - Ask yourself these questions: What are the important facts in this passage? What point is the author making? What happens in the story? What events move the story along?
2. Find the inferential meaning.
   - An *inference* is an educated guess about the content.
   - Combine information in the text with what you already know to make an inference.
   - When you make an inference, you are generalizing about the information you are reading. A *generalization* is a broad conclusion drawn from information in the text. The generalization is valid if it is based on sufficient evidence; it is invalid if the text contains exceptions to the statement.
   - Ask yourself these questions: What is implied rather than stated? What does the author expect me to know? What have I figured out that the writer does not directly state in the passage?
3. Make the evaluative leap.
   - *Evaluations* are judgments you make about the author's statements.
   - Make evaluations by deciding whether or not you agree with what the author has stated or implied in the text.
   - Make distinctions between facts and opinions to reach your own conclusions about the content.

✔ Improve your vocabulary to increase your reading speed and understanding.

✔ Analyze the structure of a passage to increase your reading comprehension.

✔ Skim a passage when you want to grasp the overall meaning quickly. Skimming alone is not an effective study technique, unless you are very short on time.

Use hand-eye techniques to track the type more efficiently.

✔ Read on the *literal,* the *inferential,* and the *evaluative* levels to grasp the author's full meaning and purpose.

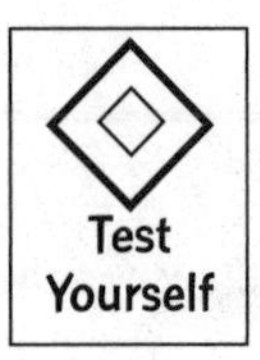

QUESTIONS

True-False Questions

1. When people say "I can't read well," they often mean, "I get stuck on the difficult words."

2. Vocabulary you know are words that you have seen before and perhaps even used in conversation and speech.
3. An *antonym* is a word that means the same as another word.
4. Definition clues encourage you to use what you already know to define the word.
5. Identifying the structure of a reading selection can help you increase your comprehension.
6. The average person reads about 250 words per minute.
7. The average speaker says about 500 to 1000 words per minute.
8. Reading fast is useless if you don't understand what you read.
9. Skimming is an effective substitute for studying a text in depth.
10. Everyone is able to read more quickly by using a marker, a pencil, or their fingers as they read.
11. When you read, the full meaning of a text emerges on three levels: the *literal,* the *inferential,* and the *evaluative.*
12. An *inference* is an educated guess about the content of a text.

Completion Questions

1. The more _________ you know and understand, the more easily you will comprehend what you read.
2. Words you know are the words you can _________ and confidently use in a sentence.
3. When you encounter words that you do not know, you can often figure them out by their _________, the surrounding words and phrases.
4. _________ clues have the meaning of the unfamiliar word right in the passage. It may come before or after the unfamiliar word.
5. _________ clues tell you what something *isn't* rather than what it is. Often, you'll find contrast clues set off with *unlike, not,* or *instead of.*
6. _________ clues encourage you to use what you already know to define the word.
7. Fiction is structured according to _________ order; the order of time.
8. _________ is often arranged in one of three ways: *chronological order, cause-and-effect order,* or *comparison-and-contrast order.*
9. _________ order shows how two people, places, or things are the same and different.
10. When you need a general idea of a text and you don't have the time to read in depth, the passage to get an overview of the content.

Multiple-Choice Questions

Using the strategies you learned in this chapter, read the following passage and answer the questions that follow.

Now estimate how few of those who do work are occupied in essential trades. For, in a society where we make money the standard of everything, it is necessary to practice many crafts which are quite vain and superfluous, ministering only to luxury and licentiousness. Suppose the host of those who now toil were distributed only over as few crafts as the few needs and conveniences demanded by nature. In the great abundance of commodities which must then arise, the prices set on them would be too low for the craftsmen to earn their livelihood by their work. But suppose all those fellows who are not busied with unprofitable crafts, as well as all the lazy and idle throng, any one of whom now consumes as much of the fruits of other men's labors as any two of the workingmen, were all set to work and indeed to useful work. You can easily see how small an allowance of time would be enough and to spare for the production of all that is required by necessity or comfort (or even pleasure, provided it be genuine and natural). . . .

Now is not this an unjust and ungrateful commonwealth? It lavishes great regards on so-called gentlefolk and banking goldsmiths and the rest of that kind, who are either idle or mere parasites and purveyors of empty pleasures. On the contrary, it makes no benevolent provisions for farmers, colliers, common laborers, carters, and carpenters without whom there would be no commonwealth at all. After it has misused the labor of their prime and after they are weighted down with age and disease and are in utter want, it forgets all their sleepless night and all the great benefits received at their hands and most ungratefully requites them with a most miserable death.

Yet when these evil men with insatiable greed have divided up among themselves all the goods which would have been enough for all the people, how far they are from the happiness of the Utopian commonwealth? In Utopia all greed for money was entirely removed with the use of money. What a mass of trouble was then cut away! What a crop of crimes was then pulled up by the roots! Who does not know that fraud, theft, rapine, quarrels, disorders, brawls, seditions, murders, treasons, poisonings, which are avenged rather than restrained by daily executions, die out with the destruction of money? Who does not know that fear, anxiety, worries, toils, and sleepless night will also perish at the same time as money? What is more, poverty, which alone money seems to make poor, forthwith would itself dwindle and disappear if money were entirely done away with everywhere.

1. In the opening lines, the speaker is critical of
   (a) Workingmen who do not suit their abilities to their jobs
   (b) The indolent upper classes
   (c) Unnatural pleasures and diversions
   (d) Essential trades
   (e) Our contempt for trades and elevation of the aristocracy
2. The phrase "any one of whom now consumes as much of the fruits of other men's labors as any two of the workingmen" refers to which of the following?
   (a) "The fruits of other men's labors"
   (b) "All those fellows"
   (c) "Unprofitable crafts"
   (d) "Useful work"
   (e) "The lazy and idle throng"

3. As used in the first paragraph, *licentiousness* most nearly means
   (a) A disregard for morals
   (b) Extravagance
   (c) Comfort
   (d) Delicacy
   (e) Self-denial
4. The "unjust and ungrateful commonwealth" in the second paragraph refers to
   (a) America
   (b) The workingmen
   (c) The vain and foolish upper classes
   (d) The current system of government
   (e) The author's proposed system of government
5. What is the speaker's bias in the second paragraph?
   (a) Toward the workingman
   (b) Against the workingman
   (c) Toward the commonwealth
   (d) Toward banking goldsmiths
   (e) Against age and disease
6. The tone of the last paragraph is best described as
   (a) Calm and dispassionate
   (b) Relaxed and self-assured
   (c) Tentative
   (d) Passionate and critical
   (e) Violent
7. Which phrase would the author most likely agree with?
   (a) A penny saved is a penny earned.
   (b) Money is the root of all evil.
   (c) Money makes the world go 'round.
   (d) You can't win it if you're not in it.
   (e) Money is essential.
8. The metaphor "What a crop of crimes was then pulled up by the roots" serves to
   (a) Make the author's abstract concept more specific and recognizable to his audience
   (b) Emphasize his main point about criminal activity
   (c) Refer to the recent outbreak of crime
   (d) Refute his critics
   (e) Compare and contrast his plan to his opponent's plan

9. The author's style is best described as
   (a) Highly abstract
   (b) Objective
   (c) Highly allusive
   (d) Informal and relaxed
   (e) Formal and elevated
10. Which is the best title for this excerpt?
   (a) The Collapse of the Commonwealth
   (b) Utopia
   (c) Economics and the Common Man
   (d) The Rich versus the Poor
   (e) Work and Play

ANSWER KEY

True-False Questions

1. T 2. F 3. F 4. F 5. T 6. T 7. F 8. T 9. F 10. F 11. T 12. T

Completion Questions

1. Words 2. Define 3. Context 4. Definition 5. Contrast 6. Commonsense 7. Chronological 8. Nonfiction 9. Comparison-and-contrast 10. Skimming

Multiple-Choice Questions

1. b 2. e 3. a 4. d 5. a 6. d 7. b 8. a 9. e 10. b

PART 4

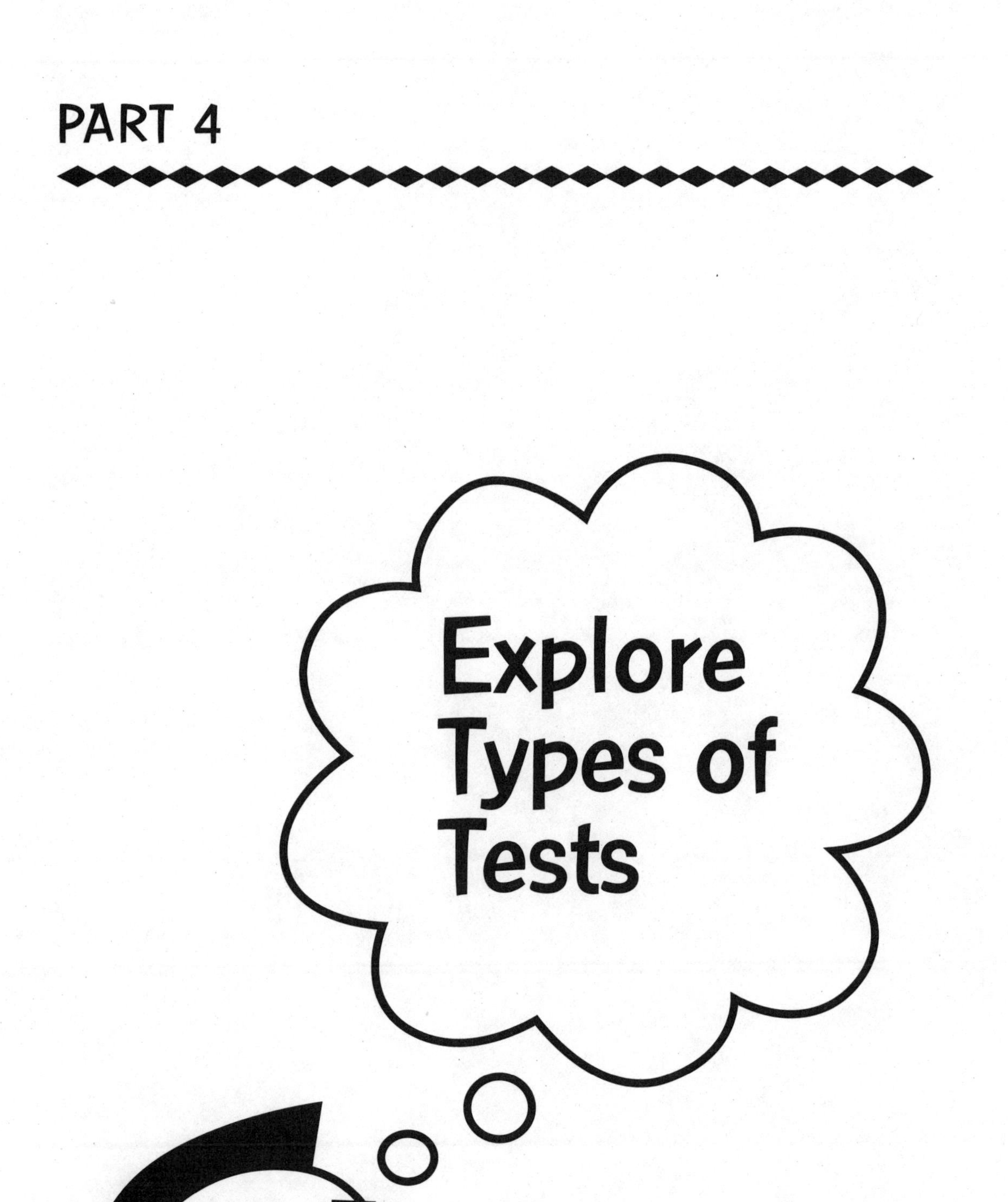

CHAPTER 12

Master Objective Tests

You should read this chapter if you need to review or learn about

- Judging the relative difficulty of objective test questions
- Earning high scores on true-false test item, multiple-choice test items, and matching test items
- Correctly solving fill-in-the-blank test items
- Doing your best on math tests

In Chapter 11, you learned how to increase your reading speed and comprehension. In this chapter, you will learn how to answer different types of short-answer questions, including true-false, multiple-choice, matching, and fill-in-the-blank test items.

Get Started

Develop a strategy for doing your best on objective items, because these are the mainstays of most standardized tests. Increasingly, standardized tests are becoming essential assessment tools in classrooms, degree curricula, and certificate programs. In addition, standardized tests are the entrance exams for quality colleges and graduate schools.

All Objective Test Questions Are *Not* the Same!

On a test, how can you determine which questions are simple and which ones are complex? Questions can be easy or difficult based on two factors: their content and their form.

- *Content* refers to the subject (i.e., the information the question tests).
- *Form* refers to the type of question (e.g., sentence completion, fill-in-the-blank, true-false, multiple-choice).

You judge the content based on the material you studied. For example, if you're being tested on vocabulary and you have memorized all the words, then the test content should be relatively easy for you. But if you didn't have the time to master the words, the content will pose serious problems.

Figure 12-1 can help you judge how difficult a question is based on its form.

Question Form and Level of Difficulty

Easier	More Difficult	Most Difficult
True-false	Analogies	Critical reading
Matching	Multiple-choice	Two-blank sentence completion
One-blank sentence completions		

Fig. 12-1 Use this chart to determine the level of difficulty of a test item.

Top 10 Hints for Scoring High on Objective Test Questions

Whether you're taking a low-stakes classroom true-false test or a high-stakes SAT, the following hints can help you do your very best.

1. *Know what to expect.* If at all possible, take practice exams so you know what you're facing when you take the real test. This is especially important with SATs, GMATs, LSATs, and other high-stake tests.

2. *Learn the directions.* On standardized objective tests, you can memorize the directions. This will help you save precious time. In addition, you won't be worrying about what's coming next on the test, because you'll be thoroughly familiar with the test format.

3. *Study.* You can't win it if you're not in it. For an important objective exam such as a college entrance test, set up a study schedule months before the exam and stick to it. Even if you're blessed with exceptionally gifted and hardworking teachers, how well you do on the test has a lot to do with the amount of reading, writing, and studying *you* do on your own.

4. *Use your time wisely.* In nearly all cases, the test questions are arranged in order of difficulty, from least difficult to most difficult. Most test takers do well on the easy questions, but few students do well on the most difficult questions. Because every question is worth the same number of points, you're better off spending your time making sure you correctly answer the easier and medium-difficulty questions rather than rushing to finish the entire test.

5. *Develop a test strategy.* There are three ways you can approach any objective test:
   - Work from beginning to end, answering every question in order. Answer every single question, even if you have to guess.
   - Answer the easy questions first, then go back and work on the harder questions.
   - Answer the hardest questions first, then go back and answer the easy ones.

None of these test-taking methods is right or wrong. However, for most people, the second method works best. If you decide to use this strategy, answer the easier questions first, then go back to figure out the more difficult ones.

6. *Mark any questions you omit.* Put a checkmark next to any question you skip. Write in pencil so you can erase the checkmarks to avoid leaving stray marks. When you get to the end of the section, go back to the beginning of the section and start answering the items you skipped.

7. *Slow down!* If you work too fast, you risk making careless errors. You're better off skipping a few questions rather than working so fast that you make costly blunders.

8. *Guess.* If you can eliminate any of the answer choices, it's always in your favor to guess. The more choices you can eliminate, the better your chances of selecting the correct

answer. If you are *not* being penalized for guessing, fill in any blanks. It costs you nothing and you might get lucky.

9. *Think before you switch answers.* Don't go back and change answers unless you're bedrock sure that your second choice is correct. Studies have shown that in nearly all cases, your first choice is more likely to be correct than subsequent choices, unless you suddenly recall some relevant information.

10. *Stay cool.* Convince yourself that you can succeed by working carefully and resolutely. If you start losing control, pause for a second to calm yourself. Take a few deep breaths, imagine a pleasant scene, and then keep working.

Tips for Earning a High Score on True-False Test Questions

True-false questions require you to recognize a fact or an idea. They also check your reading comprehension. As a result, you have to read very carefully and closely. The following suggestions can help you do your best on these test items.

1. *Pay close attention to absolute words.* When you take true-false tests, pay special attention to *absolute words* (words that are all positive or all negative). Here are some examples:

Absolutely not	*Constantly*	*None*
All	*Everyone*	*No one*
All the time	*Never*	*Not at all*
Always		

You know that answers are rarely *always* or *never,* black or white. If you see an absolute word in a test item, that item will probably not be correct. This is especially the case for true-false test items. For example,

Directions: Circle *true* if the sentence is true or *false* if it is false.

True	False	1. A sentence fragment is never acceptable in writing.
True	False	2. Water always freezes at 32° Fahrenheit.

Each of these items is false because of the absolute words *never* and *always.* Item 1 is false because sentence fragments *are* acceptable in dialogue and in casual writing. Item 2 is false because water that contains salt will *not* freeze at 32° Fahrenheit. Adding salt to water lowers the temperature required to freeze it.

2. *Look for other modifiers, too.* Scan test items for the words *usually, many, most, usually, rarely, sometimes, generally,* and *frequently* in true-false test items, as these words usually make a statement valid because they are not absolutes.

3. *Study sentence length.* For a sentence to be true, all parts of it must be true. If even one small part is false, the entire sentence is false. Therefore, the longer a sentence, the more likely it is to be false. Pay very close attention to long sentences in true-false questions. Read every part to make sure that every word is true.

4. *Be on your guard for false logic.* Two sentences can be true but connected by a word that makes them false. To prevent this type of misreading, look closely at the connecting word to make sure it doesn't lead to false conclusions. Here are some words and phrases used to connect sentences:

And	*For*	*Or*
Because	*Further*	*Since*
But	*Nor*	*Yet*
Due to	*On account of still*	

For example, *President Abraham Lincoln is famous because he was assassinated by John Wilkes Booth.* Abraham Lincoln is famous, and he was assassinated by John Wilkes Booth, but that's not what made him famous. The connecting word *because* makes the sentence false.

5. *Consider guessing.* When it comes to true-false questions, you should guess on all questions you can't answer, unless there is a penalty for guessing. You have a 50 percent chance of getting the answer right, so take the chance.

Tips for Earning a High Score on Multiple-Choice Test Questions

Multiple-choice tests require you to choose the correct choice from several options. You may have three, four, or five choices. It's especially important to approach multiple-choice test items with a logical and proven strategy, because virtually all standardized tests include a multiple-choice format. The following suggestions have proven helpful for many test takers.

1. *Use the process of elimination.* Multiple-choice test writers know that you're looking for the correct answer, so they include a lot of answers that *look* correct but are in fact wrong. Rather than looking for the *right* answer, start by looking for the *wrong* answers. Start by eliminating these ringers, because each wrong answer you knock out brings you one step closer to finding to correct answer.

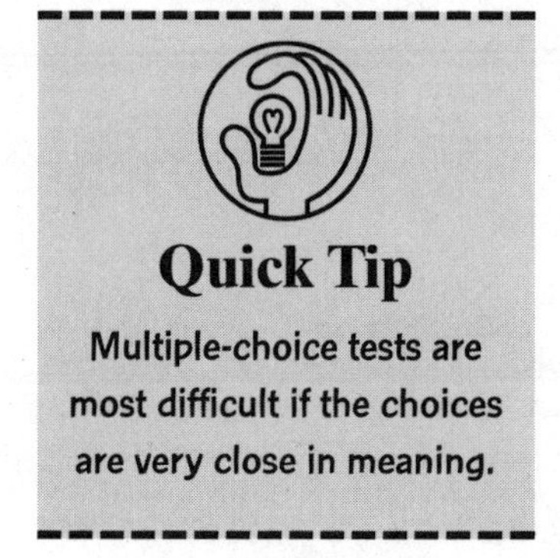

2. *Look for the words* not, except, *and* best. These questions are tricky because you're being asked to choose an answer that's the opposite of what you expect. The questions will be phrased like this:

Which is *not* an example of . . .
All the following choices are correct *except* . . .
The *best* answer is . . .

3. *Watch for the* all-of-the-above *choice.* For the answer to be *all of the above,* every part of every choice has to be correct. Verify the truth of every part of every choice before you select *all of the above* as the correct choice.

Apply the strategies you learned on the following multiple-choice vocabulary test. Select the best definition for each word.

____ 1. Cursive
a. Flowing handwriting
b. Foul language
c. Cruel
d. Commonplace

____ 2. Agitate
a. Clean
b. Tap your foot
c. Tranquilize
d. Stir up

____ 3. Adjoin
a. Separate
b. Listen closely
c. Touch
d. Disunite

____ 4. Cohabit
a. Nun's garb
b. Dependent
c. Change
d. Live together

____ 5. Concede
a. Yield
b. Build
c. Augment
d. Curtail

____ 6. Depress
a. Elevate
b. Bring down
c. Upraise
d. Invigorate

____ 7. Adjudicate
a. Subjoin
b. Deduct
c. Lessen
d. Arbitrate

____ 8. Affix
a. Withhold
b. Repair
c. Fasten
d. Injure

____ 9. Confederation
a. Southerners
b. Antagonism
c. Alliance
d. Aversion

____ 10. Collateral
a. Security
b. Far away
c. Considerably
d. Dependent

Answers

1. a 2. d 3. c 4. d 5. a 6. b 7. d 8. c 9. c 10. a

Tips for Earning a High Score on Matching Test Questions

Matching tests assess your ability to see which things go together. Thinking of these tests as a puzzle will help you match the correct pieces and eliminate choices as you go along. You'll maximize your chances for success if you have a clear test strategy. The following ideas can help you develop one.

1. *Read the list on the right first.* The questions will be listed on the left; the answers will be listed on the right. Read the answers (the right column) first, so you know the answer choices. As you read down the list you will know all the options. This can prevent you from choosing the first or second choice because it looks right, when the correct answer is further down the list.

2. *As you find each correct match, cross it off the list.* This helps you limit your choices and increase your chances of getting every answer correct.

Apply the strategies you learned on the following matching spelling test by matching each misspelled word to its correct spelling. Write the letter of the correct spelling in the space provided.

Misspelled	*Correctly Spelled*
____ 1. alin	a. autumn
____ 2. gastly	b. knack
____ 3. exilaration	c. almond
____ 4. acnowledge	d. would
____ 5. amond	e. align
____ 6. narled	f. exhibit
____ 7. gingam	g. acknowledge
____ 8. autum	h. ghastly
____ 9. tomaine	i. condemn
____ 10. condem	j. gnarled
____ 11. woud	k. design
____ 12. spagetti	l. exhilaration
____ 13. desin	m. ptomaine
____ 14. nack	n. gingham
____ 15. exibit	o. spaghetti

Answers

1. e	2. h	3. l	4. g	5. c	6. j	7. n	8. a	9. m	10. i
11. d	12. o	13. k	14. b	15. f					

Quick Tip

Standardized tests are similar to classroom tests in many ways, but they have a few significant differences. These differences change the strategies you use. First of all, the test items on standardized tests are often arranged from easier to more difficult. Therefore you will have to budget your time differently. Spend less time on the first questions and more time on the last questions.

Be prepared not to know everything you'll be asked on a standardized test. Don't be upset; this is the way the test is designed.

Tips for Earning a High Score on Fill-in-the-Blank Questions

You may or may not have answer choices with fill-in-the-blank questions. If you don't, you will have to recall the correct answer from the material you studied. If you do have choices, you will have to eliminate some and choose the best answer.

1. *Look for links in ideas.* As you read the sentence, substitute the word *blank* for the blank. This helps you figure out what is missing and how the sentence makes sense when complete. If you have been given answer choices, try to predict the answer without looking at the choices. Then look at the answer choices to find the one that best matches your prediction. If you haven't been given choices, fill in the answer based on your prediction.

2. *Look for context clues.* A fill-in-the-blank question usually contains clues to the correct answer. For example, the words *and, also, so, for, because,* and *therefore* show that the second part of the sentence supports the first part. When you see one of these words in a fill-in-the-blank question, look for answer choices that support the second part of the sentence. Other times, the blank requires a word that restates an idea already mentioned in the sentence. In this case, you will be using *summary clues* to find the missing words. The following phrases show that ideas are being summarized: *as a result, in summary, finally, in conclusion.* Finally, words such as *although, not, but,* and *however* signal contrast. If you see one of these words in the sentence, the missing word will be the opposite of the first half of the sentence.

3. *Read carefully.* One letter can change the meaning of a word, so read each answer choice carefully. *Dessert* and *desert,* for instance, may look the same if you're reading fast, but they're not the same! *Dessert* is a sweet served at the end of a meal, whereas *desert* is a dry, arid expanse of land.

4. *Check capitalization.* Some words have two meanings, depending on whether they are capitalized. For example, when capitalized, the word *Catholic* refers to a religion. However, when lowercased, *catholic* means "worldly, cosmopolitan, or wide-ranging tastes and interests."

5. *Match the grammatical form of the question and answer.* If the verb is singular, the subject or answer must be singular. If the verb is plural, the subject or answer must be plural.

6. *Check your answer by reading the entire sentence.* Rereading the answer you've chosen or written can help you decide whether it makes sense. If not, revise your answer.

7. *Use common sense to make sure your answer is logical.* If your answer doesn't match what you already know, revise it.

Tips for Earning a High Score on Math Tests

Use the following suggestions as you take tests in math. These tips also work with science tests that involve calculations, such as physics and pharmacology tests.

1. *Try to predict the answer.* As you solve the problem, try to predict the answer. This will help you avoid choosing an answer that does not make sense.

2. *Draw diagrams to help you think out problems.* Diagrams and pictures are especially helpful for math problems that involve shapes, lengths, distances, and sizes.

3. *Rephrase word problems.* Restating word problems in your own words helps you understand the problem and its different parts. Then try to relate this word problem to others you have done. This will help you see similar solutions.

4. *Be sure to show the answer in the correct mathematical form.* Even if your answer is correct, it will likely be marked wrong if it is in the wrong form (e.g., using decimals instead of fractions). Reread the test question to make sure you are stating your answer in the correct form.

5. *Show all your computations.* Be sure to show all your work, because you can sometimes get partial credit even if you made a counting error.

6. *Check your answers.* Even if you're sure that you got the correct answer, always try to make time to check your work. This can help you catch errors in counting, plus and minus signs, and logic.

7. *Use common sense.* If an answer doesn't seem right even if you found a matching answer, trust your instincts. Recalculate the problem to see where the error occurred.

It's a Wrap

✔ Objective test questions can be easy or difficult based on their *content* and their *form.*

✔ Take practice exams, learn the directions, study, use your time wisely, develop a test strategy, mark any questions you omit, work slowly and carefully, guess if there's no penalty or if you can eliminate some answer choices, think before you switch answers, and don't panic.

With true-false test items, pay close attention to absolute words and logical reasoning.

With multiple-choice test items, use the process of elimination.

With matching test items, read the list on the right first and cross off each correct match as you find it.

With fill-in-the-blank test items, look for links in ideas and context clues. Also, match the grammatical form of the question and answer.

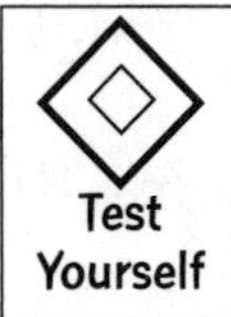

QUESTIONS

True-False Questions

1. True-false questions are usually more difficult to answer than critical-reading questions.
2. If at all possible, take practice exams so you know what you're facing when you take the real test.
3. On standardized tests, don't bother memorizing the directions, because you won't save enough time to make it worth your effort.
4. In nearly all cases, the test questions are arranged in order of difficulty, from most difficult to least difficult.
5. You're better off skipping a few questions rather than working so fast that you make costly blunders.
6. Don't go back and change answers unless you're bedrock sure that your second choice is correct.
7. Multiple-choice test writers know that you're looking for the correct answer, so they include a lot of answers that *look* correct but are in fact wrong. Rather than looking for the wrong answer, start by looking for the *right* answer.
8. When you take a matching test, read the list on the left first.
9. Standardized tests are designed to have some questions that you can't answer.
10. On fill-in-the-blank test items, match the grammatical form of the question and answer.

Completion Questions

1. Questions can be easy or difficult based on two factors: their *content* and their _________.
2. For an important objective exam such as a college entrance test, set up a _________ months before the exam and stick to it.

3. There are _________ ways you can approach any objective test.
4. Put a _________ next to any question you skip.
5. If you can eliminate any of the answer choices, it's always in your favor to _________.
6. When you take true-false tests, pay special attention to _________. These are words that are all positive or all negative.
7. For a sentence to be true, all parts of it must be _________.
8. As you read the sentence, substitute the word _________ for the blank. This helps you figure out what is missing and how the sentence makes sense when complete.
9. When a fill-in-the-blank test item requires a word that restates an idea already mentioned in the sentence, you will be using _________ *clues* to find the missing words.
10. Some words have two meanings, depending on whether they are _________.

Multiple-Choice Questions

Using the strategies you learned in this chapter, read the following passage and answer the questions.

Men are like plants; the goodness and flavor of the fruit proceeds from the peculiar soil and exposition in which they grow. We are nothing but what we derive from the air we breathe, the climate we inhabit, the government we obey, the system of religion we profess, and the nature of our employment. Here you will find but few crimes; these have acquired as yet no root among us. I wish I were able to trace all my ideas; if my ignorance prevents me from describing them properly, I hope I shall be able to delineate a few of the outlines; which is all I propose.

Those who live near the sea feed more on fish than on flesh and often encounter that boisterous element. This renders them more bold and enterprising; this leads them to neglect the confined occupations of the land. They see and converse with a variety of people; their intercourse with mankind becomes extensive. The sea inspires them with a love of traffic, a desire of transporting produce from one place to another, and leads them to a variety of resources which supply the place of labor. Those who inhabit the middle settlement, by far the most numerous, must be very different; the simple cultivation of the earth purifies them, but the indulgences of the government, the soft remonstrances of religion, the rank of independent freeholders, must necessarily inspire them with sentiments, very little known in Europe among a people of the same class of freemen, religious indifference, are their characteristics.

Exclusive of those general characteristics, each province has its own, founded on the government, climate, mode of husbandry, customs, and peculiarity of circumstances. Europeans submit insensibly to these great powers and become, in the course of a few generations, not only Americans in general, but either Pennsylvanians, Virginians, or provincials under some other name. Whoever traverses the continent must easily observe those strong differences, which will grow more evident in time. The inhabitants of Canada, Massachusetts, the middle provinces, the southern ones, will be as different as their climates; their only points of unity will be those of religion and language.

1. In the second sentence, the main effect of using parallel phrases that elaborate on one another is to
   (a) Emphasize the amount of time and effort it takes for a person to mature
   (b) Make the writing vigorous and logical
   (c) Establish the author's solemn and scholarly tone
   (d) Convince people to move to America
   (e) Temper the author's enthusiasm with unquestionable scientific facts
2. In the context of the passage, the phrase "love of traffic" most nearly means
   (a) A desire to move goods from place to place
   (b) An urge to drive
   (c) An impulsive nature
   (d) A passion for cars
   (e) A craving for new sensations
3. According to the author, our character is shaped by all of the following forces *except*
   (a) Our environment
   (b) Our government
   (c) Our career
   (d) Our genetic background
   (e) Our religious beliefs
4. The author describes people who live near the sea as
   (a) Deeply religious
   (b) Indifferent to their neighbors and other people around them
   (c) Courageous and adventurous
   (d) Pure and simple
   (e) Independent but not physically strong
5. This essay is organized by
   (a) Most to least important
   (b) Least to most important
   (c) Chronological order
   (d) Advantages and disadvantages
   (e) Spatial order, east to west
6. The author would be most likely to describe America as a
   (a) "Melting pot"
   (b) "Glorious mosaic"
   (c) "Crazy quilt"
   (d) "Salad bowl"
   (e) "Patchwork of people"
7. From what point of view is this essay written?
   (a) Third-person limited

(b) First person
(c) Omniscient
(d) Third-person omniscient
(e) All-knowing

8. Based on context clues, when was this essay most likely written?
   (a) 1400s
   (b) 1500s
   (c) 1700s
   (d) 1900s
   (e) Present-day
9. The writer predicts that
   (a) People in different parts of America will become *less* similar as time passes
   (b) People in different parts of America will become *more* similar as time passes
   (c) Americans will never get along with each other because they are too individual
   (d) People from all over the world will come to America
   (e) Americans will deplete their rich natural resources through overfarming, fishing, and mining
10. Based on the details, you can conclude that this essay reveals the author's
    (a) Gratitude that he is not an American
    (b) Belief that Americans are an easily influenced group of people
    (c) Distrust of foreigners, especially immigrants
    (d) Mild support for America and Americans
    (e) Affection for and deep faith in the promise of America and Americans

ANSWER KEY

True-False Questions

1. F 2. T 3. F 4. F 5. T 6. T 7. F 8. F 9. T 10. T

Completion Questions

1. Form 2. Study schedule 3. Three 4. Checkmark 5. Guess
6. Absolute words 7. True 8. Blank 9. Summary 10. Capitalized

Multiple-Choice Questions

1. b 2. a 3. d 4. c 5. e 6. a 7. b 8. c 9. a 10. e

CHAPTER 13

Solve Analogies on Standardized Tests

You should read this chapter if you need to review or learn about

➜ What analogies are

➜ The different relationships shown on analogy tests

➜ Techniques for solving analogies

In the previous chapter, we reviewed techniques for answering objective test items. In this chapter, you will focus on one of the most important and difficult test items, *analogies,* and you will learn techniques for answering these test items.

Get Started

Analogies **are a type of test question that assesses your ability to see relationships among words. Analogies are presented in a specific form (e.g., A:B :: C:D, read "*A* is to *B* as *C* is to *D*").**

Understanding Analogies

Analogies as test questions show different relationships among words. Every analogy question contains two pairs of words. The relationship shown in the first part parallels the relationship shown in the second part. For example,

Pair 1	**Pair 2**
carnivore : meat	herbivore : plants

A carnivore (*car*-ni-vor) eats meat. An herbivore (*er*-bi-vor) eats plants. Therefore, the two parts of the analogy show the same relationship. In this case, it's certain types of animals eating certain types of food.

Analogies are presented as mathematical equations in which : stands for *is to* and :: stands for *as.* For example,

big : small :: large : tiny

is read as

big *is to* small *as* large *is to* tiny

The relationship must *always* flow in the same direction for an analogy to be valid. For example, consider this analogy and the two choices:

couplet : poem

a. paragraph : sentence

b. sentence : paragraph

A *couplet* (*kup*-lit) is two lines that rhyme. Therefore, it is a small part of a poem. A sentence is a smaller part of a paragraph (choice *b*). However, a paragraph is *not* a small part of a sentence, so choice *a* is not valid. To be valid, the relationships must be presented in the same order.

Analogies can show many different relationships. The most common analogy relationships you will encounter on standardized tests are these:

- Synonyms
- Antonyms
- Type of
- Part to whole
- Object to function
- Lack of something
- A place for

Let's look at each type of relationship in detail.

Synonym Analogies

In this type of analogy, you'll be required to find words that are parallel in meaning. The relationship is formed between the first pair of words as well as the second pair of words. For example,

stallion : rooster :: mare : hen

In this analogy, the second pair of words must mirror the relationship shown in the first pair of words. *Stallion* is matched to *rooster* in the same way that *mare* is matched to *hen.* A *stallion* is a male horse; a *rooster* is a male chicken. A *mare* is a female horse; a *hen* is a female chicken.

Study these examples:

Example	**Explanation**
skiff : dinghy :: car : automobile	A *skiff* and a *dinghy* are both small boats, so they are synonyms. *Car* is another word for *automobile* so they are synonyms. All four words refer to a means of transportation.
parrot : sparrow :: goldfish : guppy	A *parrot* and a *sparrow* are two different types of birds. Therefore, they are synonyms for *bird.* A *goldfish* and a *guppy* are two different types of fish, which makes them synonyms for *fish.* All four words refer to creatures.

Quick Tip

In addition to mastering analogies, you can boost your score on standardized tests by using the following surefire strategies:

- Know the directions ahead of time. That way, you won't lose time on the day of the test reading the directions for the first time.
- Eliminate choices. If you can't answer a question, eliminate whichever choices you can. If you can narrow your choices to two or three items (out of five), choose the most likely answer from among the remaining choices. The odds are in your favor.
- Keep moving! If you can't answer a question, skip it and keep working.
- Check your answer sheet often to make sure that you don't mark answers in the wrong places.
- Work carefully so you don't lose points on careless errors.

Antonym Analogies

These analogies follow the same format as synonym analogies, except the words being tested are opposites of each other. As always, the relationship is formed between the first pair of words as well as the second pair of words.

foe : chum :: adversary : crony

Remember that the relationship shown in the second pair of words must parallel the relationship shown in the first pair of words. *Foe* means "enemy" and *chum* means "friend." Therefore, they are antonyms, or opposites. In the same way, *adversary* means "enemy" and *crony* means "friend." Therefore we have the same relationship between both sets of words: "enemy is to friend as enemy is to friend."

Study the following examples of analogies that show antonyms:

Example	**Explanation**
naïveté : maturity :: gullibility : sophistication	*Naïveté* (nay-eh-vit-*tay*) and *gullibility* (*guh*-luh-bil-i-tee) both mean "innocence," and *maturity* and *sophistication* both mean "experience." *Naïveté* is an antonym for *maturity* just as *gullibility* is an antonym for *sophistication.*
destitution : opulence :: indigence : luxury	*Destitution* (*deh*-sti-too-shun) and *indigence* (*in*-duh-jence) both mean "poverty." *Opulence* (*ah*-phu-lence) and *luxury* both mean "great wealth." *Destitution* is an antonym for *opulence,* and *indigence* is an antonym for *luxury.*

Quick Tip

Generally, match the grammatical form of every item in the analogy. For instance, if the first word in the analogy is a noun, the other three words must be nouns.

"Type-of" Analogies

In this form of analogy, you're being asked to show that an object belongs to a class of objects. For instance, a *smirk* is a type of smile, a *squall* is a type of storm, and a *panda* is a type of bear. Follow this example:

sword : weapon :: cudgel : club

First determine the relationship in the first pair of words. Then look for the same relationship in the second pair of words. A *sword* is a type of weapon. A *cudgel* (*kuj*-el) is a club, which is a type of weapon. As a result, each set of words shows an object that is a type of another object.

Here are two additional examples of type-of analogies.

Example	**Explanation**
mauve : color :: basil : herb	*Mauve* (mohv) is a type of color; *basil* is a type of herb.
cranial : nerve : ulna : bone	*Cranial* is a type of nerve; *ulna* (*uhl*-nah) is a type of bone.

"Part-to-Whole" Analogies

In this type of analogy, you're being asked to determine how one word in each pair is part of the other word in the same pair. For example, a *note* is part of a song, a *letter* is part of a word, and a *brim* is part of a hat. The following example shows a part-to-whole analogy:

coda : symphony : epilogue : novel

A *coda* (*koh*-dah) is a part of a symphony. An *epilogue* (*eh*-pi-log) is part of a novel. The relationship is even closer, however. A coda is the *last* part of a symphony and an epilogue is the *last* part of a novel. Finally, both a coda and an epilogue are optional: you can have a symphony without a coda just as you can have a novel without an epilogue.

The following model analogies show the part-to-whole relationship:

Example	**Explanation**
radius : circle :: spoke : wheel	The *radius* (*ray*-dee-us) is the part of a circle that extends from the center to the edge. It is shown as a line. A *spoke* is the part of a wheel that extends from the center of the wheel to the edge. A spoke is a bar. Therefore, both *radius* and *spoke* are parts of the whole. Further, both have the same shape. (Note: *Spoke* has multiple meanings. In addition to being a bar, it is also the past tense of "to speak.")
prow : ship :: nose : airplane	The *prow* is the forward part of a ship, just as *nose* is the foreword part of an airplane. Therefore, both words show a part-to-whole relationship. They also occupy the same relative position to the whole.

"Object-to-Function" Analogies

This type of analogy tests whether you can determine the function of a specific tool or item. Because this particular relationship is fairly easy to discern, test writers often include some difficult vocabulary to make the test items more challenging. I'll use common vocabulary in the following examples so you can focus on the relationship first.

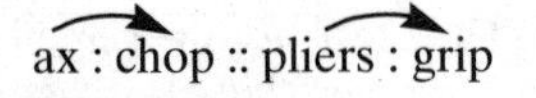

ax : chop :: pliers : grip

The function of an *ax* is to chop something, whereas the function of *pliers* (*plye*-ers) is to grip something. Both an ax and pliers are tools. Therefore, the analogy is valid.

Find the relationship in these two examples:

Example	Explanation
knife : cut :: fork : spear	The function of a knife is to cut; the function of a fork is to spear. Further, you could argue that both a knife and a fork are used with food, although a knife can be used to cut other objects, of course.
screwdriver : fasten :: awl : pierce	An *awl* is a pointed instrument used for making small holes in leather, wood, metal, and so on. The function of a screwdriver is to fasten; the function of an awl is to pierce. The analogy is even stronger because both a screwdriver and an awl have a similar shape.

"Lack-of-Something" Analogies

In this type of analogy, one word in each pair lacks some quality. The other pair must reflect the same relationship, in the same order. For example, a *recluse* (*rehk*-loos) is a loner who lacks visitors, a *coward* lacks courage, and a *pauper* (*paw*-per) lacks money.

The following examples illustrate this type of analogy:

grotto : light :: desert : water

A *grotto* is a cave, so it lacks light. A *desert* is a dry place with no moisture, so it lacks water. Therefore, both a grotto and a desert lack something.

Example	Explanation
hermit : friends :: mendicant : money	A *hermit* is someone who hides away alone, so he or she would lack friends. A *mendicant* (*men*-di-kant) is a beggar, so he or she would lack money.
miser : generosity :: traitor : loyalty	A *miser* is a cheapskate, or tightwad, so a miser lacks generosity. A *traitor* betrays his or her country, so a traitor lacks loyalty.

"A-Place-for" Analogies

In these analogies, you're figuring out where something takes place or where someone belongs. For example, an *actor* belongs on the stage, a *pilot* belongs in an airplane, and *ore* (or) belongs in a mine.

The following example illustrate this type of analogy:

horse : stable :: pig : sty

A *horse* is usually kept and fed in a *stable* in the same way that a *pig* is cared for in a *sty*. This particular relationship is easy to see, but the word *sty* might present problems if it's unfamiliar to you.

Here are two additional examples of a-place-for analogies.

Example	Explanation
birds : flock :: lions : pride	*Flock* is the specific term for a group of birds. *Pride* is the specific term for a group of lions. This particular analogy is difficult because *pride* has two entirely different meanings: (1) a group of lions and (2) self-regard. You must infer the correct meaning of *pride* from its context—the words *birds* and *lions.*
fish : school :: cows : herd	Fish travel in a group called a *school,* just as cows travel in a group called a *herd.* As with the previous example, this analogy is tricky, because *school* usually applies to a group of students and *herd* is often confused with its homonym, *heard* (to listen).

Create Precise Relationships

Knowing the seven main types of analogies can help you earn a high score on analogy tests, but analogies can be tricky. Consider the following case in point:

grain : silo ::

pilot : plane
judge : courtroom
teacher : classroom
water : reservoir
automobile : highway

At first glance, we're dealing with a place-for analogy. But when you plug in the answers, here's what you get:

A silo is a place where you find grain.

A plane is a place where you find a pilot.
A courtroom is a place where you find a judge.
A classroom is a place where you find a teacher.
A reservoir (*rez*-er-vor) is a place where you find water.
A highway is a place where you find an automobile.

Because all five answers fit, you've got a problem. The solution is to narrow down the sentence to make it more precise. Try this:

A silo is a place where grain is stored.

A plane is *not* a place where a pilot is stored.
A courtroom is *not* a place where a judge is stored.
A classroom is *not* a place where a teacher is stored.
A reservoir *is* a place where water is stored.
A highway is *not* a place where an automobile is stored.

By making the relationship more precise, the correct answer becomes apparent: A *silo* is a place where grain is stored, just as a *reservoir* is a place where water is stored. Therefore, as you work your way through analogies on standardized tests, follow these steps:

1. Start by fitting the words into one of the relationships explained here.
2. See which relationship works best.
3. Use context clues to figure out any multiple-meaning words.
4. If none of the choices make sense or you have too many seemingly correct answers, make the relationship more precise.

Quick Tip

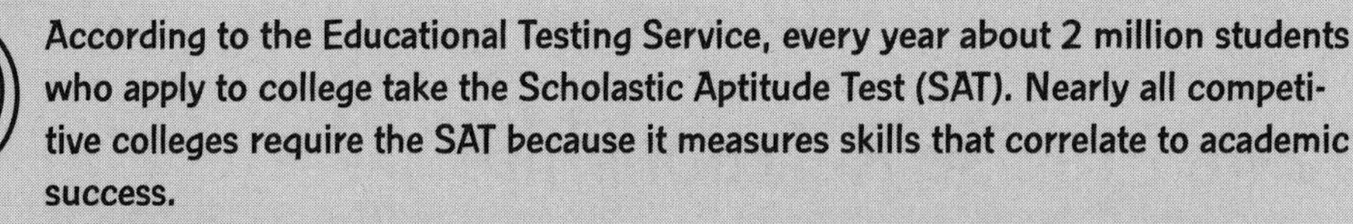

According to the Educational Testing Service, every year about 2 million students who apply to college take the Scholastic Aptitude Test (SAT). Nearly all competitive colleges require the SAT because it measures skills that correlate to academic success.

The SAT, developed and administered by the Educational Testing Service, includes both verbal and math reasoning. The test has a total of six types of questions, as follows:

Verbal	*Number*	*Math*	*Number*
Sentence completions	19	Five-choice questions	35
Analogies	19	Quantitative comparisons	15
Critical reading	40	Grid-ins	10

For additional information about the SAT, contact ETS:

Educational Testing Service
Rosedale Road
Princeton, NJ 08541
Phone: 609-771-7300; 609-921-9000
E-mail: etsinfo@ets.org
Fax: 609-734-5410; 609-530-0482

Be Creative, but Don't Overthink

The test items on standardized tests are often arranged from easier to more difficult. As you work through the test, the questions become increasingly difficult. Therefore you will have to budget your time. Spend less time on the first questions and more time on the last questions.

Protect yourself against panic by recognizing that you're not going to be able to answer every question, especially toward the end of the test. Don't be upset; this is the way the test is designed.

As the questions become more difficult, the answers will be less obvious:

Obvious Answer

shoe : foot

(a) nose : ear
(b) shirt : arm
(c) toes : foot
(d) glove : hand
(e) hat : knee

The correct answer is *d:* A glove covers your hand as a shoe covers your foot. Choice *a* is silly because a nose doesn't cover your ear. Choice *c* is wrong because toes don't cover your foot; they are part of it. Choice *e* is wrong because a hat covers your head, not your knee.

Obscure Answer

act : play

(a) line : music
(b) rhyme : poem
(c) page : novel
(d) scenery : performance
(e) chapter : book

The correct answer is *e:* An *act* is a large part of a play, just as a *chapter* is a large part of a *book.* A line is part of music (choice *a*) and a page is part of a novel (choice *c*), but neither are large parts, so they can't be correct answers.

To find the relationship between these words, you have to think creatively. Perhaps you put the words in a sentence, such as "*Act* is to *play* as . . ." Maybe you drew a diagram to find the relationship. You definitely looked at the question from several different angles to analyze it. You must use creative thinking skills to tease out the more difficult analogy relationships.

But when you think creatively, be sure not to overthink. When you overthink, you analyze your answers so deeply that you begin to see relationships that don't really exist. You might get hopelessly lost, too.

When in doubt, go for the most logical and obvious answer. If that doesn't fit, look more deeply into the question and see if you can find an answer that matches your line of thought.

Quick Tip

Are you nervous about standardized analogy tests? If so, relax! A minor case of nerves can actually help you succeed because it keeps you alert and focused.

- *Analogies* are test questions that show different relationships among words. Every analogy contains two pairs of words. The relationship shown in the first part parallels the relationship shown in the second part.
- Analogies are presented as mathematical equations in which : stands for *is to* and :: stands for *as.*
- The most seven common analogy relationships on standardized tests are synonyms, antonyms, type of, part to whole, object to function, lack of something, a place for.

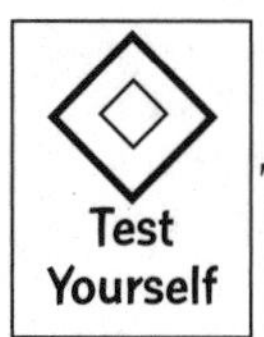

QUESTIONS

True-False Questions

1. The relationship in an analogy is formed between the first pair of words as well as the second pair of words.
2. The relationship must always flow in the same direction for an analogy to be valid.
3. All analogies show only one main type of relationship among the words.
4. In part-to-whole analogies, you'll be required to find words that have the same meaning.
5. Antonym analogies follow the same format as synonym analogies, except the words being tested are opposites of each other.
6. Generally, you do not have to match the grammatical form of every item in the analogy. For instance, if the first word in the analogy is an adjective, the other three words can be adverbs, nouns, or verbs.
7. In object-to-function analogies, you're being asked to show that an object belongs to a class of objects.
8. *Radius : circle :: spoke : wheel* is a part-to-whole analogy.

9. *Hermit : friends :: mendicant : money* is a synonym analogy.
10. As you solve analogy questions, always try to narrow your choices by making the type of relationship more precise.

Completion Questions

Select the word that best completes each sentence.

1. Spend (*more, less*) time on the first analogy questions on standardized tests.
2. Spend (*more, less*) time on the last analogy questions on standardized tests.
3. To help figure out the relationships between words in an analogy, try putting the words in (*sentence, paragraph*).
4. When in doubt about an answer, choose the most (*obscure, obvious*) answer.
5. Solve these analogies:
   watermark : paper :: birthmark : (*person, emblem*)
   beef : jerky :: grape : (*raisin, intricate*)
   magnanimous : petty :: munificent : (*miserly, generous*)
   unique : peerless :: novel : (*conventional, unrivaled*)
   divergent : identical :: anomalous : (*digressing, analogous*)
   ludicrous : laughable :: absurd : (*grave, ridiculous*)

Multiple-Choice Questions

Select the word that best completes each analogy.

1. prodigious : colossal :: infinitesimal :
   (a) copious
   (b) poignant
   (c) puny
   (d) inspiring
2. penitent : repent :: confessor :
   (a) disavow
   (b) disown
   (c) repudiate
   (d) admit
3. pagan : religion :: heathen :
   (a) belief
   (b) misgivings

(c) padre
(d) idiosyncrasy

4. gadabouts : nomads :: travelers :
   (a) vapid
   (b) tourists
   (c) fatuous
   (d) discerning
5. symptomatic : symbolic :: indicative :
   (a) indisposed
   (b) representative
   (c) contagious
   (d) endemic
6. cyclical : repetition :: circular :
   (a) broadside
   (b) termination
   (c) irksome
   (d) continuity
7. mule : intractable :: fox :
   (a) wily
   (b) quick
   (c) contumacious
   (d) comely
8. generosity : philanthropist :: mettle :
   (a) medal
   (b) metal
   (c) hero
   (d) villain
9. mellifluous : honeyed :: cacophony :
   (a) euphonic
   (b) sweet
   (c) harsh
   (d) neutral
10. freakish : change :: whimsical :
    (a) cherished
    (b) vary
    (c) dangerous
    (d) ominous

ANSWER KEY

True-False Questions

1. T 2. T 3. F 4. F 5. T 6. F 7. F 8. T 9. F 10. T

Completion Questions

1. Less 2. More 3. Sentence 4. Obvious 5. Person, raisin, miserly, unrivaled, analogous, ridiculous

Multiple-Choice Questions

1. c 2. d 3. a 4. b 5. b 6. d 7. a 8. c 9. c 10. b

CHAPTER 14

Excel at Objective English Tests

You should read this chapter if you need to review or learn about

- Understanding the American College Test (ACT) test format
- Defining Standard American English
- Identifying common errors in written English
- Correcting errors in grammar, usage, punctuation, and capitalization

In Chapter 13, you learned techniques for earning high scores on analogy tests. In this chapter, you will learn how to approach another type of standardized test: the English skills exams. These types of questions form the basis of many standardized tests, grade-level assessments, and class exams. They are a central feature of the ACT.

Get Started

Learning to recognize and correct errors in grammar, usage, and mechanics will improve your score on multiple-choice and essay exams, especially the English usage portion of the ACT.

Understand the Different Levels of Language

Successful writers and speakers suit their language to the audience and circumstances. That's because they know which words are appropriate to specific situations.

The language standard used in most academic and professional writing is called *Standard American English.* It is the writing you find in your textbooks, magazines such as *Time* and *Newsweek,* and all standard newspapers. Such language conforms to the widely established rules of grammar, sentence structure, usage, punctuation, capitalization, and spelling used by educated speakers and writers of American English.

Although most educated people know the language rules, we often violate them in our daily speech by using *colloquial language* (informal speech), *slang* (new words and phrases), and *vernacular* (the language of a particular region). Figure 14-1 provides some examples.

Colloquial language, slang, and vernacular are standard in informal discourse, but they are not used in formal written documents. As a result, it's important to study and master the rules that govern the writing and speaking of educated professionals.

Level of Language	Examples
Standard American English	I *failed* my driver's test.
Colloquial language	I *flunked* my driving test.
Slang	The *yuppie* was *hangin'* with his *buds.*
Vernacular	I ate a big *hoagie* and drank an orange *pop.*

Fig. 14-1 Levels of usage.

Discover the Test Format

Many different tests assess your mastery of Standard American English. Likely the most widely administered is the American College Test (ACT). It is a 219-question test (all multiple-choice) that tests your knowledge of four areas:

- English usage
- Mathematics
- Social studies
- Natural sciences

The test is 2 hours and 40 minutes long. Along with your high school record, teacher recommendations, and personal essays, the ACT is used for admission to many colleges and universities.

The ACT is divided into four separately timed tests in the subject areas listed. The English usage portion allows you 40 minutes to answer 75 questions. Because mastery of English is important for success on many standardized tests as well as in class assignments, we concentrate on this aspect of the ACT.

Quick Tip

The ACT is administered five times a year throughout the United States. Unlike the SAT, the ACT is usually taken only once.

The ACT English usage test requires you to

- Identify whether the underlined passage contains an error
- If so, to classify the error
- Correct the error by finding the best choice among the four given

The test contains underlined and numbered passages. Passages may consist of one word, a phrase, a clause, or an entire sentence. You will be asked not only to correct an error, but also to explain the writer's choice of rhetorical strategies, the organization of the passage, or its purpose.

Take a Practice Test

Following is a sample test. Complete it to assess your strengths and weaknesses.

Sample Test 1

The color barrier that <u>had keeped</u> major league sports white-only did not fall in
1

baseball until <u>1947 Branch</u> Rickey of the Brooklyn Dodgers brought up Jackie Robinson
2

from the <u>Minor Leagues.</u> Facing down hostility and prejudice with unshakable dignity
3

and <u>playing that was superb</u>, Robinson was named Rookie of the Year. The way was
4

opened for black <u>athletes who</u> have since enriched professional sports. Nonetheless, it
5

was not until 1966 that an African American <u>become</u> the coach of a major United States
6

professional sports team.

He <u>demonstrated quicker</u> that the move was long overdue. The man was <u>Bill Russell</u>,
7 8

and the team was the Boston Celtics of the National Basketball Association.

<u>In 1968 and 1969</u> <u>the NBA championship was won by the Celtics</u> with Russell as player-
9 10

coach. As a full-time player, the six foot nine inch center <u>lead</u> the Celtics to eight straight
11

NBA championships from 1959 to 1966. He was voted the <u>league's</u> most valuable player
12

five times.

1. (a) No change
   (b) had kept
   (c) keeped
   (d) have kept
2. (a) No change
   (b) 1947, Branch
   (c) 1947 although Branch
   (d) 1947, when Branch

3. (a) No change
   (b) minor Leagues
   (c) minor leagues
   (d) Minor leagues

4. (a) No change
   (b) playing his very best
   (c) superb playing
   (d) that playing that was superb

5. (a) No change
   (b) athletes whom
   (c) athletes which
   (d) athletes

6. (a) No change
   (b) became
   (c) had became
   (d) will become

7. (a) No change
   (b) demonstrate quicker
   (c) demonstrating quick
   (d) demonstrated quickly

8. Why does the writer place Bill Russell's name in the second sentence rather than in the first sentence, where you would normally expect to find it?
   (a) To show that Russell is a very important player
   (b) To show the parallels between Bill Russell and Jackie Robinson
   (c) To compare and contrast basketball and baseball
   (d) To make the reader curious to learn the coach's identity

9. (a) No change
   (b) In 1968 and 1969—the
   (c) In 1968 and 1969, the
   (d) In 1968 and 1969: the

10. (a) No change
    (b) won was NBA championship by the Celtics
    (c) NBA championship the Celtics was won by
    (d) the Celtics won the NBA championship

11. (a) No change
    (b) led
    (c) so as to lead
    (d) was leading
12. (a) No change
    (b) leagues'
    (c) leagues's
    (d) leagues

Check your work to see which areas of grammar, usage, and punctuation you must review.

1. (b) *Kept* is the correct past participle for *to keep.* The principal part comes after a helping verb, such as *had, is, are, was, were, had been, would have been.*
2. (d) This is a run-on sentence, because two independent clauses run together without a pause. The first clause, "The color barrier that had keeped major league sports white-only did not fall in baseball until 1947," runs into the second clause, "Branch Rickey of the Brooklyn Dodgers brought up Jackie Robinson from the minor leagues." To correct a run-on sentence, separate the two independent clauses by a period, a semicolon, or a conjunction and a comma. Choice *d* is correct because it adds the subordinating conjunction *when.* Choice *b* creates a comma splice. The conjunction in choice *c* does not make sense.
3. (c) There is no reason to capitalize "minor leagues" because it is not a proper noun.
4. (c) All elements in a sentence have to be in the same grammatical form. This is called *parallel structure.* "Superb playing" parallels "unshakable dignity" because both phrases consist of a noun modified by an adjective.
5. (a) Use the nominative (subject) form *who* as the subject of the sentence (black athletes). *Whom* in choice *b* is used as an object; *which* in choice *c* is used to refer to objects, not people. Choice *d* is wrong because the pronoun is necessary.
6. (a) The past tense *became* is required to show that the action has already taken place.
7. (d) Use the adverb *quickly* to modify the verb *demonstrated.* None of the other choices is an adverb.
8. (a) Placing Russell's name in the second sentence creates suspense and so heightens reader interest. None of the other choices makes sense in this context.
9. (c) Use a comma after an introductory phrase, such as the one here. Eliminate choice *b* because a dash is used to show a sudden shift in thought, which is not the case here. Eliminate choice *d* because a colon is used before a list or a long quotation (five lines or more), which, again, is not the case here.
10. (d) Unless the speaker is not known or you wish to avoid assigning blame ("A mistake was made") use the active voice rather than the passive voice. In the active voice, the subject is the doer of the action (". . . the Celtics won the NBA championship"). In the passive voice, in contrast, the action is done to the subject ("NBA championship was won by

the Celtics"). The active voice is considered more vigorous, clear, and succinct than the passive voice.

11. (b) *Led* is the correct past tense of the verb *to lead,* required by the meaning of the sentence.
12. (a) Because the word *leagues* is singular, add an apostrophe and an *s,* as shown in choice *a*.

Learn the Ropes

This time, concentrate on putting a name to each error. Use the grid in Figure 14-2 to help you focus on tested areas.

As you learned in previous chapters, one of the best ways to prepare for standardized tests is to practice on sample tests. As you take the following test, try to replicate test conditions. Sit in a quiet place and work all the way through the test without pausing. Then take a break and return to score your efforts.

Skill Area	Subskills
Punctuation	Apostrophes Capitalization Comma use Colon Dash Quotation marks Semicolon
Grammar and usage	Adverb/adjectives Adjectives/degree Agreement of subject and verb Possessive pronouns Who/whom Words often confused Verb tense Verb use
Sentence structure	Dangling construction Misplaced modifiers Parallel structure Sentence fragments Run-on sentences
Strategy	Arrangement of details Author's purpose Conclusions Details and examples Extraneous information Placement of topic sentence Rhetorical approach Sentence choice Topic sentence Word choice
Style	Active/passive voice Awkward sentences Conjunction choice Diction Idiomatic expressions Tone

Fig. 14-2 Review English skills.

Sample Test 2

In 1850 twenty-one-year-old [1] peddler Levi Strauss traveled from New York to San Francisco. He had to sell small items and canvas. [2] The small items sold good [3] but Strauss found himself stuck with the rolls of canvass [4] because it was not heavy enough to be used for tents. While talking to one of the miners [5]. Strauss learn [6] that sturdy pants that would stand up to the rigors of digging were [7] almost impossible to find. With a piece of string on the spot, Strauss measured the man. [8] After having worked all day, the pants were finished [9]. For six dollars in gold dust, Strauss sewed the leftover canvas into a pair of stiff and [10] rugged pants. The miner liked the results, word [11] got around about "those pants of Levis." [12] They were the most unique pants. [13] Strauss wrote to his two brothers in New York to send more canvas. He received instead a tough brown cotton cloth made in Nimes, France, called *serge de Nimes.* [14] Almost at once, the foreign term was shortened to *denim.*

1. (a) No change
   (b) In 1850: twenty-one-year-old
   (c) In 1850—twenty-one-year-old
   (d) In 1850, twenty-one-year-old

2. What should be done to this sentence?
   (a) No change
   (b) Join it to the previous one with a comma.
   (c) Delete "He had" and join it to the previous one with a comma.
   (d) Add "because" and join it to the previous one with a comma.

3. (a) No change
   (b) sold well

(c) sold very good
(d) sold nice

4. (a) No change
   (b) crevasse
   (c) canvas
   (d) credenza

5. What should be done to this sentence?
   (a) No change
   (b) Join it to the previous one.
   (c) Join it to the following one with a comma.
   (d) Change *talking* to *talk.*

6. (a) No change
   (b) learned
   (c) was learning
   (d) learnt

7. (a) No change
   (b) rigors of digging was
   (c) rigors of digging is
   (d) rigors of digging are

8. (a) No change
   (b) On the spot, Strauss measured the man with a piece of string.
   (c) Strauss, with a piece of on the spot string, measured the man.
   (d) The man was measured on the spot with a piece of string by Strauss.

9. (a) No change
   (b) After having worked all day, they were finished.
   (c) After having worked all day, Strauss finished them.
   (d) After Strauss worked all day, he finished the pants.

10. (a) No change
    (b) but
    (c) plus
    (d) together with

11. (a) No change
    (b) the results word

(c) the results, yet word
(d) the results, and word

12. (a) No change
(b) Levis'
(c) Levi's
(d) Levis's

13. (a) No change
(b) They were very unique pants.
(c) They were extremely unique pants.
(d) They were unique pants.

14. Does the example fit here?
(a) Yes, because it explains how Levi's jeans came to be made of denim and why they are sometimes called "denims."
(b) Yes, because it made the writer's point about Levi being resourceful and hardworking.
(c) No, because it has nothing to do with the topic, the history of an American institution.
(d) No, because it interrupts the flow of the narrative.

15. Which of the following sentences would best conclude this paragraph?
(a) Levi was a true genius.
(b) These were the humble beginnings of a fashion that would take the world by storm.
(c) France has given America many other important things as well, including fine cheese, wine, and music.
(d) A surprisingly large number of words have entered English from other cultures.

Check your work to see which areas of grammar, usage, and punctuation you must review.

1. (d) Use a comma to set off an introductory phrase. Choice *b* is wrong because colons are used to set off lists or long quotes. Choice *c* is wrong because dashes are used to show a sharp change in thought.
2. (c) Choice *a* is wrong because it creates a stilted, redundant style. Choice *b* is wrong because joining this sentence to the previous one with a comma would create a comma splice. Choice *d* is wrong because the conjunction *because* is illogical. Only choice *c* makes logical sense.
3. (b) Use the adverb *well* to modify or describe the verb *sold.* Choice *d* is wrong because *nice* is both clinched and an adjective rather than the adverb (*nicely*) required by this sentence.

4. (c) *Canvas* is a noun meaning "fabric." *Canvass* is a verb meaning "campaign." This sentence requires *canvas,* fabric. (Choice *b* refers to a canyon; choice *d* refers to a piece of furniture.)
5. (c) Join this sentence to the next one to create a complex sentence: *While talking to one of the miners, Strauss learned that sturdy pants that would stand up to the rigors of digging were almost impossible to find.* Joining it to the previous sentence (choice *b*) creates an illogical sentence. Choice *d* does nothing to correct the fragment.
6. (b) Use the past tense (learned) to be consistent with the tense already established in the essay.
7. (a) The sentence is correct as written, for the plural verb *were* agrees with the plural subject *pants.* Don't be confused by the word *rigors.* Choices *c* and *d* can be eliminated because they change from the past to the present tense.
8. (b) This is a misplaced modifier. The modifier *on the spot* has to be placed as close as possible to the word it modifies, *measured.* Only choice *b* does this. Choice *c* is illogical: What is "spot string"? Choice *d* changes to the passive voice, a less vigorous construction.
9. (d) As written, this is a dangling construction, because it states that the pants—not the man—worked all day. Choice *d* best corrects this error.
10. (b) *But* is a better conjunction in this context because it shows the contrast between *stiff* and *rugged.*
11. (d) This is a *comma splice,* two independent clauses run together without the correct punctuation or conjunctions. Only choice *d* corrects this error logically.
12. (c) Add an apostrophe and an *s* to show ownership: *Levi's.* Only choice *c* punctuates correctly.
13. (d) Because *unique* is already superlative in degree, it cannot be further modified.
14. (a) The passage tracks the development of Levi's jeans. The final step in this evolution occurred when the fabric changed from the original canvas to the familiar denim. Choice *b* is wrong because that is not the writer's point—even though Levi does possess those qualities. The same is true of choice *c*. Choice *d* is wrong because the example does not interrupt the flow of the narrative; rather, it fits right in as a relevant example.
15. (b) This sentence restates the writer's main point: that Levi's jeans had a modest beginning but grew to be a key cultural element. Choices *c* and *d* are clearly off the topic. Choice *a* does not reflect the content of the essay: Levi's success is partly due to accident and partly to his intelligence.

✔ Review the rules of standard English grammar, usage, and mechanics.

✔ Familiarize yourself with the format of the ACT.

✔ Practice to improve your skills.

QUESTIONS

True-False Questions

1. Successful writers and speakers suit their language to the audience and circumstances.
2. Everyone uses Standard American English when speaking casually to their friends.
3. Standard American English is used by newscasters.
4. The newly coined words *phat, rad,* and *groovy* are examples of Standard American English.
5. People in New York who call an overstuffed sandwich a *hero* are using a kind of regional language called *vernacular.*
6. Colloquial language, slang, and vernacular are standard in informal discourse, but they are not used in formal workplaces and documents.
7. ACT stands for "A Common Testing Program."
8. The ACT is five hours long.
9. The ACT is used as the sole criteria for admission to many colleges and universities.
10. The ACT and other tests like it assess your knowledge of grammar, usage, spelling, and punctuation.

Completion Questions

1. The set of language standards used in most academic and professional writing is called _________.
2. Informal speech is also called _________.
3. _________ is the term for new words and phrases.
4. The language of a particular region is called _________.
5. The ACT contains _________ questions test, all multiple-choice.
6. The ACT tests your knowledge of _________ different subject areas.
7. These areas include _________ 8. _________ 9. _________ 10. _________.

Multiple-Choice Questions

Each year it seems to get harder to pay for a college education because a college

education costs so much and it has been difficult to get scholarships. Although it has been
1 2

estimated that at least $500 million in private-sector money is available to help teens pay

for the college education. According to some sources nearly $250 million in scholarship
3

funds goes unclaimed every year. College financial aid officers claim the money would all be used if applicants looked more thorough [4] for funds. Other people, in contrast, [5] argue that it is very hard for students and their parents to find these financial aid sources on their own. A new industry used computers to locate [6] possible sources of financial aid. They know that most of the private funding comes from traditional sources such as religious organizations, veterans groups, labor unions, and businesses [7]. But there are also sources targeted for specific applicants. That's why it's [8] important to do your research when it come to applying for scholarships. First, born on a certain day for [9] students there are college scholarships for them. [10]

1. (a) No change
   (b) scholarships are difficult to get.
   (c) and it is being difficult to get scholarships.
   (d) it be difficult to get scholarship money.
2. (a) No change
   (b) Since
   (c) In spite of the fact that
   (d) However
3. (a) No change
   (b) sources: nearly
   (c) sources, nearly
   (d) sources—nearly
4. (a) No change
   (b) more thoroughly
   (c) more, thorough
   (d) more thorougher
5. The writer is developing ideas through which method?
   (a) Compare and contrast
   (b) Cause and effect
   (c) Reasons and causes
   (d) Personal experience

6. (a) No change
   (b) would be using computers to locate
   (c) has been using computers to locate
   (d) uses computers to locate
7. Are the underlined examples appropriate to this passage?
   (a) Yes, because they back up the writer's point about the difficulty of obtaining funding.
   (b) Yes, because they illustrate the writer's point about conventional sources for scholarships.
   (c) No, because they have nothing to do with the thesis.
   (d) No, because they are too vague to be effective.
8. (a) No change
   (b) That's why its
   (c) That's why its'
   (d) Thats why its
9. The writer wishes to add information here that will explain and further support the point made in the preceding sentence. Which of the following sentences will do that best?
   (a) For instance, you can get scholarships for many different skills, abilities, talents, and achievements.
   (b) That is why it is very important to read all the scholarship literature very carefully.
   (c) But it is crucial that applicants file for scholarships early and fill out all the forms exactly as required.
   (d) For instance, there are scholarships for people who have specific last names, who are twins, who are children of New England fishermen, or who are left-handed.
10. (a) No change
    (b) First, on a certain day for students born there are college scholarships.
    (c) First, there are college scholarships for students born on a certain day.
    (d) For students born first on a certain day there are college scholarships.
11. This essay would be of interest to readers who want to know
    (a) How to apply for admission to a college
    (b) More about securing financial aid for college
    (c) Which colleges are most highly ranked and why
    (d) Why it is important to get a college education in the twenty-first century
12. Suppose the writer wanted to add more information to this essay. Which of the following additions would be most relevant to the passage as a whole?
    (a) An example of a person who won an unusual scholarship
    (b) A description of a large coeducational college
    (c) An account of freshman year in a state college
    (d) A reliable way to select a college

ANSWER KEY

True-False Questions

1. T 2. F 3. T 4. F 5. T 6. T 7. F 8. F 9. F 10. T

Completion Questions

1. Standard American English 2. Colloquial language 3. Slang 4. Vernacular 5. 219 6. Four 7. English usage 8. Mathematics 9. Social studies 10. Natural sciences

Multiple-Choice Questions

1. (b) This is the best choice because it is neither wordy nor awkward.
2. (d) *However* shows contrast, required by the sentence. *Although* (choice a) and *In spite of the fact that* (choice *d*) both create fragments. *Since* (choice *c*) is not logical.
3. (c) Use a comma after an introductory subordinate clause.
4. (b) Use an adverb (*thoroughly*) to modify or describe an adjective (*more*).
5. (a) The signal words *in contrast* show that ideas are being developed through comparison and contrast.
6. (d) The other choices violate the tense (or time) in the passage.
7. (b) The underlined examples are appropriate to this passage because they are all examples of traditional sources for scholarships.
8. (a) *That's* is a contraction for "that is"; *it's* is a contraction for "it is." Both are required by the sentence.
9. (c) This choice is the least awkward and wordy. Choice *d* is wrong because it completely changes the meaning.
10. (c) The other choices are wordy, illogical, or confusing.
11. (b) The entire passage is concerned with exploring alternative methods for obtaining financial aid for college.
12. (a) Because the entire essay concerns financial aid, choice *a* would provide the most useful information.

CHAPTER 15

Ace Sentence Completion Tests

You should read this chapter if you need to review or learn

- What sentence completion questions look like
- How to answer sentence completion questions that have one blank
- How to answer sentence completion questions that have two blanks
- Tips for avoiding common sentence completion pitfalls and traps

In Chapter 14, you practiced taking standardized tests that require you to analyze passages for errors in grammar, usage, punctuation, and logic. In this chapter, you'll learn how to earn a high score on sentence completion test questions, a stock item on many standardized tests such as the SAT.

Get Started

Sentence completion questions appear on many standardized tests, including the verbal section of the SAT, along with reading comprehension and analogy questions. Solve sentence completion test items by looking for context clues, contrast clues, summary clues, and cause-and-effect clues.

What Are Sentence Completion Test Items?

Sentence completion questions test two areas of English language proficiency:

- A broad range of vocabulary, measured by your ability to understand the meaning of the sentences
- The ability to understand the logic of sentences, measured by your ability to insert the correct words

One or two parts of a sentence will be omitted and replaced by blanks. When one part is omitted, each answer choice will provide *one* different word. When two words are omitted, each answer choice will provide *a pair* of words. Here's what a typical sentence completion question looks like (we'll analyze this question later):

Through his _________ he managed to cheat his partners out of their earnings.

(a) Inefficiency
(b) Ineptness
(c) Machinations
(d) Regime
(e) Dealings

The Basic Five-Step Plan

Use the following five steps to solve sentence completion test items:

1. Read the sentence through to get a general sense of its meaning. As you read, ask yourself the following questions:

- What does the sentence mean?
- What word will best fill in the blank (or blanks)?
- What part of speech is necessary to complete the sentence correctly? The part of speech may be a noun, verb, adjective, or adverb, for example.

2. Anticipate the answer. Determine whether the missing word (or words) must support or contrast with another idea in the sentence.

- Words such as *so, for, because, therefore,* and *as a result* signal support.
- Words such as *although, not, but,* and *however* signal contrast.

3. Read the five answer choices. Always review *every* choice. Remember that the instructions for all the verbal questions ask you to choose the *best* answer. One choice may appear to fit, but it might not be the *best* of the five choices. You have to review all the choices to find the best one.

4. If you have to guess, use these methods:

- First eliminate all choices that don't make sense.
- As a last resort, select a difficult vocabulary word. More on this later.

5. Check your answer by reading the entire sentence with the word or words you have selected in place. This will help you confirm that the sentence makes sense.

It's time to go back to the sample question you looked at already. This time around, try approaching the question using the five-step approach you just learned. Then read the explanation that follows.

Through his __________ he managed to cheat his partners out of their earnings.

(a) Inefficiency
(b) Ineptness
(c) Machinations
(d) Regime
(e) Dealings

(c) After you have read the sentence through for sense, ask yourself, "Through *what* (blank) does one cheat?" The word *cheat* is a clue that the sentence is dealing with underhanded behavior, deception, or dishonesty. Further, the missing word must be a noun (a thing) to make sense in the sentence. In addition, the missing word must support the main idea of the sentence; there is no contrast here. Therefore, you might come up with answers such as this one: "Through *unfair means, evil planning, or conspiracy,* he managed to cheat his partners out of their earnings."

Then read the five answer choices, looking for the *best* answer. Try each choice, like this:

(a) *Inefficiency* would fit the general meaning of the sentence, but is it the best choice? *Inefficiency* doesn't imply a deliberate attempt to cheat.
(b) *Ineptness* is the same as choice *a*; neither word implies the deliberate attempt to defraud implicit in the word *cheat.* Since both choices are essentially the same, why would *b* be a better choice than *a?* It's not.
(c) *Machinations* is the best choice so far, because it is the only word that implies an intentional effort to deceive.
(d) *Regime* is a noun, but it does not fit the meaning of the sentence as shown in the word *cheat.*
(e) *Dealings* is even more neutral than choices *a* and *b,* so it clearly doesn't fit with *cheat.*

Quick Tip

Even though you may feel sure of your answer, don't neglect to check it by rereading the entire sentence with the word or words you have selected. This step helps you double-check that the sentence makes sense.

Strategies for Tackling Sentence Completion Questions

The strategies you'll learn about here apply to any sentence completion question. You can revisit these tips as we look at more sample questions later in this chapter.

1. *Pace yourself.* Sentence completion questions become more difficult as the test progresses, so allocate your time carefully. If you spend too much time on the earlier, easier questions, you won't have enough time to complete the final, more difficult items.

2. *Know your vocabulary.* Define the answer choices and the most important words in the sentence. These key words will usually be nouns, verbs, adjectives, or adverbs. Look for roots, suffixes, and prefixes as you decode words.

3. *One letter can make all the difference, so read each answer choice carefully.* *Dessert* and *desert,* for instance, may appear the same on first glance, but *dessert* is a sweet served at the end of a meal and *desert* is a dry, arid expanse of land.

4. *Always understand the sentence before you try out the choices.* You *must* understand the meaning of a sentence before you can start filling in the blanks. Otherwise, most of the words will seem to fit.

5. *Check capitalization.* Some words have two meanings, depending on capitalization. For example, with a capital *C,* the word *Catholic* refers to a religion, but when the same word is written with a lowercase *c,* it means "worldly, cosmopolitan, or having wide-ranging tastes and interests."

6. *Look for words that have the same meaning.* If the words mean the same thing—as with *inefficiency* and *ineptness* in the sample question—then obviously neither word can be the correct choice. As a result, you can safely eliminate both words and concentrate on the other choices.

7. *Check part of speech and verb tenses.* Effective sentences are parallel: the grammatical elements are in the same form. For example, all the verbs in a sentence will end in *-ing* or *-ed.* When you are considering answer choices, look for those that fit in with the rest of the sentence.

8. *With two blank questions, test the first word in each pair to save time.* When the test item has two blanks, first read the sentence all the way through. Then try the first word of each answer pair in the first blank in the sentence. If it doesn't make sense, eliminate the entire pair of words without trying the second word at all.

9. *Don't be thrown by nonsensical answer choices.* Some answer choices will simply not make sense. Don't waste your time puzzling over a choice to determine exactly *why* it doesn't make sense. If you have better choices, just eliminate it.

10. *Look for the* best *choice, not the* perfect *choice.* Sometimes the best choice from among the five choices given is not the word that you would have chosen if you had written that sentence yourself. Nevertheless, if it is the *best* choice available, that's the one you want.

Using Contrast Clues to Answer Sentence Completion Questions with Two Missing Words

As you try to fill in the blanks by anticipating which word fits best, determine whether the missing words *contrast* with another idea stated in the sentence. The following words and phrases are used most often in standardized sentence completion questions to show contrast:

Although, though	*Yet*	*Conversely*	*Despite*
Not	*On the other hand*	*In contrast*	*Even though*
But	*Nevertheless*	*On the contrary*	*In spite of*
Rather than	*Nonetheless*	*However*	*Instead of*

Quick Tips

Answer two-blank questions one blank at a time. Work on the first blank, then the second blank.

If you spot any of these words or phrases in a sentence completion question, look for an answer that *contrasts* with an idea stated elsewhere in the sentence. Try it now:

Although the concert had been enjoyable, it was overly _________ and the three encores seemed _________.

(a) extensive . . . garrulous

(b) protracted . . . excessive

(c) inaudible . . . superfluous

(d) sublime . . . fortuitous

(e) contracted . . . lengthy

(b) The contrast word *although* tells you that the second half of the sentence will state an idea that is the opposite of the idea stated in the first half. The first half the sentence states that the concert had been enjoyable; therefore, you should look for words that suggest the opposite of *enjoyable.* The phrase *overly protracted* tells you the concert was drawn out and thus too long. This would clearly decrease the listener's enjoyment. *Excessive* encores are overdone and not necessary. This, too, is something the audience would not find enjoyable.

Extensive in choice *a* fits the first half of the sentence but not the second half, because *garrulous* means very talkative. Eliminate choice *b* because *inaudible* does not make sense with *enjoyable;* the same is true with *sublime* (inspiring) in choice *c* and *contracted* in choice *e.*

Using Support Clues to Answer Sentence Completion Questions with Two Missing Words

Below are the words used most often to show supporting statements between main clauses:

So	*As a result*	*Due to this*
For	*Thus*	*Additionally*
Because	*Consequently*	*And*
Therefore	*Accordingly*	*Also*
Moreover	*Likewise*	*Furthermore*
Besides	*In addition*	

When you see one of these words or phrases in a sentence completion question, look for answer choices that support the other part of the sentence. The correct choice will most often be a synonym or near-synonym for a key word or words in the sentence. Try it now:

The rocking of the boat made him feel _________ so he soon felt the onset of an attack of _________.

(a) oily . . . anger

(b) bionic . . . acrimony

(c) energetic . . . panic

(d) queasy . . . nausea

(e) immature . . . remorse

(d) The rocking of the boat made him feel *queasy* (sick to his stomach). As a result, he felt *nausea* (as though he was going to vomit). Eliminate *a* and *b* because the first word in each does not fit the context. The same is true of *c;* people rarely feel *energetic* (full of energy) when a boat rocks. In contrast, a rocking boat is usually soothing. Finally, choice *e* is illogical. The motion of a boat has nothing to do with maturity.

Using Summary Clues to Answer Sentence Completion Questions with Two Missing Words

Sometimes the blanks require a word that condenses an idea already mentioned in the sentence. In this case, you will be using summary clues to find the missing words. The following transitions show that ideas are being summarized:

As a result
Hence
Concluded
In conclusion
Realized
Decided
In short
In brief
In summary
Finally
On the whole

Look for a summary word as you work through this test item:

After seeing shocking films of animals maimed and tortured by traps set by unscrupulous hunters, Marissa concluded that buying a fur coat would be _________, even _________.

(a) repulsive . . . immoral
(b) mandatory . . . immortal
(c) subliminal . . . sinful
(d) glamorous . . . priceless
(e) redundant . . . exorbitant

(a) Summarizing the first part of the sentence, you know that the films of the creatures were "shocking" because they showed the "animals being maimed and tortured by traps." Therefore, the summary must show something highly offensive. Only *a* shows this: the speaker feels that purchasing a coat would be not only *repulsive* but also *immoral* (not moral). Choice *b* is wrong because *mandatory* means the exact opposite of what is required by the sentence. The same is true of *glamorous* in choice *d. Subliminal* (choice *c*) has nothing to do with the sentence; neither does *redundant* (superfluous) in choice *e.*

Using Cause-Effect Clues to Answer Sentence Completion Questions with Two Missing Words

The cause is *why* something happens. The effect is the *result,* what happens due to the cause. Writers use specific signal words to identify cause-and-effect relationships. Here are some of the most common ones you will encounter on the sentence completion items:

Accordingly
Because
Consequently
Therefore
Due to
Thus
For
Hence
If . . . then
As a result
So
When . . . then
In order to
So . . . that
Therefore
Since
So that

Quick Tip

Some signal words, such as *because, for,* and *thus,* can be used to show more than one type of relationship. As a result, you always have to analyze the sentence and the choices *completely* to make sure that you have found the correct relationship among ideas.

If you _________ your energy wisely, then you will never _________ for it.

(a) burn . . . cauterize
(b) use . . . want
(c) husband . . . economize
(d) expend . . . wish
(e) economize . . . alter

(b) The *cause* is stated in the first part of the sentence; the *effect,* or result, is stated in the second part. If you *use* your energy wisely, then you will never *want* for it. It may be easier to see the cause-and-effect relationship if you replace the pronoun with the noun: "then you will never *want* for energy [it]." You can eliminate (A) because it is illogical: *burn* and *cauterize* mean the same thing and so do not show cause and effect. The same is true of *c.* Choice *d* is wrong because *expending* your energy wisely doesn't mean that you will never *wish* for it again. Similarly, choice *e* does not make sense.

Quick Tip

On harder questions, resolve close judgment calls in favor of more difficult vocabulary words. This is especially true with the last questions in each set of nine or ten.

- ✔ Sentence completion test items assess your knowledge of vocabulary and your ability to understand the logic of a sentence.
- ✔ Use context clues, contrast clues, summary clues, and cause-and-effect clues.
- ✔ For test items with two blanks, work on one blank at a time. Solve the first blank and then the second one.

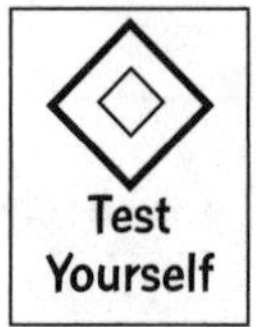

QUESTIONS

True-False Questions

1. During the Revolutionary War, Hessian troops fought on the British side not as _________, but as _________. They were paid in money, not glory. The missing words are *allies . . . mercenaries.*
2. Professor Martin spent his entire career as a teacher trying to _________ his students to appreciate the _________ of poetry. The missing words are *encourage . . . beauty.*
3. Although the movie was panned by all the major critics, audiences around the country seemed to find it _________. The missing word is *reprehensible.*
4. Peter was _________ by the repeated rejections of his novel; as a result, he _________ to submit his manuscript to other publishers. The missing words are *undaunted . . . continued.*
5. Since there is a stigma attached to this job, it is _________, even at a(n) _________ salary. The missing words are *enticing . . . fabulous.*
6. A week of sun and exercise had a _________ effect; due to this, the dark circles under her eyes were _________ and her skin took on a rosy glow. The missing words are *peremptory . . . reinstated.*
7. A system of education should be _________ by the _________ of students it turns out; in summary, quality is preferable to quantity. The missing words are *judged . . . caliber.*
8. Don't get involved with _________ politicians because you'll get caught in a _________ from which you'll never extricate yourself. The missing words are *venal . . . anathema.*
9. The press secretary had more _________ than a Philadelphia lawyer; consequently, he could never be pinned down to a _________ answer. The missing words are *lubricity . . . substantive.*
10. If he hasn't yet _________ the importance of speaking well of others, he must be quite _________. The missing words are *rejected . . . arcane.*

Completion Questions

1. The party boss shrewdly shifted party lines; hence, he was able to _________ any voting bloc out of _________.
2. The restaurant itself was beautiful and the service excellent, but the food was _________.
3. He was the chief _________ of his uncle's will; in short, he was left with a(n) _________ of $200,000.
4. When his temperature _________ above 104°, then he became _________.
5. Although he was never at the scene of the crime, his complicity was uncovered; he had _________ and _________ at the robbery by acting as a fence.
6. The offenders then prostrated themselves and _________ for mercy.
7. If you find peeling potatoes to be _________, then perhaps you'd _________ to scrub the floors?
8. The film was completely devoid of any plot or character development; it was merely a _________ of striking images.
9. She delivered her speech with great _________, gesturing flamboyantly with her hands and smiling broadly from her opening remarks to her conclusion.
10. Despite the flawless _________, I was _________ to read the letter since it was written in Hungarian.

Multiple-Choice Questions

1. Louis XIV was the _________ of _________ elegance because he wore a different outfit for practically every hour of the day.
   (a) epitome . . . sartorial
   (b) paragon . . . tawdry
   (c) acme . . . gourmet
   (d) architect . . . gastronomic
   (e) root . . . European
2. Joan was abrasive and curt with her clients; as a result, her supervisor put a letter in her file citing her _________ and _________.
   (a) enthusiasm . . . impertinence
   (b) lethargy . . . stamina
   (c) diligence . . . acumen
   (d) rudeness . . . abrasiveness
   (e) discourtesy . . . incompetence
3. The ship was in a(n) _________ position having lost its rudder; therefore, it was subject to the _________ of the prevailing winds.
   (a) inexcusable . . . direction

(b) unintended . . . rip tides
(c) dangerous . . . breezes
(d) untenable . . . vagaries
(e) favored . . . weaknesses

4. A good trial lawyer will argue only what is central to an issue, eliminating _________ information or anything else that might _________ the client.
(a) seminal . . . amuse
(b) erratic . . . enhance
(c) extraneous . . . jeopardize
(d) prodigious . . . extol
(e) reprehensible . . . initiate

5. We waited patiently for the storm to slacken but it _________ refused to _________.
(a) persistently . . . strengthen
(b) stoutly . . . abate
(c) consistently . . . perambulate
(d) wanly . . . sublimate
(e) sternly . . . mollify

6. Giving preference to his brother's son for that office smacks of _________ to me!
(a) nihilism
(b) chauvinism
(c) sycophancy
(d) pleonasm
(e) nepotism

7. Favoring one child over another will only intensify _________ rivalry.
(a) fraternal
(b) sororal
(c) parental
(d) sibling
(e) maternal

8. The general _________ his order; he had the traitor shot instead of _________.
(a) countermanded . . . hanged
(b) reinforced . . . hung
(c) confirmed . . . roasted
(d) rescinded . . . hung
(e) reviewed . . . canonized

9. The _________ from the factory was _________; consequently, the thick, black smoke was evil-smelling and noxious.
(a) effluvium . . . noisome

(b) overflow . . . salubrious
(c) outflow . . . aromatic
(d) view . . . provoking
(e) effluent . . . redolent

10. She was known for her _________; in short, no one was more _________ than she.
    (a) virtue . . . wanton
    (b) economy . . . profligate
    (c) altruism . . . selfless
    (d) conservatism . . . leftist
    (e) communism . . . conservative

ANSWER KEY

True-False Questions

1. T 2. T 3. F 4. T 5. F 6. F 7. T 8. F 9. T 10. F

Completion Questions

Here are some possible responses. Synonyms are acceptable as long as they maintain the same relationship and have the same connotation.

1. gerrymander . . . existence 2. inedible 3. beneficiary . . . inheritance
4. climbed . . . delirious 5. aided . . . abetted 6. begged 7. onerous . . . prefer
8. montage 9. verve 10. calligraphy . . . unable

Multiple-Choice Questions

1. a 2. d 3. d 4. c 5. b 6. e 7. d 8. a 9. e 10. c

CHAPTER 16

Excel at Essay Tests

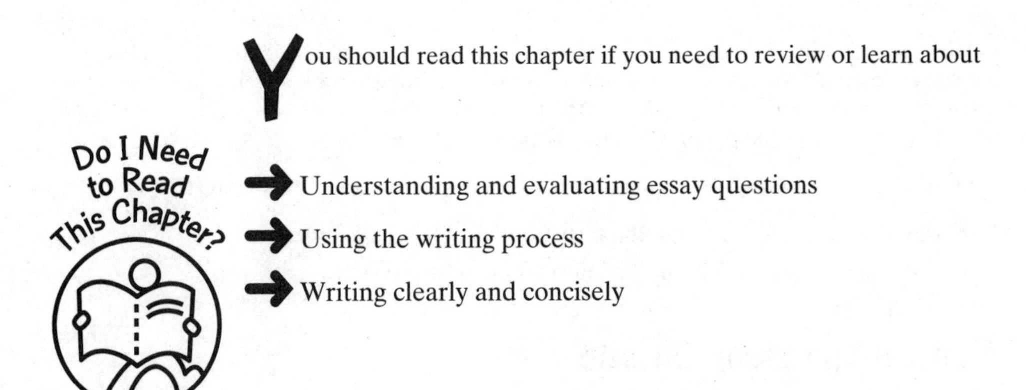

You should read this chapter if you need to review or learn about

- Understanding and evaluating essay questions
- Using the writing process
- Writing clearly and concisely

Get Started

Earning a high score on essay tests is easier if you prepare, practice, and learn some test taking strategies, especially the writing process.

All Essay Tests Are *Not* the Same!

There are four main types of essay questions that you may be called upon to answer: *recall, analyze, evaluate,* and *synthesize.* Let's look at each one in turn.

Recall-Type Essay Questions

On these tests, your instructor wants to find out what facts you have learned. As a result, you must remember facts and summarize them in a logical essay. Here are some typical recall questions:

- Write an account of the American Revolution as if you were a bystander.
- Explain how to set up a web page using HTML or FrontPage Express.
- Describe how a bill becomes a law.
- Trace how the continents were formed.

How can you tell whether the essay question focuses on recall? Read the exam closely to see if it is designed to find out whether you've *read* the material or whether you can *extend* what you learned. If it's the first choice, then you're dealing with a recall essay. In that case, you should write an essay filled with facts, details, and examples.

Here are two good ways of arranging the information on a recall writing test:

1. *Order of importance.* Present the facts from most to least important.
2. *Chronological order.* Present the information in time order.

Analyze-Type Essay Questions

With these essay questions, your instructor wants to find out how well you've made sense of what you've heard in class and read at home. When you *analyze,* you separate something into parts, examine each part, and show how they relate to the whole. This shows the teacher that you understand the main idea.

Essay tests that ask you to analyze usually contain one or more of these key words:

Analyze　　Explicate
Assess　　Explore
Clarify　　Interpret
Classify　　Probe
Describe　　Review
Determine　　Show
Examine　　Support
Explain

Here are some typical analysis questions:

- Analyze what happens in the story "The Lottery" by Shirley Jackson.
- Explore the causes and effects of the Industrial Revolution.
- Show why it is important to recycle.

Evaluate-Type Essay Questions

Here's where the instructor asks you to make judgments by applying what you believe to the topic. You back up your opinion with details and examples from your reading and notes.

Here are some essay questions that ask you to *evaluate:*

- Lawyers are expected to provide free legal services at some time in their careers. Argue that doctors should or should not have the same obligation at some time in their careers to provide free medical care to people who cannot afford it.
- Should juvenile offenders be treated differently from adult offenders? Why or why not?
- Are computers being overemphasized in our schools? Argue yes or no.
- If there were limited room on the last spacecraft to depart from a doomed Earth, someone would have to select the passengers. Among the characters you have met in the readings we have done this year, nominate two whom you feel would qualify for consideration. Justify why each character deserves to be aboard the spacecraft.

Synthesize-Type Essay Questions

Synthesizing generally requires the most creativity because it includes all the other tasks—recall, analysis, and evaluation. Here are some essay questions that ask you to synthesize information:

- While shopping with a friend and your younger sister, you see another shopper slip a small article into a shopping bag. What do you do and say?
- Would you rather be popular with an entire group without forming a really close friendship or have one very close friend but not be popular with the group? Explain your answer.
- If you could choose any special power you wished, what would it be and why? How would you use this power?
- In your opinion, what pressures create difficulties in second marriages for the new spouse, children, and stepchildren in terms of fairness, finances, and other issues?

To earn a high score on these tests, use the facts to analyze the question and reach a conclusion. You will be graded on your logic and original thinking. You can arrange your information this way:

- Open with your main idea. Give an overview of the point you'll be making.
- Support your point with details and examples.
- Reach a logical and intelligent conclusion.

Top 10 Essay Test Strategies

Here are my winning strategies for earning high scores on essay tests.

1. *Analyze the question.* Before you do anything else, make sure that you understand exactly what is required of you. Rephrase the question in your own words to make sure that you comprehend it and grasp any subtle points.

It's often the little words that trip up test takers. Watch especially for *how* and *why* embedded in the writing prompts. These crucial little words are frequently misread by hurried test takers, but such a slip can result in a completely misdirected essay.

2. *Underline key words.* Underline any key words in the question to help you understand what you have to do. Writers under pressure often forget to answer an important part of a question. Underlining the key words in the question helps you safeguard against this problem. For example, if the question states, "Summarize the key events in the French Revolution," underline *summarize* and *French Revolution.*

3. *Answer the question.* *Follow directions exactly and do exactly what you're asked to do.* Be sure to address every single part of the question. No matter how impressive your writing, you will not receive any credit if you don't answer the question. For example, if the question calls for you to write about a play or a novel, you'll receive no credit for writing about a short story—no matter how brilliant your analysis. You will receive only partial credit if you answer part of the question. If you grasp no other point from this chapter, make it this: directly answer the question you're given and follow the directions exactly.

4. *Get the guidelines.* Go back over the instructions to get the essay's guidelines. Here's what you want to know before you start to write:

- *Audience:* Who will be reading my writing? What do they expect from me?
- *Purpose:* Why am I writing? The reasons for testing in pressure-writing situations are threefold:

  To convince someone that your opinion is correct
  To convey information about a topic
  To tell a story
- *Length:* How long should my essay be? Do I have to write a paragraph, three paragraphs, four paragraphs?
- *Time:* How much time do I have to write? The amount of time I have determines how I plan and write.

5. *Use your time well.* There's no rule that you have to write the essays in order. Say you have to write three essays. If you hit a blank on question 1, immediately move on to question 2 or 3 and get started. In a test situation, you don't have the time to sit thinking about a question for 10 minutes.

6. *Start writing.* It's natural to start your essay at the beginning with the introduction, but if you're stuck for an opening, don't waste time agonizing. Instead, start where you can, with the body paragraphs. Although it's vital that essays be well organized and logical, it's equally vital that you complete the essay in the time you have been allocated. The best essay in the world won't earn any points if you don't get it down on paper within the time limit.

7. *Keep writing.* If you get stuck, skip some lines and keep on going. If you get more stuck, take a few deep breaths and keep on going. Staring blankly at the paper with rising panic only wastes time.

Write neatly. If you're writing is illegible, the scorer won't be able to read your paper. If it's merely messy, your scorer might misread a crucial point. Much as we don't like to admit it, neat papers *do* predispose scorers to smile more kindly. If you suspect that your handwriting is hard to read, print neatly and carefully.

8. *Edit and revise.* After you have a first draft hammered out, go back and edit the paper. Look for unclear statements, missing information, and repeated information. Cut unnecessary sections, add needed material, and move sentences that are in the wrong place. If you don't have time to edit and revise after you have completed a draft, do it as you go along. Some student writers are unwilling to edit because they don't like having cross-outs on their paper. It's *always* better to edit your paper to than let an awkward or incorrect statement stand.

If you're writing on a computer, run the spelling and grammar checkers, but don't rely on them. The spelling checker won't catch wrong words (e.g., *inn* or *ion* for *in*) and the grammar checker homogenizes stylistic elements.

Quick Tip

Special note to lefties: Avoid erasable pens, because the ink tends to smear as you drag your hand across the page.

9. *Proofread.* This can be one of the most important steps in any paper, for no matter how valid your points, how dear your examples, if you have made a great many careless writing errors, you will lose credit. Try to leave your paper for a few moments, perhaps look over the short answers or another essay, and then go back to it refreshed. Always make sure that you have time to proofread, and be as careful as you can to read what is there, not what you *think* is there.

10. *Deal with panic.* You can psych yourself up or down—it's all in your head. Convince yourself that you can succeed by working carefully and resolutely. If you start to lose your composure, pause for a second to calm yourself and then keep soldiering on.

Quick Tip

As you did when you studied for short-answer tests, create your own essay test questions and write the answers. Look over the textbook, your notes, and any past tests you took to predict what topics the teacher will ask this time. Then practice writing the test within the specific time you will be given on the test. This is especially helpful if you have trouble writing in a set time. Once you've prepared for the test, you'll feel more self-assured.

And, as you have already learned, never leave the test early. Use the time to check your work.

Use the Writing Process

Using the writing process on essay tests helps you approach the writing task logically. As a result, you'll be more likely to include all the important facts and examples in the correct order. You'll be more likely to avoid panic, too, since you're organized.

There are three main steps in the writing process:

1. Planning
2. Drafting
3. Revising

When you *plan* your essay you . . .

- Prewrite by listing ideas, making charts and diagrams, and asking yourself the five Ws and H (*who, what, when, where, why,* and *how*).
- Choose which ideas to include and which ones to omit
- Arrange your ideas in a logical way

When you *draft* your essay you . . .

- Write your first copy

When you *revise* your essay you . . .

- Add facts that you need to make your point
- Cross out details that are off the topic
- Rearrange information so the essay is more logical and unified
- Correct errors in spelling, punctuation, capitalization, grammar, and usage
- Write your final copy (if you have enough time)

Use Specific Details

As you learned in Chapter 10, *details* take the form of facts, examples, statistics, reasons, definitions, and descriptions. Use details to convince your reader that you know the subject. Details also makes your writing vivid and specific.

The following essay was written under pressure for a literature exam. It earned an A.

Question: *"Failure in human relationships results when one avoids the normal responsibilities of one's position in life." Show how this is true for any one character from any work of recognized literary value that you have read.*

When a person avoids the normal responsibilities of his or her position in life, human relationships will likely collapse. This is true of Macbeth in William Shakespeare's play, *Macbeth.* In the beginning of the play, Macbeth is a loyal warrior to his king, Duncan, but as the play progresses he shuns his responsibilities and thus fails in human relationships.

As King Duncan's kinsman, Macbeth is one of the most trusted generals. His reputation was burnished by his many loyal and brave acts during battle. When Macbeth upholds his reputation by fighting bravely for the king against the traitorous Thane of Cawdor's armies, Duncan rewards him with the title of the defeated Thane of Cawdor. This shows how Duncan is a fair and decent King, rewarding his men justly and generously for their bravery. It also shows how Macbeth fights with distinction in the beginning of the play, fulfilling the expected responsibilities as a loyal thane. But all this changes right after the battle, when Macbeth encounters three witches.

As they journey home from battle, Macbeth and his friend Banquo come upon three weird sisters. The witches tell Macbeth that he shall have a glorious future as Thane of Cawdor (he does not yet know he is to receive the title) and eventually King. Intrigued, Macbeth continues on his journey home to learn that he has indeed been given the title of the disloyal thane. This sparks his ambition and he first begins thinking about killing the King to hasten any chance he may have to become King himself. He tells his wife, Lady Macbeth, what has happened and she fans his ambition, plotting how to kill Duncan. They accomplish the heinous deed that night, stabbing the good and generous King and planting the daggers on his guards. Macbeth has clearly deviated from his normal responsibilities as a loyal servant to his King, for killing one's king is treacherous indeed. From this point on, the play describes the destruction of all of Macbeth's relationships.

All suspected enemies are killed to help Macbeth maintain his shaky power base. Macbeth even has his close friend Banquo murdered, for the witches had prophesied that Banquo's heirs would become king. He had intended to kill both Banquo and his son, Fleance, but Fleance escaped the murderers during the fray. He also murders Macduff's family in Act IV, scene 2, for the loyal Macduff, another of Duncan's original soldiers, organized the rebellion against the now power-crazed Macbeth. The scene where Macbeth's soldiers murder Macduff's family—all the little "chickens"—shows us again how far Macbeth has moved away from his responsibility, how fully he has failed in human relationships.

Macbeth's denial of his normal responsibilities as a loyal soldier to the good King Duncan result in the destruction of all human relationships. By the end of the play he has become a murderous tyrant, devoid of all humanness. Fortunately, few people cause as much devastation as Macbeth did when he shattered individual families and left Scotland in ruins. However, irresponsible people can still cause havoc and sorrow when they avoid their expected responsibilities.

Evaluation: The introduction divides the answer into two parts: (1) Macbeth's loyalty to the good King Duncan in the beginning of the play and (2) his later denial of his proper role as kinsman and thane.

This structure is maintained throughout the essay, as paragraph 2 discusses the first point and paragraph 3 the second point. The student explains Macbeth's behavior during battle and describes how the good king rewards him. This is crucial, for it must be shown that Macbeth is slaying a good king and thus committing a heinous deed. The setting aside of normal responsibilities would make no sense if Macbeth were killing an evil person—witness Macduff's actions in the end of the play. The final part of this paragraph is especially good, as the writer specifically says, "This shows how . . ." Include phrases such as "This proves . . ." "This illustrates . . ." "This is an example of . . ." to keep yourself on topic.

In paragraph 3, the writer does a very good job of showing that in killing the king, Macbeth has violated the duties of any subject, much less a sworn supporter. The sentence "Macbeth has clearly deviated from his normal responsibilities as a loyal servant to his King . . ." is especially good, for it ties up the rest of the paragraph and makes the point. The final sentence explains that the rest of the essay will show how all of Macbeth's relationships are destroyed.

The student proves the rest of the thesis by showing how Macbeth's relationships with Banquo, Fleance, and Macduff were destroyed when Macbeth set aside his normal and expected human responsibilities. The reference to "chickens"—recalling Macduff's impassioned speech on hearing of the murder of his family—is an effective specific detail. The final sentence restates the topic and makes the point clear.

Quick Tip

Be sure to proofread. No one expects a *perfect* paper in a pressure-writing situation, but sloppy errors undercut your thinking and can sink even the best papers.

Link Ideas with Connecting Words

Connect related ideas with linking words. These words and phrases tie your ideas together and create logic. Figure 16-1 shows some of the most useful connecting words. The relationship is listed on the left; the connecting words on the right.

Write Clearly, Concisely, and Carefully

The most successful essays always fulfill their purpose, address their audience, and have a logical organization. This is true whether the essay is written at home or during a test.

Relationship	Connecting Word(s)	
Addition	Also	In addition
	Too	And
	Besides	Further
	Next	Then
	Finally	Moreover
Example	For example	For instance
	Namely	Specifically
Contrast	Nevertheless	Nonetheless
	Yet	In contrast
	But	Still
	However	On the other hand
Comparison	In comparison	Similarly
	Likewise	In the same way
Concession	Naturally	Granted
	Certainly	To be sure
	Of course	
Place	Nearby	In the distance
	Here	There
	At the side	Next to
	Adjacent	In the front
	In the back	
Result	Due to this	So
	Accordingly	Consequently
	As a result	Therefore
Summary	Finally	In conclusion
	In summary	In brief
	As a result	Hence
	On the whole	In short
Time order	First	Second
	Third	Fourth (etc.)
	Next	Subsequently
	Immediately	Later
	Eventually	In the future
	Currently	Now
	During	Meanwhile
	Before	Soon
	Afterward	At length
	Finally	Then

Fig. 16-1 Useful transitions and linking words.

Quick Tip

If you run out of time before you can finish writing your essay, jot down what you were going to say in a few complete sentences. Your instructor may be able to give you some extra credit even through you didn't finish writing the entire essay.

Following is an essay on language acquisition written in a college linguistics class as part of a midterm exam.

Is language innate in humans? I say, at least in part, yes it is. We can say that if a major component of language—grammar—is innate, then language itself should be as well. "Complex language is universal because *children actually reinvent it,* generation after generation," says Pinker. Based on this, I will examine several cases of spontaneous grammar formation by children. If children are capable of creating grammar without any instruction, then such grammar must pre-exist in their brains.

A new language can come into being as a *pidgin.* A pidgin is a makeshift jargon containing words of various languages and little in the way of grammar. Some of the best examples of the innate formation of a grammar system are linguist Derek Bickerton's studies of such pidgins. Bickerton noted that indentured workers on plantations in the South Pacific needed to communicate with each other in order to carry out practical tasks. However, the slave masters of the time were wary of their laborers being able to communicate with each other, so they formed mixed groups of laborers who spoke different languages. These laborers created their pidgin from rough mixtures of their own language and the language of the plantation owners. But this formation was not a sudden, conscious act. The formation of a pidgin is gradual shift from speaking a few words of the owner's tongue to speaking a new language. Pidgins typically have ". . . no consistent word order, no prefixes or suffixes, no tense or other temporal and logical markers, no structure more complex than a simple clause, and no consistent way to indicate who did what to whom," according to Pinker. A pidgin is not a full, complex, grammatically specific language.

The leap into a "true" language is made when the pidgin speakers have children. These children learn the pidgin as their native language. Amazingly, though, the language they speak has much greater grammatical complexity. Such children use a consistent word order, prefixes or suffixes, tenses to indicate past or future events, complex sentence structures, and similar grammatical devices the pidgin lacked. This newly formed, "true" language is called a *creole.*

According to Bickerton, since the children have created the creole largely on their own, without formal training or even complex language input from their parents, they must have some innate mental machinery that forms grammar. As evidence of this, he also notes that creoles that are mixtures of different languages tend to be uncannily similar, sometimes even to the point of having the same basic grammar. Additionally, the mistakes some children make while learning more established languages show this basic grammar as well, suggesting that there is an underlying grammatical structure imprinted on the human mind—one that children "default" to.

While there are currently no societies where we can observe creolization occurring with a spoken language, we can observe the creolization of sign languages for the deaf. Since 1979, in Nicaragua, children at schools for the deaf have essentially formed a pidgin. None of them had a real signing system, so they pooled their collections of makeshift gestures into what is now called the Lenguaje de Signos Nicaragüense (LSN). Like any spoken pidgin, LSN is a collection of jargon that has no consistent grammar, and everyone who uses it uses it differently.

When younger children joined the school, after LSN existed, they creolized it into what is called Idioma de Signos Nicaragüense (ISN). While LSN involves a lot of pantomime, ISN is much more stylized, fluid and compact. And children who use ISN all use it the same way—the children had created a standardized language without need for textbooks or grammar classes. Many grammatical devices, such as tenses and complex sentence structures, that didn't exist in LSN, were introduced by the children into ISN.

Jenny Singleton and Elissa Newport's study of a deaf boy they called Simon, who was born of two deaf parents, shows that only one child is needed to creolize a language. Both of Simon's parents had learned American Sign Language later in life, and had not fully mastered many of the complex grammatical features of the language. Simon grew up being exposed to his parents problematic signing. Simon was very similar to the child of pidgin speakers, and true to Bickerton's theories, he essentially created grammar where there was none. His signing was far better than his parents', including grammatical devices they had never mastered but he used perfectly and effortlessly. For example, while his parents were unable to properly combine verb inflections, Simon essentially reinvented the ASL system of superimposing two inflections onto a single verb in a specific order.

As these examples show, children can create grammar—and the grammar created by different children is very similar. If this is possible, the grammar must exist in their minds from birth, hard-wired into the complex computer that is the human mind. And if grammar pre-exists in the brain, the basis of complex language must as well.

It's a Wrap

- ✔ There are four main types of essay questions: *recall, analyze, evaluate,* and *synthesize.*
- ✔ Always begin an essay test by analyzing the question and considering your parameters (audience, purpose, length, and time). Use the writing process.
- ✔ Include details to convince your reader that you know the subject. Details also make your writing vivid and specific.
- ✔ Connect related ideas with linking words.

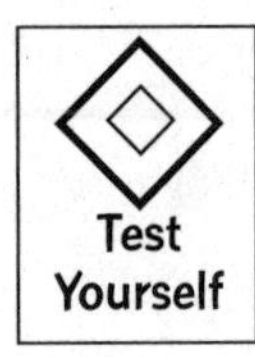

QUESTIONS

True-False Questions

1. There are four main types of essay questions that you can be asked to answer: *recall, analyze, evaluate,* and *summarize.*

2. Recall essays are filled with facts, details, and examples.
3. *Evaluating* generally requires the most creativity because it includes all the other tasks—recall, analysis, and assessment.
4. Before you write a single word on an essay test, make sure that you understand exactly what is required of you.
5. No matter how impressive your writing, you cannot receive credit if you don't answer the question.
6. If you have to write more than one essay, it's always a good idea to write the essays in the order in which they are presented on the test. Writing the second essay first, for instance, is a bad idea.
7. Always start by writing the introduction, even if you have to sit and wait for inspiration to strike.
8. Never leave the test early. Use the time to check your work.
9. Connecting words and phrases tie your ideas together and create logic in your writing.
10. The most successful essays always fulfill their purpose, address their audience, and have a logical organization.

Completion Questions

1. When you remember facts and summarize them in a logical way, you are writing a _________ essay.
2. _________ is a method of organization in which you present facts from most to least important.
3. _________ is a method of organization in which you present the information in time order.
4. When you _________, you separate something into parts, examine each part, and show how they relate to the whole.
5. When you write an essay that makes judgments by applying what you believe to the topic, you are _________ the topic.
6. _________ in your own words to make sure that you comprehend it and grasp any subtle points.
7. It's often the little words that trip up test takers. Watch especially for _________ and _________ embedded in the writing prompts.
8. Your _________ are the people who will be reading your essay, the instructor or scorer.
9. In addition to considering your audience, purpose, and the length of your essay, you must also consider how much _________ you have in which to write.
10. It's vital that you _________ when you finish writing to catch any spelling errors, punctuation mistakes, or omitted words.

Multiple-Choice Questions

1. What type of question is "Trace how the electoral college was formed"?
   (a) Synthesize
   (b) Evaluate
   (c) Analyze
   (d) Recall
2. Essay tests that ask you to analyze usually contain one of the following words *except*
   (a) Summarize
   (b) Analyze
   (c) Explore
   (d) Explain
3. What type of question is "Describe the causes and effects of the Triangle Shirtwaist Factory Fire"?
   (a) Summarize
   (b) Recall
   (c) Analysis
   (d) Restatement
4. In which order should you follow these steps to write an excellent analysis or synthesis essay?
   1. Reach a logical and intelligent conclusion.
   2. Open with your main idea. Give an overview of the point you'll be making.
   3. Support your point with details and examples.

   (a) 1, 2, 3
   (b) 2, 3, 1
   (c) 2, 1, 3
   (d) 3, 1, 2
5. After you read and analyze the test question, you should next
   (a) Edit your writing and revise unclear portions
   (b) Write neatly
   (c) Proofread
   (d) Underline any key words in the question
6. All of the following purposes can be tested in a pressure-writing situation *except*
   (a) Writing clearly and neatly
   (b) Convincing someone that your opinion is correct
   (c) Conveying information about a topic
   (d) Telling a story

7. In order, the three main steps in the writing process are
   (a) Planning, drafting, revising
   (b) Planning, writing, outlining
   (c) Shaping, editing, proofreading
   (d) Outlining, writing, rewriting
8. When you *plan* your essay you . . .
   (a) Proofread it
   (b) Prewrite by listing ideas and making charts and diagrams
   (c) Cross out details that are off the topic
   (d) Edit it
9. When you *draft* your essay, you . . .
   (a) Arrange your ideas in a logical way
   (b) Choose which ideas to include and which ones to omit
   (c) Write your first copy
   (d) Rearrange information so the essay is more logical and unified
10. When you *revise* your essay, you do all of the following *except*
   (a) Add facts that you need to make your point
   (b) Think of ideas to include
   (c) Write your final copy (if you have enough time)
   (d) Correct errors in spelling, punctuation, capitalization, grammar, and usage

ANSWER KEY

True-False Questions

1. F 2. T 3. F 4. T 5. T 6. F 7. F 8. T 9. T 10. T

Completion Questions

1. Recall 2. Order of importance 3. Chronological order 4. Analyze 5. Evaluating 6. Rephrase the question 7. How, why 8. Audience 9. Time 10. Proofread

Multiple-Choice Questions

1. d 2. a 3. c 4. b 5. d 6. a 7. a 8. b 9. c 10. b

PART 5
The Moment of Truth: Test Time

CHAPTER 17

Get a Running Start

You should read this chapter if you need to review or learn about

- Preparing for a test
- Laying the groundwork for test success
- Studying alone versus studying in groups

Get Started

When does the test start? When the instructor or proctor walks into the room? When the bell rings and the papers are handed out? When you start answering the test questions? Actually, the test starts long before you think.

Tests begin when you study and prepare for them. The groundwork takes place days before the actual test. To do your best on any test, you have to be ready.

Before you can prepare for a test, you have to know what you're preparing *for.* That's because each test is different. Knowing what to expect helps reduce test jitters, too. Follow these steps.

Fab Five Test Prep Hints

1. Get test information from your instructor.

   - Find out the test *format.* Will the test be true-false, multiple choice, fill-in, essay, or some combination of these formats?
   - Find out the test *content.* What information will you need to know?
   - Find out how much of the test is based on your notes, how much on the textbook, and how much on classwork.
   - Listen to what the instructor says. Ask questions if you are confused.

2. Speak to other students in your class. See how they interpret the instructions the instructor has given. This is a good way to check your comprehension, too.

3. Review tests you've already taken in this class. These tests will show you the types of questions the instructor asks. You'll find out what information the instructor emphasizes, too, so you can make sure you're on target when you study.

4. Pay close attention to the material the instructor writes on the board. Copy it all down. Instructors write down the material they think is important, so you can be sure some or all of it will appear on a test.

5. Go to extra-help classes the instructor offers. Instructors often review for tests during these sessions.

However, if you're taking a standardized test, there's no "instructor" to ask. In these cases, you can request sample questions from the company that administers the test. Usually, a few of these sample questions will be given to you in a booklet when you sign up for the test. You can also find standardized sample questions online at the address listed in the test booklet.

Quick Tip

Today, many instructors set up Web sites. Be sure to check these often, especially as tests approach. The instructor might have posted lectures, which will help you complete your notes, for example.

Study on Your Own

Now that you know what you will be tested on, gather your textbook, notes, handouts, and other materials. Arrange them in the order in which the material was presented. Highlight important ideas and focus on them.

Skim the textbook and take notes on any information you might be missing in your notes. Add this information to your notes. Be sure to review it as you study.

Many textbooks contain review questions at the end of each section or chapter. Even if the instructor hasn't assigned these questions, answer them as you prepare for the test. You can find the answers by going back over the chapter. When you look for the answers, you are also rereading the chapter.

To make the most of your study time, get into a study routine. Try these hints:

- Study at the same time in the same place every day. Sit at your desk in your study center to get into the study habit.
- Study your most difficult material first, when you are least tired.
- Use the memory techniques you learned in Part 1 to fix important concepts and ideas in your mind.
- As you study, give yourself a break. Stretch every 15 minutes or so.

Practice on similar tests to find out your strengths and weaknesses. For example, if you have trouble writing an essay in the time allocated, concentrate on learning this skill. (Taking essay tests is covered in detail in Chapter 16.) Completing similar tests helps you learn how to make the best use of your time.

Quick Tip

Don't take real standardized tests "just for practice" because they go on your permanent record. Instead, practice with previously published standardized tests, which are available in review books.

If you don't have enough old tests to use because it's early in the year, make up your own tests. Use the material for the upcoming test. You can trade tests with a classmate or a small group of classmates to increase your "test bank."

Study in Groups

Studying with classmates can help you in many ways.

- Group members can take turns summarizing the material aloud or quizzing each other on important topics. Some group members can ask questions to help clarify confusing points and other group members can provide the answers.
- Group members can pass around their notes, too, which helps fill in gaps in everyone's notes.
- Since everyone looks at a topic in his or her own unique way, group members can help you analyze the readings and class notes from different angles.

Study groups can be helpful at any time in the study process. Depending on the test and your individual time constraints, you might wish to start studying with classmates a week before the test or a few days. You can even meet for a refresher study group the day before the test or the morning of the test.

Some people like studying in groups, but others prefer to work alone. You may like to study in a group because you feel that it helps you review the material more completely. On the other hand, you might avoid study groups because you find that you always do more work than other study group members. Figure 17-1 shows some of the advantages and disadvantages of studying in groups.

Advantages of Study Groups	Disadvantages of Study Groups
Build confidence	Cause insecurity or panic for some students
	Reviewing material you might have missed can be very distracting
Can help you focus	Waste time if you're prepared and others aren't

Fig. 17-1 The advantages and disadvantages of study groups.

Studying in groups may be right for you if you can concentrate on your work even though others go off track. Group study is also helpful if you have missed some classes and don't understand all the information. Avoid group work if you find it hard to stay on track in groups or if your friends don't do their share of the work. In addition, group study might not work for you if you often measure your progress against others and find yourself coming up short.

Quick Tip

Study groups are most effective when they're small, no more than three to five students.

To Cram or Not to Cram?

A full-day conference at work. A holiday celebration. A hot date. Help! You're pressed for time. Why not leave all your studying to the last minute and cram it all in? Here's why not: Cramming doesn't work. It also tends to make you panic when you realize that there's no way you can learn a week's worth of information in an hour. Instead of wasting your time cramming, try the effective study plan shown in Figure 17-2.

Power Study Plan	
Four days before the test	Reread your notes and the textbook.
Three days before the test	Skim your notes and the textbook. Recite important points aloud.
Two days before the test	Without looking at your notes or the textbook, recite the key points. Look back at your notes and the text to check your success.
The day before the test	Make a sample test and answer the questions or have someone quiz you. Skim your notes and the textbook to find the most important points.
The day of the test	If the test is in the morning, you may not be able to study. If you do have a few minutes, however, skim your notes one last time. Be sure to relax before the test.

Fig. 17-2 Make a study plan.

Super Test Strategies

There's even more you can do to increase your chances of success on any test. Try these strategies to become a super test taker:

1. *Prepare the night before.* Lay out your clothing, pens or pencils, watch, lunch, and other school supplies. You don't want to be rushing around in the morning.

2. *Choose comfortable clothing.* Avoid itchy sweaters or starchy pants. Your clothes should be loose enough so you're comfortable.

3. *Get a good night's sleep.* Yes, I know you've heard it before, but it really works. A solid eight hours of z's can recharge your batteries and give you the winning edge on *any* test.

4. *Be sure to eat breakfast.* Eat a nourishing breakfast of cereal, fruit, and toast. You might want to have eggs, French toast, or pancakes. Don't make do with a toaster pastry or donut.

5. *Avoid soda.* Too much caffeine can give you the jitters, so avoid caffeinated colas.

6. *Wake up!* If you're a morning sleepyhead, wake yourself up with a hot shower or brief exercise. A short jog works well (and you can walk the dog at the same time).

7. *Leave yourself enough time in the morning.* Figure out how much time you need in the morning to get ready—and then add an extra 15 minutes. If an emergency arises, you'll have time to deal with it. If everything goes smoothly, you can review your notes for a few extra minutes.

8. *Build your self-confidence.* Getting yourself all upset before a big test will make you feel more nervous. It can also rob you of the confidence you need to succeed. Remind yourself that you have prepared well so you will do well. A positive attitude yields great results.

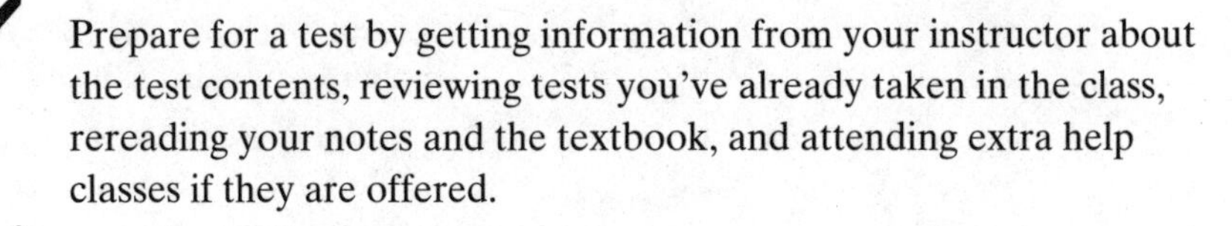

✔ Prepare for a test by getting information from your instructor about the test contents, reviewing tests you've already taken in the class, rereading your notes and the textbook, and attending extra help classes if they are offered.

✔ Consider studying in groups as well as on your own.

✔ Don't cram. It's a waste of time.

✔ Prepare the night before, choose comfortable clothing, get a good night's sleep, eat breakfast, avoid soda, leave yourself enough time in the morning, and adopt a positive attitude.

Test Yourself

QUESTIONS

True-False Questions

1. Preparing completely for a test helps calm your nerves and reduce test jitters.
2. If you don't understand what's going to be on a test, don't ask questions. This will help you look intelligent rather than foolish.
3. To check your comprehension of pretest instructions, you can speak to other students in the class to see if they interpreted the information the same way you did.
4. It's a waste of time to answer the review questions at the end of each section or chapter in your textbook unless your instructor assigns them.
5. Study your most difficult material first, when you're least tired.
6. It's an especially good idea to take standardized tests for practice because they don't go on your record.
7. Group study is helpful if you've missed some classes and don't understand all the information.
8. You might avoid study groups because you find that you are always doing more work than other group members.
9. From some people, cramming can be an effective way to study.
10. Four days before the test, you should reread your notes and the textbook.

Completion Questions

1. Review _________ you've already taken in this class. These tests will show you the types of questions the instructor asks on tests.
2. Pay close attention to the material the instructor writes on the _________.
3. Go to the _________ offered by the instructor. Instructors often review for tests during these sessions.
4. Before a test, always check any _________ the instructor has set up because instructors often post test information before a major exam.
5. Skim the _________ and take notes on any information you might be missing in your notes. Add this information to your notes. Be sure to review it as you study.
6. To make the most of your study time, get into a _________, a regular course of study.
7. As you study, give yourself a _________. Stretch every 15 minutes or so.
8. Group study might not work for you if you often _________ against others and find yourself coming up short.
9. Before a test, you should always eat _________.
10. Avoid _________ before a test because it can make you very jittery.

Multiple-Choice Questions

1. Before a classroom test, you should speak to your instructor to find out all of the following *except*
   (a) What form the test will take
   (b) How you can do extra credit to raise your grade
   (c) What will be tested
   (d) How much of the test comes from your notes and how much from the textbook
2. If you're taking a standardized test, you can *best* prepare for the test by
   (a) Talking to your classmates about the content of the test
   (b) Requesting sample questions from the company that administers the test
   (c) Studying a textbook on the topic
   (d) Writing sample essays
3. Place the following test study steps in the correct order.
   1. Highlight important ideas and focus on them.
   2. Gather your textbook, notes, and handouts, and other materials.
   3. Arrange the material in chronological order.

   (a) 1, 2, 3
   (b) 2, 3, 1

(c) 3, 1, 2
(d) 3, 2, 1

4. Studying with your classmates can help you
   (a) Only if everyone is fully prepared
   (b) Summarize the material aloud
   (c) Only if you have outstanding group members
   (d) Do more work than anyone else so you get extra credit from the instructor
5. Study groups are not a good idea if
   (a) You get easily distracted
   (b) You have not taken any notes
   (c) You have missed some classes
   (d) The test is far off
6. Study groups are most effective when they are
   (a) Held the day before the test
   (b) Large, at least 5 to 10 students
   (c) Small, no more than three to five students
   (d) Held the week before the test
7. Arrange the steps of the following study plan in the correct order.
   1. Relax.
   2. Reread your notes and the textbook.
   3. Make a sample test and answer the questions or have someone quiz you.
   4. Skim your notes and the textbook.

   (a) 1, 2, 3, 4
   (b) 4, 3, 2, 1
   (c) 3, 1, 4, 2
   (d) 2, 4, 3, 1
8. Do all of the following before a test *except*
   (a) Lay out your clothing
   (b) Get a good night's sleep
   (c) Schedule some last-minute cramming
   (d) Leave yourself enough time in the morning to get ready
9. When you take a test, especially an important one, you should wear
   (a) Dress clothes
   (b) Comfortable clothing
   (c) Old clothes
   (d) Itchy sweaters or starchy pants

10. You can build your self-confidence before a test by
    (a) Preparing well
    (b) Talking to other people in the class
    (c) Remembering how much the test counts in your future
    (d) Winging it

ANSWER KEY

True-False Questions

1. T 2. F 3. T 4. F 5. T 6. F 7. T 8. F 9. F 10. T

Completion Questions

1. Tests 2. Board or web site 3. Extra help classes 4. Web site 5. Textbook
6. Study routine 7. Break 8. Measure your progress 9. A good breakfast
10. Caffeine

Multiple-Choice Questions

1. b 2. b 3. b 4. b 5. a 6. c 7. d 8. c 9. b 10. a

CHAPTER 18

The Moment of Truth: Taking Tests

You should read this chapter if you need to review or learn about

- Maximizing your chances for success in test situations
- Budgeting your time
- Developing a test strategy
- Guessing on test questions

Get Started

Being well prepared can help you do your best on tests. So can learning to use your time wisely, approaching a test logically, and checking your work.

You have read all your textbooks, listened carefully in class, taken notes, and reviewed your notes. Perhaps you have studied with a group of friends, too. You have made up your own test questions to test your knowledge of the material.

It's not enough to know the material, however; you also have to know *how* to take tests. That's what you learn in this chapter.

Put Your Best Foot Forward

Be Prepared

Be sure to have everything you need for the test: pens, pencils, erasers, calculators, rulers, and so on. Since you put all these materials in your backpack the night before, you should be well prepared on the day of the test. Grab your backpack and you're all set to test.

Arrive at the Test Early

Get to the classroom or test center with time to spare. Allow yourself enough time to settle in the seat, lay out your pens and pencils, and relax. If you're sitting in your chair early with everything set to go, you'll have time to calm down and focus on the task at hand. So be sure to leave yourself at least five extra minutes so you're not dashing in at the last minute, huffing and puffing. So many of my students find themselves in this bind. They come racing in, all disheveled, and lose precious time getting settled.

Choose Your Seat Carefully

Sitting near friends during a test can be disrupting. If you see your friends handing in their papers early, you may feel pressured to do the same, even if you are not finished with the test. Therefore, try not to sit near your friends. Choose a seat in the front of the room, so you can clearly see and hear the instructor.

Also stay away from fellow test takers who read the questions aloud to themselves, chew gum and crack it loudly, or play with their pens and pencils as they take tests. These distractions can make it difficult for you to concentrate.

Quick Tip

Always carry extra batteries for your calculator. Calculators (and other battery-operated study aids such as electronic spellcheckers) have a nasty habit of running out of battery power just when you need them most.

Be Cool

Since you have arrived at the test early and you are fully prepared for success, you should be relaxed. If you still have some last-minute jitters, take a few deep breaths and focus on a pleasant scene. Imagine being at the lake, beach, or park, for example.

Remind yourself that you are well prepared for this test, because you *are*. Convince yourself that other students have aced this test and you can, too.

Keeping yourself focused can also reduce tension. Try not to think about anything but the test in front of you. If you find your mind wandering, return to the test—but don't forget to pat yourself on the back for staying in control. Refocusing on the test shows that you have stopped yourself from wasting time.

Pay Close Attention to *All* Directions—Spoken and Written

The test directions will usually be given orally and in writing. The instructor or proctor will announce some directions after everyone has settled down and then direct students to read the directions written on the test. Pay very close attention to what is said and what you read, because following the directions closely can make the difference between a high grade or a low one.

As you read the directions, ask yourself these questions:

- "How many questions do I have to answer?" On some tests you have to answer all the questions; on other tests, only a few. For example, if you overlook the sentence, "Choose one of the four possible essay topics," and you try to write all four essays, you will run out of time and give incomplete answers.
- "Where do I have to write my answers?" You might have a special answer sheet, a text booklet, or your own paper.
- "Will I be penalized for guessing?" The instructor might subtract points for incorrect answers. If there is no penalty for guessing, never leave an answer blank. (More information later on guessing.)
- "How much information do I have to include?" You might have to show every step in a math problem, for example, or include four paragraphs in your essay.

If you still have questions after the instructor speaks and you have read all the directions, raise your hand and get the answers you need. Be sure you completely understand the directions before you plunge into the test.

Budget Your Time

Before you start working on the test, figure out how much each part of the test counts. On some tests, every question is worth the same number of points—1 point each, 4 points each, or 5 points each, for instance. On other tests, however, some sections may be weighted differently.

For instance, the first section may have 10 questions that count 1 point each (for a total of 10 points), the second section may have 20 questions that count 3 points each (for a total of 60 points), and the third section may require an essay that counts 30 points. The amount that each question or section is worth affects the time you should spend on each part of the test.

Time-Budgeting Rules

- Spend the most time on the sections that count the most.
- Spend the least time on sections that count the least.

For example, say you have one hour for the test. The test contains 20 short-answer items worth 25 points and an essay worth 75 points. Spend the bulk of your time—at least 45 minutes—writing the essay.

If you don't complete a question in the time you have allotted, leave it and move on. You can return to the question if you have extra time at the end of the test. If you do skip a question and move on, be very careful to mark your answer sheet correctly.

You also have to budget your time if you are writing an essay. Decide how much time you can spend planning, drafting, and revising. Don't make yourself frantic trying to stick to your schedule, but do keep an eye on the time and try to stay on track. Follow the guidelines in Figures 18-1 and 18-2 to allocate your time.

If you have half an hour in which to write an essay . . .	
Planning	3 minutes
Drafting	15 minutes
Revising and editing	10 minutes
Proofreading	2 to 3 minutes

Fig. 18-1 Budgeting time for a half-hour essay.

If you have an hour in which to write an essay . . .	
Planning	5 minutes
Drafting	40 minutes
Revising and editing	12 minutes
Proofreading	2 to 3 minutes

Fig. 18-2 Budgeting time for a one-hour essay.

If you have time left over, spend it . . .

- Double-checking your answers
- Returning to questions you could not answer the first time
- Proofreading your essay for errors in grammar, usage, and punctuation
- Recopying messy parts of your essay

As You Work . . .

Provide All Student Information

As soon as you have read the directions and skimmed the entire test, write your name, date, and class on the paper. Also include any other information the instructor wants, such as your student number. It's amazing how many test papers are turned in without names. Identifying yourself is especially important on statewide assessments, which may not be scored by your own instructor. It's equally vital on standardized tests such as SATs and ACTs. Otherwise, your score may go unreported since no one will know who you are.

Read the Entire Test

Before you start writing, take a few minutes to skim the test. Remember, when you skim a passage, you read it very quickly to get the main idea. Here's what to look for:

- The types of questions (short-answer, true-false, etc.)
- The content of the questions
- Which questions look easy and which ones look difficult

Knowing what's on the test helps you develop a test strategy, explained in the next section. It also reassures you that you studied the right material and are well prepared for the test.

Jot Down Notes and Key Facts

Write down any important details or facts while they are still fresh in your memory. These notes may help you answer questions later on. In addition, having some notes reduces test anxiety because it reminds you that you have learned a lot.

Depending on the test content, here are the kinds of notes you may wish to jot down:

- Multiplication tables
- Math formulas
- Science facts
- Key historical dates and events
- Important fictional characters or real-life people
- Literary terms (e.g., *rhyme, simile, metaphor*)

- Geographical places and features (lakes, rivers, oceans, etc.)
- Foreign language words and their definitions
- Vocabulary words and their meanings
- Spelling words

Write your notes on scrap paper, inside the test booklet, or in the test margins. Always be sure that you are permitted to write in these places before you do so. After all, you don't want your notes being counted as an answer.

Develop a Test Strategy

There are three ways you can approach any test:

1. Work from beginning to end, answering every question in order. Answer every question, even if you have to guess.
2. Answer the easy questions first, then go back and work on the harder ones.
3. Answer the hardest questions first, then go back and answer the easy ones.

None of these test-taking methods is right or wrong, but for most people, method 2 works best. If you decide to use this test strategy, answer the easier questions first and then go back to figure out the more difficult ones. This strategy helps you in many ways:

- You use your time well by getting the most correct answers down fast.
- You build confidence as you write down the correct answers.
- You often think of clues that help you answer the more difficult questions.
- You may find the correct answer to a hard question revealed in another test question.
- You build momentum, which prepares your mind for the test mode.
- You leave time for the harder questions.
- You reduce any penalty you might have for guessing (more on this later).

As you work from the beginning to the end, put a checkmark next to any question you skip. Write in pencil so you can erase the checkmarks in case you are not allowed to write on the test. When you get to the end of the test, go back to the beginning and start answering the questions you skipped.

Quick Tip

Keep moving so you stay within your time limit. Never let yourself get bogged down on one or two questions, especially if they are not worth many points.

Work Carefully

Imagine that you come to question 25. It's a multiple-choice question with four choices, A, B, C, D. You read the test stem and choice A. "Ah ha!" you think. "The correct choice is clearly A." Should you write A on your answer sheet? No!

Even if you think you have spotted the correct answer immediately, read every answer to make sure that you are correct. You might have misread the question, a common mistake. People tend to see what they expect, not what is really on the page. This is especially true in a high-pressure situation such as a test. Take a close look at *every* choice before you make your decision and mark your answer.

Consider Getting Clarification

What happens when you read a question several times and it just doesn't make sense? You skip the question and move on. When you return to the question, however, it still may not make any sense, so you read it for a third time. Perhaps it's still murky.

If you really don't understand a question and you have read it several times, raise your hand and ask the instructor or proctor for clarification. In some cases, the instructor will be able to point you in the right direction. In other cases, however, the instructor will be forbidden from offering any assistance. This is especially true on standardized statewide tests. In these instances, you will have to do the best you can by analyzing the test question. Read on to find out some ways to do this.

Quick Tip

Never ask a classmate to clarify a question for you. If you do, you might be accused of cheating. Speak only to the instructor or person administering the test.

Don't Second-Guess Yourself

"The short-answer pattern really matters," some people say. "You can never have two Cs (As, Bs, etc.) in a row," you may have heard. Not true. The pattern of letters on the answer sheet doesn't matter at all. You may have an ABCDABCD pattern, an AABBCCDD pattern, or any other pattern—or no pattern at all. It's irrelevant.

If you do see a pattern, don't be fooled into changing your answers. Your grade will always be higher if you answer questions based on what you know rather than on the way the answers look on the page. If you start to think that you've chosen the incorrect answer, analyze the question rather than the answer pattern. If you can't think of a good reason to change the answer, leave it alone. Studies show that your first analysis is more often the correct one.

Be Creative, but Don't Overthink

Sometimes, the answer isn't obvious, so you have to think outside the box by looking at the question from different angles to analyze it. You have to use creative thinking skills on many tests.

But when you think creatively, be sure not to *overthink*. When you overthink, you analyze your answers so deeply that you create relationships that don't really exist. You might get hopelessly lost, too.

When in doubt, go for the most logical and obvious answer. If that doesn't fit, look more deeply into the question to see if you can find an answer that matches your line of thought.

Should You Guess?

Some tests penalize you for guessing; others do not. In general, many standardized tests try to discourage guessing by taking off points for incorrect answers.

If there is *no* penalty for guessing, fill in every single answer—even if you have to guess. After all, you have nothing to lose and everything to gain! Most statewide assessments do not penalize you for guessing.

If there *is* a penalty for guessing, try to reduce the odds. For example, if every multiple-choice question gives you four possible answers, you have a 25 percent chance of being right (and a 75 percent chance of being wrong) each time you have to guess. But if you can eliminate a single answer, your chance of being correct rises to 33 percent. If you can get your choices down to two answers, you have a 50 percent chance of being right. Even if there is a penalty for guessing, pick an answer if you can reduce your choices to two, because 50 percent odds are good enough. The PSAT, SAT I, and SAT II tests penalize you for guessing.

Before you give up on any question, always try to eliminate one or more of the answer choices. Remember, the more choices you can eliminate, the better your odds of choosing the right answer.

Pace Yourself to Avoid Making Careless Errors

Make sure you are wearing a watch or can see a clock. This will help you keep working at the right pace. You want to work quickly, but not so quickly that you throw away points by working carelessly. It's an awful feeling to lose points on questions that you really can answer. There are several types of careless mistakes that can result in incorrect answers:

- Misreading a question
- Miscalculating a math problem
- Marking an answer wrong (e.g., marking B instead of C because you're working too fast)

To prevent these careless errors, after you fill in your answers, check the answer sheet against the choices on the test. Read the answer and the letter to yourself. Say the letter in your head.

When you are working on math problems, check that your answers make sense. Are they logical? For example, if you are figuring a discount, make sure that it's not more than the original price. If you're calculating the average age of a fourth grader, make sure it's not 65 years old!

Check Your Work

When you finish the test, always check your work. Even if you have just a minute or two, use your time to look over your papers.

Ask yourself these questions as you check fill in the blank, short answer, and essay tests:

- Have I included all necessary words? People often omit words when they are in a hurry.
- Have I spelled all the words correctly? Check easy words as well as more difficult ones.
- Is my punctuation correct?
- Have I checked my grammar and usage, too?
- Can my writing be read easily?

Quick Tip

If your writing is difficult to read, consider printing. Don't use all block capitals, however. Instead, use the accepted mix of uppercase and lowercase letters.

Ask yourself these questions as you check short-answer tests:

- Have I written my responses in the correct places on the answer sheet?
- If I am not being penalized for guessing, did I fill in each blank?
- If I had to fill in circles, are my responses neat?
- If I had to write letters or numbers, can my answers be read easily?
- On standardized tests, did I erase stray marks that might be misread?

Losing your place on an answer sheet is a major disaster that you want to avoid. Here's how it happens:

- You're working from the beginning to the end of the test. You get stuck on a few test items, so you skip them and keep on working.
- You focus on the next question and forget to skip a space on the answer sheet. As a result, you fill in the correct answer—but in the wrong spot.
- When you get to the last spot on the answer sheet, you have two spaces left. You suddenly realize that when you skipped questions, you forgot to skip corresponding spaces on the answer sheet—even though you put checkmarks next to the questions!

You can avoid this disaster by checking your answer sheet each time you skip a question. Keeping your answer sheet next to the text booklet can help you remember to keep checking.

Use All Your Time

Never turn in your paper and leave early. Use all the time you have been given—every single minute. Check over your work and think about your answers. If you are sure you're completely finished, set your test aside and take a brief break. A few minutes later, look back at the test and your answers. Errors often pop right out when you've stepped away from the test. You don't want to be out the door and suddenly realize that you have finished early because you forgot to write one of the essays.

Quick Tip

Reread the test questions and compare your answers against them. This will help you make sure that you have answered every part of each question.

- Have all your materials, arrive at the test center with time to spare, choose your seat carefully, try to relax, pay close attention to all directions, and budget your time.
- Provide all student information, skim the entire test before you start working, and jot down notes and key facts.
- Develop a test strategy that works for you.

- Don't second-guess yourself or overthink, guess if you can eliminate choices or if you will not be penalized, pace yourself, and use all your time.

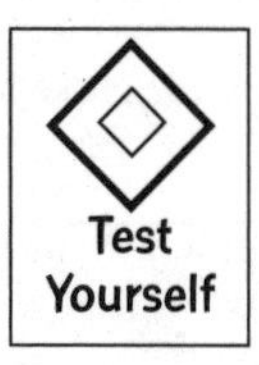

QUESTIONS

True-False Questions

1. Get to the classroom or test center with time to spare. Allow yourself enough time to settle in the seat, lay out your pens and pencils, and relax.
2. Try to sit near your friend during a test because it is comforting to have a friendly face near you. This is especially important during high-stakes standardized tests.
3. The test directions are always given in writing but rarely orally as well. Therefore, it's more important to read the directions than to listen to the proctor.

4. If you still have questions after the instructor speaks and you have read all the directions, raise your hand and get the answers you need.
5. Answer each and every question, no matter how much time it takes you.
6. Before you start working on the test, figure out how much each part of the test counts.
7. When you first start working on the test, write down any important details or facts while they are still fresh in your memory.
8. Never let yourself get bogged down on one or two questions, especially if they are not worth many points.
9. If you think you have spotted the correct answer immediately, mark it and move on.
10. The short answer pattern really matters, so pay close attention to the order of answers.

Completion Questions

1. Choose a seat in the _________ of the room, so you can clearly see and hear the instructor.
2. During a test, always carry extra _________ for your calculator.
3. Keeping yourself focused can help reduce _________.
4. If you do _________ a question and move on, be very careful to mark your answer sheet correctly.
5. _________ is especially important on statewide assessments, which may not be graded by your own instructor.
6. Before you start writing, take a few minutes to _________ the entire test.
7. As you work from the beginning to the end, put a _________ next to any question you skip.
8. When you _________, you analyze your answers so deeply that you create relationships that don't really exist. You might get hopelessly lost, too.
9. If there is *no* penalty for guessing, _________ every single answer—even if you have to guess.
10. Before you give up on any question, always try to _________ one or more of the answer choices.

Multiple-Choice Questions

1. As you read the test directions, ask yourself all of the following questions *except*
   (a) "How many questions do I have to answer?"
   (b) "Where do I have to write my answers?"
   (c) "Am I really prepared for this test?"
   (d) "Will I be penalized for guessing?"

2. Follow this rule for budgeting your time during a test:
   (a) Spend the most time on sections that count the most and the least time on sections that count the least.
   (b) Spend the least time on sections that count the most and the most time on sections that count the least.
   (c) Spend some time on sections that count the most and the rest of the time on sections that count the least.
   (d) Spend the same time on all questions, regardless of their point value.
3. If you have half an hour in which to write an essay, you should draft for about
   (a) 5 minutes
   (b) 10 minutes
   (c) 30 minutes
   (d) 15 minutes
4. If you have an hour in which to write an essay, you should plan (or prewrite) for about
   (a) 1 minute
   (b) 5 minutes
   (c) 20 minutes
   (d) 30 minutes
5. If you have time left over after you complete your essay, spend it doing all the following *except*
   (a) Double-checking your answers
   (b) Proofreading your essay for errors in grammar, usage, and punctuation
   (c) Recopying messy parts of your essays
   (d) Second-guessing your response
6. Which is the *best* test strategy?
   (a) Whatever strategy works best for you on any given test.
   (b) Work from beginning to end, answering every question in order. Answer every question, even if you have to guess.
   (c) Answer the easy questions first and then go back and work on the harder ones.
   (d) Answer the hardest questions first and then go back and answer the easy ones.
7. Sometimes the answer isn't obvious so you have to . . .
   (a) Give up in despair
   (b) Ask another test taker for help
   (c) Use creative thinking skills
   (d) Forget about ever answering that question

8. If there is a penalty for guessing,
   (a) Do not guess, no matter how tempted you feel
   (b) Take a wild guess
   (c) Try to reduce the odds by eliminating choices
   (d) Skip any confusing questions and return to them later, when you have time
9. Place the steps in the correct order to help test takers prevent careless errors as they check their work:
   1. Say the letter in your head.
   2. Check the answer sheet against the choices on the test.
   3. Read the answer and the letter to yourself.

   (a) 2, 3, 1
   (b) 3, 2, 1
   (c) 1, 2, 3
   (d) 3, 1, 2
10. If your writing is difficult to read,
   (a) Print, using all block capitals
   (b) Print, using the accepted mix of uppercase and lowercase letters
   (c) Write in pencil
   (d) Write in erasable pen, so you can correct all cross-outs

ANSWER KEY

True-False Questions

1. T 2. F 3. F 4. T 5. F 6. T 7. T 8. T 9. F 10. F

Completion Questions

1. Front 2. Batteries 3. Tension 4. Omit or skip 5. Identifying yourself
6. Skim or read 7. Checkmark 8. Overthink 9. Fill in 10. Eliminate

Multiple-Choice Questions

1. c 2. a 3. d 4. b 5. d 6. a 7. c 8. c 9. a 10. b

CHAPTER 19

Calm Test Jitters

You should read this chapter if you need to review or learn about

- Techniques for reducing panic before and during tests
- Ways to overcome math and science anxiety

Get Started

In Chapter 18, you learned ways to maximize your chances for success in test situations by budgeting your time and developing a test strategy. Now learn to calm your nerves during a test.

Do you feel stomach butterflies long before exam day? Do you feel panic the day of the exam? Does test anxiety cause you to perform below your abilities? If so, you are not alone. Everyone feels some panic before a test. And if they claim they don't, they're liars!

Five Ways to Conquer Assessment Anxiety

"The only thing we have to fear is fear itself," said President Franklin Delano Roosevelt. President Roosevelt was right, but try telling that to all the butterflies in your stomach the night before a big test. Fortunately, there are many effective ways to deal with assessment anxiety. Here are five of my most effective techniques for overcoming test panic.

1. *Downplay the test.* It's natural to feel nervous before a high-pressure situation; in fact, some scientists think that we're hardwired to get an adrenaline rush when we're in tight spots. These scientists theorize that tension under pressure comes from ancient days when we faced bison and other gigantic creatures. The adrenaline gave us the power we needed to run away. Now, however, we can't run away; we have to stay and face the pressure. So how can you deal with this flood of tension? Start by downplaying the test.

Instead of thinking of the test as "The Worst Day of My Life," "Doomsday," "The Kiss of Death," or "My Personal Waterloo," think about the test as one more hurdle to overcome. Be casual when you talk about it, and don't let your classmates, parents, or instructors push your panic button.

2. *Don't dismiss your fears.* In your attempt to downplay the test, don't go to the opposite extreme of saying "Oh, this old SAT [ACT, PSAT, MCAT, LSAT, etc.] doesn't mean a thing. I can still go to Harvard [become a brain surgeon, be master of the universe, etc.] if I bomb the test." Recognize that tests *do* matter, some more than others. Nonetheless, even in the most pressurized test situations, the test will never be the sole measure of your qualifications. And a test certainly has nothing to do with your worth as a human being.

3. *Build familiarity.* You can't do your best if you don't know the test's ground rules. Be prepared, as you learned in Chapter 18. Studying your notes in detail can help you feel confident. Knowing what's going to be on the test and the form it will take can go a long way to reducing test anxiety, too. It's very helpful to work through practice tests and memorize all the directions, as we've already discussed.

4. *Learn (and use!) relaxation techniques.* Use visualization and breathing techniques to overcome your fear of failure. Visualize or imagine yourself doing well—filling in the blanks or writing the essays with confidence. Imagine the instructor handing back your test with a big A on top. Visualizing success puts you in control.

Breathing techniques can also help, especially during a test. If you feel yourself losing control, take slow, deep breaths to calm yourself. If you have time before the test, try to get in some exercise. It's a great way to reduce tension. Even 10 minutes of jogging can take the edge off.

5. *Be optimistic.* We can't all be little rays of sunshine, especially when faced with a big important test. Nonetheless, studies have clearly shown that people who approach tense

situations with an upbeat attitude do better than those who trudge in feeling defeated. Imagine yourself achieving success rather than failing.

Playing the what-if game can also help you be more confident. Verbalize your worst-case scenario, because putting your fear into words can help you gain a more realistic attitude. Ask yourself, "What if I took this test and didn't know anything?" This will help you put the test into perspective and so lift your spirits.

Quick Tip

Right before a big test, stay away from people who bring you down by reinforcing your stress and anxiety. You don't need them pulling you down with their doom-and-gloom scripts.

More Effective Ways to Deal with Test Panic

What if none of my suggestions work for you and panic strikes during an important test (or even a minor one)? Start by recognizing that panic is a natural reaction to a pressure situation. Nonetheless, panic can prevent you from doing your best on tests, so let's reduce or banish it. Here are some techniques that can help you deal with panic:

Don't panic if . . . some questions seem much harder than others. They probably are! That's the way the test was designed. This is especially true on standardized tests. Accept this and do the best you can. On standardized tests, remember that you don't have to answer each question to do well. That's because you're not being marked against yourself; rather, you're being judged against all other test takers. Furthermore, they're feeling the same way you are.

Don't panic if . . . you can't get an answer. Just skip the question and move on. If you have enough time, you can return to the question later. If you run out of time before you can return to it, you were still better off answering more questions than wasting time on a question you didn't know.

Don't panic if . . . you blow the test all out of proportion. It is true that some tests are more important than others, especially standardized college admission tests. But any test is only one factor in your overall education. Remind yourself that you have been working hard in class and keeping up with all your homework. Keep in mind that how you do on one test will not affect your entire academic career.

Don't panic if . . . you freeze and just can't go on. If this happens, remind yourself that you have studied and so you are well prepared. Remember that every question you have answered is worth points. Reassure yourself that you're doing just fine. After all, you are. Stop working and close your eyes. Take two or three deep breaths. Breathe in and out to the count of five. Then go on with the test.

Quick Tip

Take comfort from the fact that a minor case of nerves can actually help you do well on a test (especially a standardized test) because it keeps you alert and focused on the task at hand.

You know that you have to pace yourself to do your best. But did you also know that you can improve your score by taking a short break if you feel you're losing your concentration? Look up from the test, stretch, and take a few deep breaths. Often, just a brief pause of a minute or two can refresh you and give you a second wind.

Overcome Math and Science Anxiety

Speaking now as a classic math phobic, I can sympathize with the surprising number of capable students who turn to jelly when they're confronted by a test in math and/or science. I know that I once did. The following suggestions can help you cope with this aspect of test panic.

Start by recognizing that many people are victims of math and science myths. These incorrect assumptions deal with the way people learn math and science. People often fall into patterns of fallacious thinking, as shown in Figure 19-1.

Myth	Test Fear
Math calls for logic, not creativity.	You can't do well if you're a creative rather than a logical thinker.
Math problems can be solved only one way.	You can't pass the test if you don't know the "right" way to solve each problem.
Science experiments have only one right answer.	If you don't get the "right" answer, you're doomed to failure.
Good math and science students have broken the secret code for success.	If you don't have the secret decoder ring, you're doomed to math test hell.

Fig. 19-1 Common math and science misconceptions.

Fortunately, each of these myths can be easily shattered.

1. First of all, mathematicians and scientists recognize and embrace the need for creativity in their work. This means that when you are taking a math or science test, you can often look at a problem in different ways and come up with imaginative—and correct—solutions.

2. Math problems can be solved in a variety of ways. For example, you might use mental math by figuring the solution in your head. Or you can use a calculator to arrive at the answer. Often, you can draw a picture or diagram to help you see the answer. Here's where the creativity comes into play.

3. Thank goodness scientific experiments have more than one right answer; otherwise, we wouldn't have such important discoveries as penicillin—a lifesaving medicine discovered by accident!

4. Here's the secret to doing well on math and science tests (and classes): *hard, consistent effort and good study skills.* It's the same "secret" you use on all your other tests.

To do well on math and science tests without gnashing your teeth or pulling out your hair, be sure to prepare fully. Try these ideas:

- *Read and reread your textbook.* As you study for a test, accept the fact that it may take you as long as 15 minutes to read and understand a single paragraph in your textbook. Take the time; it will pay off when you ace the test.
- *Participate in class.* Some students are so convinced that they're not going to do well in math and science that they subconsciously adopt a self-defeating attitude. Instead, as you would do in all your other classes, sit near the front of the room, answer questions the instructor asks, and pay close attention to what is said.
- *Ask questions.* If you're ashamed of looking ill prepared or stupid, remember that you're in school to learn. You're not there to impress other students or the instructor. If you don't get the information you need in class, you will not be able to do your best on the test.
- *Most important, believe in yourself.* Don't buy into the fiction that "girls can't do math" or "only boys have a natural aptitude for science" Nonsense!

✔ Downplay the test, but don't dismiss your fears.

✔ Become familiar with the test and its contents, use relaxation techniques, and envision yourself doing well on the test.

✔ Quell panic by recognizing that you likely won't be able to answer every test question. Try not to make the test more important than it is.

✔ Overcome math and science anxiety by recognizing the role of creativity in both fields, preparing for your tests, and believing in yourself.

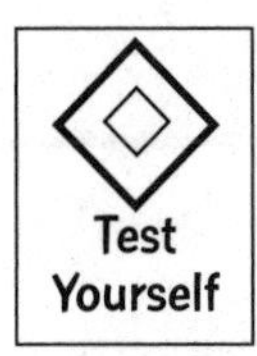

QUESTIONS

True-False Questions

1. It's natural to feel nervous before a high-pressure situation; in fact, some scientists think that we are hardwired to get an adrenaline rush when we are in tight spots.

2. The most pressurized test situations serve to validate your existence, because these tests are often the sole measure of your qualifications.
3. Knowing what's going to be on the test and the form it will take can go a long way toward reducing test anxiety.
4. Extreme panic can help you do your best on some standardized tests.
5. On standardized tests, you don't have to answer all the questions correctly to do well.
6. When you take a standardized test, you are being marked against yourself rather than being judged against all other test takers.
7. You are always better off answering more questions than wasting time on a question you didn't know.
8. Mathematicians and scientists recognize and embrace the need for creativity in their work.
9. Nearly all math problems can be solved in only one acceptable way.
10. The secret to doing well on math and science tests is hard work and strong study skills.

Completion Questions

1. You can reduce test anxiety by _________ the test so that it doesn't seem as important.
2. In your attempt to downplay the test, don't _________ your fears.
3. You can't do your best if you don't know the test's _________.
4. _________ or imagine yourself doing well, as you fill in the blanks or write the essays with confidence.
5. Studies have clearly shown that people who approach tense situations with a(n) _________ attitude will do better than those who trudge in feeling defeated.
6. Playing the _________ game can also help you be more confident during a test.
7. According to some scientists, _________ is a natural reaction to a pressure situation.
8. It is true that some _________ are more important than others, especially standardized college admission tests.
9. A minor case of nerves can actually help you do well on a test (especially a standardized test) because it keeps you _________.
10. You can improve your score by taking a short _________ by pausing for a few seconds if you feel you are losing your concentration.

Multiple-Choice Questions

1. When you talk about an upcoming test, you should
   (a) Push the panic button to mobilize your mind for success
   (b) Never share knowledge with a classmate so they don't do better than you do

(c) Be casual to reduce your fears
(d) Blow the test all out of proportion to get that helpful adrenaline rush

2. You can become more confident about a test by doing all of the following *except*
   (a) Studying your notes in detail
   (b) Knowing what's going to be on the test
   (c) Cramming the night before the test
   (d) Memorizing all the test directions
3. During a test, you can use relaxation techniques that include
   (a) Memorizing and underling key passages
   (b) Visualization and deep breathing
   (c) Cramming and deep breathing
   (d) Visualizing and studying
4. You can help put the test into perspective and so lift your spirits by
   (a) Verbalizing your worst-case scenario
   (b) Imagining yourself repeating the class because you failed the final exam
   (c) Talking to your classmates during the test
   (d) Creating a doom-and-gloom script to help you plan for failure
5. When you are taking a test, try not to panic if
   (a) You have studied hard and you can answer all the questions
   (b) The test starts on time
   (c) The test questions are all the same level of difficulty
   (d) Some questions are more difficult than others
6. If you can't answer a question,
   (a) Panic because it shows that you are not well prepared
   (b) Don't move on until you can
   (c) Skip it and move on
   (d) Recognize that it really matters
7. If you freeze during a test and can't go on,
   (a) Pause and take a few deep breaths
   (b) Get up and leave the room
   (c) Ask the proctor or a classmate for help
   (d) Check your notes briefly for reassurance
8. People often incorrectly think that
   (a) Math problems can be solved many ways
   (b) Math calls for logic, not creativity
   (c) Science experiments have many right answers
   (d) Math calls for creativity, not logic

9. To do well on math and science tests,
   (a) Try not to ask questions in class so you don't appear foolish or ill prepared
   (b) Attend class when you have the time
   (c) Read and reread your textbook
   (d) Try not to participate in class so you don't interrupt the flow of the lecture
10. Always remember that you are in school to
   (a) Learn as much as you can
   (b) Look smart in front of other students
   (c) Act intelligent
   (d) Impress the instructor

ANSWER KEY

True/False Questions

1. T 2. F 3. T 4. F 5. T 6. F 7. T 8. T 9. F 10. T

Completion Questions

1. Downplaying 2. Discard or dismiss 3. Rules 4. Visualize 5. Optimistic
6. What-if 7. Panic 8. Tests 9. Alert and focused 10. Break

Multiple-Choice Questions

1. c 2. c 3. b 4. a 5. d 6. c 7. a 8. b 9. c 10. a

CHAPTER 20

After the Test

You should read this chapter if you need to review or learn about

- Learning from the test-taking experience
- Improving your score on subsequent tests

Get Started

In Chapter 19, you learned techniques for calming your assessment anxiety. In this chapter, discover how to use tests as a springboard for even greater academic success.

After you complete the test, use it to improve for next time. If you got an A, congratulations! If you didn't get the top grade, don't despair. Instead, use it as a learning

experience. Don't compare yourself to your friends and classmates. Instead, focus on the things you did well to prepare and take the test. Remind yourself that next time you'll do better.

Here are some ways to get the most from your test-taking experience.

Evaluate What You Did Right and What You Can Do Better

With each test you take, you can become a better test taker—if you analyze your strengths and weaknesses. Think of yourself as an athlete in training. You practice and work out, of course, and you can improve by studying your performance in detail. Here are some questions you can ask yourself:

- *What was my biggest problem on this test? How do I know?* You can figure out your biggest problem by seeing which questions you missed. Look for a pattern of errors. Perhaps you missed all the mathematical word problems or forgot to include specific details in the essay.
- *What caused my mistakes? For example, did I run out of time? Did I misread questions? Did I study the wrong material or not study carefully? Was I rushing? Did I make careless mistakes?* Look back at the pattern of errors and analyze their cause. Be honest with yourself; take responsibility for your future *now.*
- *How can I overcome these problems?* Perhaps you will decide to take practice tests to learn how to allocate your time better. You might practice the reading comprehension techniques you learned in Part 3. Or you might decide to work with a study group to make sure you cover all the important information you may be missing on your own. You could write practice essays, read outside material, and go to extra-help classes, too.

Check for Grading Errors

Instructors sometimes make mistakes when they grade tests. Perhaps the instructor misread your answer, seeing a *b* for a *d.* Or you might have solved the math problem in a different way, and the instructor didn't understand what you were doing. There might even be a poorly designed question that has two valid answers.

Quick Tip

Even standardized tests such as SATs and ACTs can have mistakes in grading and question design. Such errors are very infrequent, but they have been known to occur.

Don't bother the instructor to try to get points that you don't really deserve. But do talk to the instructor if you think your test may have been misgraded. You may be able to get a higher score if you can show that your answer is correct or even reasonable.

Your instructor might be willing to give you additional credit for a partially correct answer. That's why it is important to show your work in math and science problems. If you're not allowed to show your work on the answer sheet or the test booklet, show it on scrap paper. Be sure to turn in the scrap paper with the answer sheet.

Talk with Your Instructor

Most instructors really want to help their students succeed. This is even more true if you are clearly putting effort into your work. Instructors know that how well you learn depends in part on your attitude: if you approach school in a positive way, you're far more likely to do well when you study and take tests. When your instructor helps you, you'll feel more connected to your education.

Ask your instructor to evaluate your test to point out your strengths and weaknesses. See what suggestions your instructor makes. Compare these to what you have figured out on your own. If they match, you know where you have to put your effort. If they don't, look back at the test and see why there's a difference of opinion. Are you being honest with yourself?

There are times when we avoid being honest with ourselves because, well, honesty can be painful. Instead of assessing our strengths and weaknesses candidly, we retreat behind excuses like these:

- "I can never succeed because the instructor hates me."
- "It's hopeless. I'll never be a good test taker."
- "I'm just too stupid to pass."
- "What's the use? The system is stacked against me."

Don't fall into this trap of substituting excuses for action. Instead, see what you did well on the test and where your work needs improvement. Then act on your analysis by strengthening your knowledge and test-taking skills.

Study Smarter

Adjust your study methods based on your self-assessment, your test score, and your instructor's advice. For example, if you find that your notes were weak, you might want to take notes in a different way. If you've been jotting down ideas, you might want to try making outlines. You can also photocopy your textbook and then highlight key points. Write comments in the margins, too.

If you find that you lost points because of careless errors, you can practice working more carefully and checking your work. If you got a lower score than you expected because you really didn't understand the questions on the test, you should seek extra help. Misunderstandings have a way of snowballing. If you don't understand the material on this test, you're going to have hard time building on it for the next test . . . and the ones after that.

Quick Tip

College instructors are required to offer extra help. They must meet with students during specific times, called *office hours.*

Get Some Help

For years, you've been doing great studying on your own. Suddenly, you find that your math grade is in the basement because you just don't understand the material. Perhaps you can't get above a C on any essay-type questions, when you've always gotten As on them before. Maybe physics is your Waterloo (it sure was mine). Whatever classes you are finding difficult, you are not alone. Very often, students encounter major problems in making the grade when they move from high school to college or from college to graduate classes.

If you've tried the instructor's extra help and you're still confused, ask a friend to tutor you until you grasp the concept. If your friend isn't willing to help (or is having the same problems you are), check out the school's tutoring service. Most schools have student tutors who work for free as part of their community service. Other schools have tutoring centers staffed by professionals. You might be able to get extra help from your parents, relatives, and older brothers and sisters, too.

I strongly suggest that you try all of these methods before you pay a lot of money for live or online tutoring. As a high-priced tutor myself, I certainly welcome the extra income. However, I firmly believe that most students can succeed with free extra help from their instructors, classmates, or school tutoring services.

Resolve to Do Better Next Time

Right now, you might feel like crumpling the test paper into a tight ball and throwing it into the garbage. Even though you're frustrated, don't give up.

Tests are designed to see how well you know a specific subject. Think of the test in a positive way and you'll get more from the experience. Use what you learned to be the best student you can be.

It takes courage to learn from a painful experience, but you've come this far already, so you're in the home stretch. With a bit more effort, you can raise your grade. Test taking and studying are skills that can be learned. It takes time and effort to become an excellent test taker, but your investment will pay off now and in the future. You'll do better in school today, and you'll have the tools you need to shape the future you want—and deserve.

Take a minute to congratulate yourself. You've set goals for yourself and planned ways to make them come true. You've started getting organized and have taken responsibility for your own learning. Perhaps you've already arranged for a study partner and set up your study center. You've learned how to take good notes and make the most of your time.

Now you know some powerful techniques for reading more effectively, too. You prepare carefully for a test by organizing and reviewing your notes and the textbook. You've learned ways to calm test jitters. You know how to prepare, budget your time, and develop a test strategy for short-answer and essay tests. After a test, you evaluate what you did right and what you can do better so you can study even smarter next time.

Anything worth doing requires hard work. Becoming a super student and great test taker is no exception. Some of the world's most successful people were struggling students who learned how to read, study, and take tests more effectively. Now you, too, have the keys to the kingdom of success.

- ✔ After you receive your graded test, evaluate what you did right and what you can do better on the next test.
- ✔ Check for grading errors and talk with your instructor.
- ✔ Study smarter and get some extra help.
- ✔ Decide to do better next time.

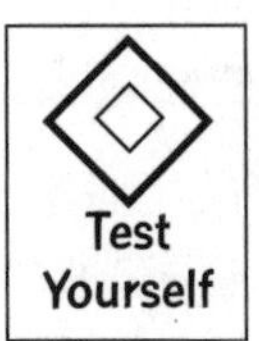

QUESTIONS

True-False Questions

1. With each test you take, you can become a better test taker—if you analyze your strengths and weaknesses.
2. Instructors rarely if ever make mistakes scoring tests, especially now that many instructors give computer-based tests.
3. Don't bother the instructor to try to get points that you don't really deserve.
4. Your instructor might be willing to give you additional credit for a partially correct answer.
5. Few instructors care whether their students succeed; after all, they get paid anyway and most have job security through tenure.
6. Ask your instructor to evaluate your test to point out your strengths and weaknesses.
7. If you don't understand the material on this test, you're not going to have a hard time building on it for the next test. That's because every test is separate from every other test.

8. If you find that you lost points because of careless errors, you can practice working more carefully and checking your work.
9. Few people feel frustrated after doing poorly on a test because they anticipated earning a low score.
10. Test taking and studying are skills that you can learn.

Completion Questions

1. You can figure out your biggest problem on a test by seeing which questions you ________.
2. As you evaluate your test performance, it is most important that you are ________ with yourself and take responsibility for your future.
3. You may be able to get a higher score if you can show that your answer is ________ or even reasonable.
4. If you're not allowed to show your math or science calculations on the answer sheet or the test booklet, show them on the ________.
5. Instructors know that how well you learn depends in part on your ________: if you approach your studies in a positive way, you're far more likely to do well when you study and take tests.
6. Adjust your ________ based on your self-assessment, your test score, and your instructor's advice.
7. If you got a lower score than you expected because you really didn't understand the questions on the test, you should seek ________.
8. Even though you're frustrated, don't ________.
9. Think of the test in a ________ way and you'll get more from the experience.
10. There's no doubt that it takes ________ to learn from a painful experience, but you can do it!

Multiple-Choice Questions

1. After you take every test, ask yourself all the following questions *except*
   (a) "What was my biggest problem on this test?"
   (b) "What caused my mistakes?"
   (c) "Why is this happening to me?"
   (d) "How can I deal with my specific test problems constructively?"
2. If you suspect that your test has been misgraded,
   (a) Talk to the instructor to see if an error has occurred
   (b) Suck it up and don't bother the instructor
   (c) Demand the points that you earned
   (d) Accuse the instructor of deliberately trying to cheat you

3. Asking your instructor for assistance in understanding material helps you in all the following ways *except*
   (a) Making you feel more connected to your work
   (b) Guaranteeing you a higher grade
   (c) Improving your comprehension
   (d) Showing that you are invested in your work and determined to succeed
4. After you conference with your instructor about your test paper, you should
   (a) Throw out the test
   (b) Compare the instructor's suggestions to what you have figured out on your own
   (c) See what grades everyone else got to find out if the instructor is a fair grader
   (d) Drop the issue for now but determine to do better in the future
5. Some students don't learn from tests because
   (a) The system is stacked against them
   (b) They will never be good test takers
   (c) Their instructor hates them
   (d) They are not willing to be honest with themselves as they assess their strengths and weaknesses
6. Consider improving your next test score by using each of the following methods *except*
   (a) Writing comments in the margins of your notes
   (b) Photocopying your textbook and then highlighting key points
   (c) Continuing to study the same exact way you have in the past
   (d) Changing the way you take notes
7. If you have gone to the instructor's extra-help sessions and you are still confused,
   (a) Get some help from a friend or the tutoring center
   (b) Give up because it is obvious that you will never pass
   (c) Drop the class and pick it up next semester or next year with a different instructor
   (d) Go back to the instructor for extra help
8. You might consider getting extra help from all of the following sources *except*
   (a) A pricey online tutoring service
   (b) A classmate who is earning higher grades
   (c) Your school's tutoring services
   (d) Your relatives
9. After the test, take a minute to congratulate yourself because
   (a) You didn't cry when you got a low score on the test
   (b) You understand that tests never matter in the big picture

(c) You've set goals for yourself and planned ways to make them come true
(d) You let others determine your school success

10. Becoming an excellent student and test taker requires all of the following *except*
(a) hard work
(b) keen intelligence
(c) determination
(d) good study skills

ANSWER KEY

True/False Questions

1. T 2. F 3. T 4. T 5. F 6. T 7. F 8. T 9. F 10. T

Completion Questions

1. Missed or answered incorrectly 2. Honest 3. Correct 4. Scrap paper 5. Attitude 6. Study methods 7. Extra help 8. Give up 9. Positive 10. Courage

Multiple-Choice Questions

1. c 2. a 3. b 4. b 5. d 6. c 7. a 8. a 9. c 10. b

Index